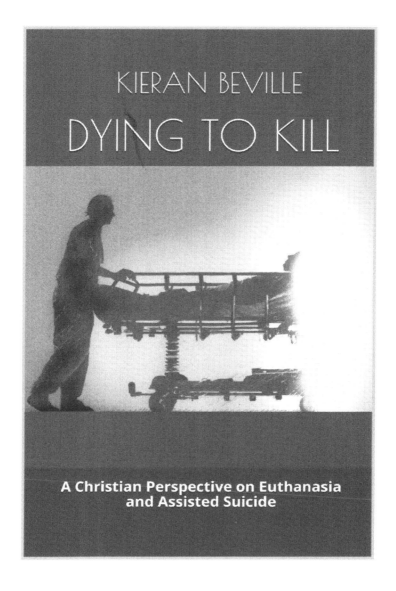

KIERAN BEVILLE
DYING TO KILL

A Christian Perspective on Euthanasia and Assisted Suicide

D1525341

DYING TO KILL

A Christian Perspective on Euthanasia and Assisted Suicide

Kieran Beville

Christian Publishing House
Cambridge, Ohio

Christian Publishing House
Professional Christian Publishing of the Good News

DYING TO KILL A Christian Perspective on Euthanasia and Assisted Suicide

Publishing by Christian Publishing House

ISBN-13: 978-0692339190

ISBN-10: 0692339191

Endorsements

'Kieran Beville has assembled a huge amount of information on the subject of euthanasia and how it is dealt with around the world. The result is a very sobering account of attempts to legitimate assisted suicide in our society, something that Christians must be prepared to resist. He discusses the issues that this raises sensitively, biblically and uncompromisingly. This book will be of great help to Christian believers who want to understand better what is happening in this area and will assist them in developing a biblical response.' **Robert Strivens, Principal, London Theological Seminary**

'"Dying to Kill" is a clearly written, well-researched, cogently argued, shocking wake-up call. It presents the reader with the "Humane Holocaust" that threatens, as Malcolm Muggeridge wrote last century, "to transform a war crime into an act of compassion," via the often well-intended mercy killing/euthanasia lobby, in its various guises and disguises. It reminds us that time is running out. Read, mark, learn, weep and pray. For the issues are, quite literally, a matter of life and death for everyone. May all who value the sanctity of life raise the alarm and act now. **Dr Steve Brady, Principal, Moorlands College, Christchurch, U.K.**

Table of Content

Endorsements 4

Acknowledgements 15

Foreword 18

Introduction 21

England and Wales 21

Scotland 21

Changing Tide 22

Falconer Bill 23

Definition of Terms 23

Opposition 30

Basic Ethical Principles 31

Social and Spiritual Values 33

Preliminary Concerns 35

Care at the End of Life 37

Addressing Ignorance and Fear 38

The Injured Young 39

Treating Depression 41

Spiritually Naked 41

Legitimate Concerns 43

Advice from the General 44

Qualified to Comment 46

Scorn Not His Simplicity 47

CHAPTER 1 "You shall not Kill" 52

Suicide 55

Assisted Suicide 56

Euthanasia 62

Abortion 64

Media Bias 64

CHAPTER 2 Background to Euthanasia in the
Netherlands 66

The Remmelink Report 68

Falsified Death Certificates 71

Inadequate Pain Control and Comfort Care 71

Broadening Interpretations of Euthanasia Guidelines. 72

Policy and Practice 73

The Irony of History 74

The Burden over Posed Compassion 76

Dwell in the Whole Counsel of God 77

Implications of the Dutch Euthanasia Experience 77

Current Law 79

Oversight is by Non-Judicial Committees 80

Change in the Burden of Proof 81

Residency not Required 81

CHAPTER 3 Society at Death's Door 86

Dispatching the Demented 90

Britain 91

The Dutch Model 94

CHAPTER 4 Brave New World 98

Increasing Numbers..98

Death on Wheels 99

CHAPTER 5 The Pied Piper of Hamelin 111

Vulnerable 117

Loneliness 117

Dutch Doctors Support Euthanasia.......................118

National Survey 119

American Research..120

Terminally Ill Seldom Consider Euthanasia or Assisted
Suicide 121

CHAPTER 6 Dancing with Death...................... 124

Normalisation...126

A Good Death for Louise....................................130

Empowerment for Whom?...................................137

CHAPTER 7 Sick Society 140

The Hippocratic Oath 141

Changing Criteria 145

Physician Sentiment..148

Outcome of the Consultation Process 153

CHAPTER 8 Politics of Death 156

Subjectivity 160

The Reaper and the Dog 161

Vacuum and Vortex 164

Popping your Clogs...169

Euthanasia for Minors 170

Advance Directives 171

Follow the Leader 172

Dying to Kill.. 172

Maine Referendum.. 173

The Oregon Experience 173

Opposition Coalition Formed.................................... 174

Polls Tell the Story.. 176

CHAPTER 9 Dutch Disease..............................178

Australia.. 179

Indecent Haste 180

Removing Food and Fluids is not a Violation of Human Rights Act... 180

Zurich Allows Assisted Suicide in Homes for the Elderly 182

Equality 182

Deep-Continuous Sedation 182

Termination Without Request or Consent 183

CHAPTER 10 Ethical Definitions and Historical Debate..188

Definition.. 189

Classification of Euthanasia 195

Voluntary Euthanasia.. 195

Non-Voluntary Euthanasia..................................... 196

Involuntary Euthanasia 196

Passive and Active Euthanasia 196

Doctrine of Double Effect 196

Intentional Harm Versus Side Effects 197

Medicine 198

Criticisms 200

History 201

Beginnings of the Contemporary Euthanasia Debate 203

Early Euthanasia Movement in the United States 205

1930s in Britain 208

Nazi Euthanasia Programme (Action T4).............. 209

Euthanasia Debate..212

Theological and Philosophical Support for Euthanasia 213

CHAPTER 11 Dignitas **216**

History and Operation.......................................216

Suicide Method..217

Statistics 218

Costs and Finances 218

Suicide Tourism...219

Allegations by Dignitas Ex-Employee....................219

Reaction of Local Swiss People and Organisations .. 220

Patient Selection...220

Cremation Urns in Lake Zurich 220

Dignitas in the Media 221

CHAPTER 12 Dignity in Dying.................**226**

Origins...227

1950s to 1980s 230

1990s...233

2000 to Present 234

Diane Pretty..235

Partnership...236

Arguments and Opposition....................238

Practicalities 241

Advance Decisions...............................242

CHAPTER 13 Exit International........... 243

Activities 243

Philip Nitschke 245

Dying with Dignity 249

Palliative Care 249

Younger People and Suicide..................250

References in Pop Culture.....................254

Australian Censorship 255

Euthanasia Techniques 257

Barbiturate Testing Kit 258

Nitrogen Canisters...............................259

Awards and Recognition.......................260

CHAPTER 14 Doctor Death................ 262

Most of Kevorkian's "patients" had no Terminal Illness
....263

Early life..264

Career 265

Criticism and Kevorkian's Response 268

Art Career... 270

Trials 271

Conviction and Imprisonment 271

Activities after His Release from Prison 277

2008 Congressional Race 278

Death 279

Legacy 279

Heroism 281

Contemporary Crisis 283

CHAPTER 15 Palliative Care or Slippery Slope....285

Scope of the Term....................................... 286

Comparison with Hospice Care 288

History 289

Assessment of Symptoms 292

Symptom Management 292

Dealing with Distress 293

People Involved... 296

Funding 297

Acceptance 298

Palliative Sedation..................................... 298

The Liverpool Care Pathway 299

General Practice.. 301

Drugs Used 301

Sedation vs. Euthanasia..................................302

Slippery Slope 303

Action T4..307

CHAPTER 16 A Biblical View of Life and Death ..310

Body, Mind and Spirit 316

Help for the Hopeless.......................................317

Biblical Perspective 317

The Purpose of Pain 319

The Vulnerability of the Mind..........................319

Becoming Equipped as Comforters.......................320

Triumphant in Trouble 321

Regaining Perspective 322

Injuries of the Soul...323

Transcending our Limitations 325

Death is Inevitable..325

Longing for Home...328

Beyond the Horizon..330

The Resurrection 330

Reasons to Believe in the Bible.............................335

Does Science Contradict the Bible? 339

Good News for Dying People...............................344

Conviction Comes before Conversion 345

The Great Exchange..346

APPENDIX A The Sixth Commandment in the 21st Century 353

Death Penalty and War 355

Abortion 358

Thoughts, Words and Deeds 358

Capital Punishment 359

APPENDIX B Religious Views 369

Buddhism 369

Roman Catholicism 370

Protestantism 370

Hinduism 371

Islam 371

Jainism 372

Judaism 372

Shinto 373

APPENDIC C Legality of Euthanasia 374

Australia 375

Legalisation in the Northern Territory 377

Reaction to Act 378

Organisations 378

Christians Supporting Choice for Voluntary Euthanasia
.... 379

Belgium 379

Canada 379

Quebec 380

China 381

New law 381

France 384

India 385

Ireland 385

Israel 388

Japan 389

Luxembourg 390

Mexico 391

Netherlands 392

New Zealand 393

Norway 394

Switzerland 394

Turkey 394

United Kingdom 395

USA 396

Non-Governmental Organisations 397

Oregon Ballot Measure 16 (1994) 398

The law 399

Analysis of Impact 400

Attempts to Repeal 400

Washington Death with Dignity Act 402

Specific Provisions in the Initiative 403

Other Books by This Author **415**

Select Bibliography.....................................**417**

Acknowledgements

I wish to express my sincere thanks to Dr Andrew Fergusson who wrote the Foreword. Dr Fergusson qualified at St Thomas's Hospital in 1975 and after hospital medicine worked in general practice in South-East London from 1979-89. He became Assistant General Secretary to the Christian Medical Fellowship in April 1989 where he understudied his predecessor until October 1990 when he became General Secretary until end of December 1999. He sat as an elected member of the General Medical Council from 2000-2003, was President of the Centre for Bioethics and Human Dignity in Deerfield, Illinois in 2005-6, and returned to Christian Medical Fellowship from 2007-11. He has written several hundred articles and two books (*Euthanasia: An Edited Collection of Articles from the Journal of the Christian Medical Fellowship*, 1994 and *Hard Questions About Health and Healing, Christian Medical Fellowship*, 2005) and edited half a dozen others on subjects at the interface of medicine and Christianity, and is a regular broadcaster on radio and TV. He chaired the anti-euthanasia coalition HOPE (Healthcare Opposed to Euthanasia) from 1990-2000. HOPE was the precursor of Care Not Killing. In semi-retirement now, he chairs the Advisory Group of Care Not Killing of which he has been a Board member since 2010. Dr Fergusson is also a committed evangelical Christian with a desire that the biblical case against euthanasia and assisted suicide be heard more clearly in the church and society. Evidently, he is eminently qualified to comment on euthanasia and assisted suicide. It is a very great privilege to have him involved in this writing project. He lives in Faversham, Kent and relaxes by reading classic detective fiction and supporting Millwall Football Club, (nobody is perfect!).

Sincere thanks also to Dr Steve Brady, principal of Moorlands College for his endorsement of this work. Steve was born and educated in Liverpool where he was converted in his teens. He trained at what is now the London School of Theology. There he met Brenda, his wife of nearly forty years, who has bravely battled and coped with Multiple Sclerosis nearly all that time, and now resides in full-time care. They have two married children and four grandchildren. He has held pastorates in Buckinghamshire, Leicester, London and Bournemouth. He serves as Principal of Moorlands College, which trains men and women for Christian service in the UK and overseas. He has spoken at conferences and conventions throughout the UK and internationally, serves as a Trustee of the Keswick Convention, and is Chair of the Association of Bible College Principals. He holds a Ph.D. degree in theology and is the author, contributor and editor of over a dozen books. Steve hates gardening but he is a keen sportsman and has an unrepentant attachment to Everton Football Club!

I am indebted to Dr Robert Strivens, for taking time to read my manuscript and write a commendation. Dr Strivens is the principal of London Theological Seminary, located in North London, which trains men for pastoral and preaching ministry. He teaches Church History and some New Testament at LTS. In 2012, he completed his doctoral research on Philip Doddridge, a prominent Dissenting minister in England in the early 18th century. Before working full-time at LTS in 2007, Robert was pastor of Banbury Evangelical Free Church (1999-2007), having trained for the pastorate at LTS (1997-99). Prior to that, he was a solicitor, working in the City of London and in Brussels for about 15 years. Robert is married to Sarah and they have three sons. He has wisely not disclosed an allegiance to any football club. Draw your own conclusions!

It is useful to have a medical doctor in the family and I want to express my gratitude to my brother-in-law, Dr Graham Joy for reading the manuscript. He made some very helpful suggestions and corrections. Graham is a General Practitioner and devout Christian. He gained his medical degree from Guys hospital medical school, London. After a series of hospital jobs he trained for general practice, and has been a partner in a group practice in Margate for 30 years. He has also been involved in training hospital doctors to become General Practitioners. His expertise was most helpful.

Whereas I am grateful to the people mentioned above for their contributions, I want to make it clear that any errors, which might remain, are entirely my responsibility.

Some of Chapter 1, "You shall not kill", as well as "Appendix A: The Sixth Commandment in the Twenty-First Century", have been excerpted and adapted from my book *The Commandments in Contemporary Culture*. ISPCK, 2010 and used here with permission.

In the chapter, "A Biblical View of Human Life" the section dealing with depression has been excerpted and adapted from my article entitled "When the Preacher Gets Discouraged", which featured in *Preaching* (a magazine published by Salem Publishing Inc., Nashville Tennessee, USA) in May/June, 2013. Thanks to the executive editor Michael Duduit for allowing me to use it here.

Foreword

I never sought end-of-life issues and the debate about legalising euthanasia and assisted suicide as my specialist subject, but as an experienced GP I arrived to lead the staff at Christian Medical Fellowship in 1989 just as media, public and parliamentary debates about liberalising the law took off. By 1990, I was chairing a hastily formed coalition called HOPE, Healthcare Opposed to Euthanasia. More than twenty years on, in retirement, I find myself active several days a week in the much more professional and much larger coalition, the Care Not Killing Alliance (www.carenotkilling.org.uk).

Both HOPE in the 1990s and CNK since 2005 had to take two key strategic decisions: the coalitions would be single issue and not touch on other areas like abortion and embryo research, and they would not use faith-based arguments and language in campaigning. The evidence-based case against legalisation of euthanasia and assisted suicide (which is simply euthanasia 'one step back') is very strong but to win the public policy argument the coalition had to recruit as many supporters as possible. Specifically Christian language would have been unhelpful.

But how often, addressing church audiences, have I longed to be able to be more specifically Christian! An extended biblical Christian case against euthanasia and assisted suicide is overdue, but with Kieran Beville's book, it is now here.

He is well qualified to write. A Baptist minister in Ireland, he has confronted suffering, bereavement and grief pastorally. A lecturer in Intercultural Studies and Practical

Ministry at Tyndale Theological Seminary in Badhoevedorp in the Netherlands, he has been able to research on the ground the tragic consequences of that country's practice of euthanasia. In family terms, he grew up with two siblings with Down's syndrome; and he shares courageously about a sustained period of severe depression that led him seriously to consider his own suicide.

Kieran amasses evidence from around the world of the consequences of legalisation; summarises legal and philosophical arguments; paints comprehensive pen portraits of the two main candidates for the global title of 'Dr Death' (the American Dr Kevorkian and the Australian Dr Nitschke); and adds anecdotes and case histories that make the whole argument against seem so much more real and so much more human.

However, it is for his Christian case we are most indebted. Some might argue that we need no more than the four words of the Sixth Commandment, 'You shall not murder', and indeed I have often in frustration held back from using those four words with the 'misguidedly merciful' in many Christian congregations. However, he gives us much more, with reflections on suffering, dying and death set in a thoroughly biblical Gospel context.

We have been well advised elsewhere to consider all such difficult subjects from the perspectives of God's two books – the more reliable one, the Bible, and the evidence from the experiences of fallen man. No Christian who studies these two books thoroughly can support euthanasia or assisted suicide.

We called our first coalition HOPE, seeking a media-friendly acronym. However, I will never forget the Christian palliative care consultant lecturing on these matters many years ago. He put up a slide featuring that well-known cliché

'Where's there's life, there's hope' and then shocked the medical audience by negating it with the words 'I don't believe it; I've been in many clinical situations where that's just not true. But I do believe this:' and his next slide read 'Where there's hope, there's life'.

Kieran says No to euthanasia and assisted suicide, but a loud Yes to Christian hope, for both this world and the next.

Dr Andrew Fergusson

Introduction

Assisted suicide has been on the agenda in the UK repeatedly over the past 20 years, sometimes beneath the surface but now front and centre in the media, amongst think tanks and increasingly in parliament. There is quite a lot of public interest in this issue and a growing desire (if not demand) that it be made legal.

England and Wales

Lord Falconer – a Labour member of the House of Lords – has been at the forefront of parliamentary efforts to see assisted suicide legalised in England and Wales. Having tabled an amendment to the Coroners and Justice Bill in 2009 and subsequently chaired a so-called 'Independent Commission on Assisted Dying' in 2012, Lord Falconer introduced a Bill in the 2013/14 parliamentary session. This Bill would have legalised assisted suicide for mentally competent adults with less than six months to live. Due to the constraints of the parliamentary timetable, the Bill did not get past its preliminary stage (First Reading).

Scotland

Attempts to change the law in Scotland to legalise assisted suicide in recent years have been led by Margo Macdonald MSP. The Assisted Suicide (Scotland) Bill is the latest legislative proposal and was brought before the Scottish Parliament on 13 November 2013. Although Ms Macdonald died on 4 April 2014, her Bill continues under the leadership of Patrick Harvie MSP who was named as an additional 'member in charge' of the Bill when it was tabled.

The Bill would make it legal for people with the potential to live for decades to opt for assisted suicide. Rather than requiring there be objective evidence of serious physical suffering, the Bill merely mentions an 'unacceptable quality of life' as qualification for assisted suicide.

Mr Harvie's Bill contains much of the same content as the End of Life Assistance (Scotland) Bill, which was heavily defeated by the Scottish Parliament in 2010 by 85 votes to 16.

Changing Tide

Former Archbishop of Canterbury Lord Carey has supported legislation that would make it legal for terminally ill people in England and Wales to receive help to end their lives. Lord Carey dropped his opposition to the Assisted Dying Bill "in the face of the reality of needless suffering".[1] But the current Archbishop of Canterbury Justin Welby has called the bill "mistaken and dangerous".

Tabled by Labour peer Lord Falconer the legislation would make it legal for adults in England and Wales to be given assistance ending their own life.[2] It would apply to those with less than six months to live. Two doctors would have to independently confirm the patient was terminally ill and had reached their own, informed decision to die.

---

[1] James Chapman, "Carey: 'I've changed my mind on right to die", *Daily Mail*, 11 July, 2014.

[2] Debated extensively in the House of Lords on 18 July, 2014 with an indecisive outcome.

Insisting it would not be "anti-Christian" to change the law, Lord Carey said the current situation risked "undermining the principle of human concern which should lie at the heart of our society".[3] He added: "Today we face a central paradox. In strictly observing the sanctity of life, the Church could now actually be promoting anguish and pain, the very opposite of a Christian message of hope."[4]

When Lord Carey was still the Archbishop of Canterbury he was among the opponents of Lord Joffe's Assisting Dying for the Terminally Ill Bill, which was successfully blocked in the House of Lords in 2006.

Falconer Bill

The assisted dying bill, introduced by former Labour cabinet minister Lord Falconer has been debated in the House of Lords. It is one of the more contentious issues in modern ethics and politics. Falconer's draft legislation, which would allow doctors to prescribe a lethal dose to terminally ill patients judged to have less than six months to live, is a private member's bill and so unlikely to become law. But it is inevitable that the issues of assisted dying will be debated in the House of Commons.

Definition of Terms

Euthanasia as it is generally understood means knowingly and intentionally performing an act that is explicitly intended to end another person's life. It usually includes the following elements: the subject is a competent, informed person with an incurable illness who has voluntarily asked for his or her

---

[3] Ibid

[4] Ibid

life to be ended; the agent knows about the person's condition and desire to die and commits the act with the primary intention of ending the life of that person; and the act is undertaken with sympathy and compassion and without personal gain. Euthanasia, therefore, is a deliberate, intentional act to terminate life. Do sympathy and compassion justify such actions? Is the consent and desire of the euthanized sufficient grounds to warrant such action? These questions and many others will be addressed in this work.

Assistance in suicide means knowingly and intentionally providing a person with the knowledge or means or both required to commit suicide, including counselling about lethal doses of drugs, prescribing such lethal doses or supplying the drugs.[5]

Euthanasia and assisted suicide, as understood here, must be distinguished from the withholding or withdrawal of inappropriate, futile or unwanted medical treatment or the provision of compassionate palliative care, even when these practices shorten life.

Currently there is widespread opposition to euthanasia and physician-assisted suicide from professional medical associations in many countries and many of these bodies have made public statements asserting that opposition. Following a thorough consultation process the Royal College of General

---

[5] Providing information on how to commit suicide is not illegal in many countries, hence Exit International can host seminars throughout the world. Assisted suicide is legally permissible in some countries in Europe, namely, the Netherlands, Belgium, Luxemburg and Switzerland. In the USA it is lawful in Oregon, Montana and Washington. In Latin America is legal in Columbia. Because it is lawful many people think it is a legitimate entitlement but there is a difference between the law and morality in this matter.

Practitioners (RCGP) in the UK announced (n February 2014) their continuing opposition to changes in the existing law which prohibits assisted suicide and euthanasia.

In 2013, the Canadian Medical Association voted overwhelmingly against becoming pro-euthanasia. Delegates at the Canadian Medical Association (CMA) annual general meeting in Calgary passed a motion calling on the organisation to "support the right of any physician to exercise conscientious objection when faced with a request for medical aid in dying". The CMA's existing policy, adopted in 2007, states that, "Canadian physicians should not participate in euthanasia or assisted suicide." The CMA's affirmation of its existing policy came four months after the World Medical Association reaffirmed its own declaration against euthanasia and physician-assisted suicide, calling such practices "unethical" and "in conflict with basic ethical principles of medical practice."

It is a fundamental principle of medicine that a doctor should not kill or offer to assist in killing. What is needed (and being provided in many instances) for people nearing the end of life is palliative care services - at home if so desired and feasible and in hospices. Doctors should be involved in killing pain, not killing people. Society should not entrust the legal power to administer death to patients into the hands of physicians and it seems to be quite bizarre that some people in society do not see a problem with this. Death is not just a legal and medical issue and so the debate should not be confined solely to legal and medical professionals.

Death is also a spiritual matter. Assisted dying lobbyists often seek to frame the debate in terms of "choice" and as such it is the ultimate form of consumerism. End of life issues have a moral dimension and so pastors and chaplains should have a voice in this discussion. Most ordinary decent people who want a good death (who doesn't) are not pro-euthanasia. Individualism has to some extent displaced communal values, which require consensus and co-operation. This is part of the problem because the issue of euthanasia and physician-assisted suicide should be discussed in the context of the overall good for society.

The British Medical Association reaffirmed its opposition to assisted suicide in 2009. The American Medical Association (AMA), New Zealand Medical Association (NZMA) and the World Medical Association are all officially opposed. In 2012 the Massachusetts Medical Society reaffirmed its opposition to physician-assisted suicide as did the National Hospice and Palliative Care Organisation the same year. Other professional medical bodies which are opposed are the American Medical Directors Association, Royal College of Physicians, Royal College of Nursing, American Nurses Association (ANA), Royal College of Psychiatrists, The Royal College of General Practitioners (RCGP), Christian Medical & Dental Society, American Geriatrics Society and the National Spinal Cord Injury Association.

Many noted physicians have expressed their opposition, such as the former Surgeon General, in the USA, C. Everett Koop. In reality, Oregon is atypical of the USA. Doctors who advocate for euthanasia are a minority and they are actually assisting the suicide of their own venerable profession.

In a society that has abandoned Christian values, it is no wonder that pro-euthanasia physicians are beginning to infiltrate the ranks of the medical profession. The majority of doctors (worldwide) are not willing to kill a patient by euthanasia if requested but one fears that this could change in time, preserving only (and perhaps initially) a doctor's right to "conscientious objection" when faced with a patient request for death. The relationship between law, liberty and morality is a fragile one. It ought to be a matter of concern, not only for doctors, that euthanasia might become legal in Britain, the USA and many other parts of the world. Once euthanasia and physician-assisted suicide become legal, conscientious objection becomes increasingly difficult to defend.

There is nothing dignified about suicide and there is nothing dignified about a doctor killing his/her patient. Legal approval will legitimise and normalise the sinister culture of death. Killing patients is not good medical practice. The Greek physician Hippocrates, who lived 400 years before Christ, also practiced at a time when the value of human life was disregarded, as it is today. Hippocrates vowed that he would "never give a deadly drug to anybody who asks for it." Surely, it must remain unethical to do so. A doctor cannot be both a healer and a killer without losing the trust of society.

Legislation to allow euthanasia and physician-assisted suicide may state that these services ought to be available to patients who have been diagnosed with terminal illness. "Terminal" might be further defined as "six months or less" to live. But these kinds of predictions are notoriously inaccurate. Doctors are sometimes mistaken in diagnosis and prognosis. Where euthanasia and physician-assisted suicide is legally permitted there is often a lack of basic safeguards. Or where adequate safeguards are proposed they are frequently ignored in practice.

People would be well advised to be careful what they vote for because there could come a day when a relative or an heir could request the termination of their lives. Follow-up monitoring of the patient is often not required so that the prescribing doctor would not know if a patient changed their mind. It's possible that once the lethal drugs are dispensed, they could be given without a patient's knowledge or consent. Because assisted-suicide is relatively inexpensive, insurers may influence patients by refusing to provide coverage for life-extending procedures. Potentially people could be killed as part of a cost-cutting measure. On the other hand, one may opt for it if one does not have an adequate pension plan. What is even more sinister is the possibility that it will be imposed on such people without their consent as they will be perceived as a burden on society and may even view themselves in this way, as a burden to loved ones. Such a sinister prognosis may seem like nightmarish fiction but some societies in the Western world have already started on a journey that seems to be leading to that place. Many people who are not terminally ill are already availing of euthanasia and assisted suicide, especially in Holland, but elsewhere too. Do people really want to see a doctor who can kill them?

Physicians who assist in suicide are forced to lie because they are often required to list the underlying condition on the death certificate, rather than "suicide". Assisted suicide, in the future, will likely expand to include people with manageable conditions such as HIV infection or diabetes. Eventually this could devolve into involuntary euthanasia resulting in the elderly being afraid to go to hospital.

In spite of the fact that the American Medical Association is opposed to doctor-assisted suicide this practice has been legal in Oregon since 1994, where it has been an unmitigated disaster with several controversial cases.

One Oregon woman suffered a stroke. Her daughter asked her doctor to discontinue life support. When the patient survived, the doctor administered morphine and valium. Later, he placed a magnet over her pacemaker in an attempt to disrupt it. Finally, he administered a paralytic drug to kill her. After the case was publicised, the doctor lost his licence for sixty days. He is currently practicing medicine. Another woman chose suicide because it was covered, while medical care was not.

The issues of euthanasia and physician-assisted suicide are often presented as being about compassion and choice. But this is misleading. There is nothing compassionate about killing. Those who work in hospice and palliative care offer real compassion to the dying and they assist people to die with dignity. Pro-euthanasia pressure groups and assisted suicide lobbyists have hijacked the phrase "dying with dignity" but a dignified death is already available in all developed countries of the world without euthanasia and assisted suicide.

Generally, doctors do not wish to play a role in assisting a patient's death. Assisting patients to die prematurely is not part of the moral ethos or the primary goal of medicine. If the legislation were to be changed, it would have serious negative consequences on the relationship between doctors and their patients. It remains vital that access to the best quality palliative care is available in order to ensure that terminal suffering is properly managed. Doctors perform a crucial role of healing and saving life. Having a dual role of taking life, while at the same time protecting life, would undermine their credibility and the sacred trust that exists between a patient and doctor. What is needed is better education for doctors on hospice and palliative care so that they can provide responsible alternative treatment in end of life situations. This is possibly the best way to eliminate the quest for euthanasia. Doctors should not become executioners. In a world of economics without ethics, it is inevitable that euthanasia and assisted suicide will become part of cost-cutting measures.

To some extent ignorance and fear is driving the pro-euthanasia debate. The education of more doctors in alternatives to doctor-assisted suicide is crucial in addressing this. They need to be provided with intensive training in pain control, compassionate care and alleviation of fears. Thus educated, doctors will in turn enlighten their colleagues and communities regarding effective palliative care.

There is a lot of documented evidence that an aggressive drug regimen can effectively protect dying patients from pain and doctors will not have any trouble prescribing medication if they are careful and document their actions. During the dying process, a doctor should be encouraging and bolstering his patients.

Doctor-assisted suicide in the Netherlands has expanded to include euthanasia even without a patient's knowledge or consent. Doctors in The Netherlands often resort to euthanasia when it appears that their efforts to cure the patient have been unsuccessful. Holland has shown that once the doctor has accepted the fact that he can end life, no amount of rules or regulations will protect the public.

Death needs to be regulated, with protocols for the use of life-sustaining treatments, in a manner that upholds the sanctity of life. When patients are offered a reasonable alternative, they will reject euthanasia. People who opt for euthanasia and assisted suicide often do so out of fear and anxiety. If that is addressed the desire for euthanasia and assisted suicide will diminish. A code of ethics based on the sanctity of human life is needed.

Opposition

Euthanasia and assisted suicide are opposed by almost every national medical association and prohibited by the law codes of almost all countries. A change in the legal status of these practices would represent a major shift in social values and behaviour. For the medical profession to support such a change and subsequently participate in these practices, a fundamental reconsideration of traditional medical ethics would be required.

Physicians, other health professionals, academics, interest groups, the media, legislators and the judiciary are all deeply divided about the advisability of changing current legal prohibitions of euthanasia and assisted suicide. Because of the controversial nature of these practices, their undeniable importance to physicians and their unpredictable effects on the practice of medicine, the relevant professions and society must approach these issues cautiously and deliberately.

Basic Ethical Principles

Although euthanasia and assisted suicide have traditionally been interpreted as contrary to standard codes of medical ethics in most countries there is nevertheless a need to have these practices mentioned explicitly in such codes. Many of them were written at a time when it was assumed that euthanasia and assisted suicide were wrong and therefore no such clarity needed to be expressed overtly.

Such a code should be informed by consideration of the well-being of the patient. This means that the care of patients who are terminally ill or who face an indefinite life span of suffering must be the physicians' first consideration. The notion that a life is meaningless is a moral judgement outside the scope of a physician's remit. Doctors have the moral responsibility to provide appropriate care for their patients. This includes their physical comfort and psycho-social support, even when cure is no longer possible.

The doctor must provide patients with the information they need to make informed decisions about their medical care and answer their questions to the best of their ability. This involves respecting the right of a competent patient to accept or reject any medical care recommended. This will mean ascertaining, wherever possible, and recognising the patient's wishes about the initiation, continuation or cessation of life-sustaining treatment. A medical professional must accept a share of the profession's responsibility to society in matters relating to legislation affecting the health or well-being of the community. Patients have a right to be informed when a physician's personal morality would influence the recommendation or practice of any medical procedure that the patient needs or wants. Doctors who are opposed to euthanasia and assisted suicide should make that clear to their patients if such requests are presented to them. Such requests are being made and some doctors in the UK are facilitating assisted suicide in other jurisdictions. The balance between patient well-being and autonomy, responsibility to society, and physician autonomy is important. But personal autonomy ought not to drive this agenda. There is an important absolute principle at the core of this issue.

It is not a good moral argument to say that because something is desired and widely practiced that it should be legalised in order to monitor and control it. This argument has prevailed in Holland with regard to the use of cannabis, prostitution, euthanasia and physician-assisted suicide. But where does such a pragmatic and unprincipled approach ultimately lead and who is to say where the boundaries are to be drawn. For example, paedophilia is desired and practiced by many so that if the same pragmatic approach is adopted then it could conceivably be legalised at some future time in some "liberal" society on the basis that it is the democratic (majority) wish. This would be completely morally wrong!

Social and Spiritual Values

Physicians should not participate in euthanasia and assisted suicide and their legitimate concerns about legalisation of such practices must be heeded. Ultimately, it is the prerogative of society to decide whether the laws dealing with euthanasia and assisted suicide should be changed. Physicians, like everybody else, should participate responsibly in that debate, where governments allow for a consultation process. All of societies' citizens should consider such matters very seriously and wherever changes to the law are made by way of referendum, people should vote responsibly. However, medical doctors have a particularly relevant contribution to make to the shaping of perspective in these matters. Nevertheless, these matters should not be left to the sole discretion of medical practitioners as there are important legal, social and ethical issues pertinent to euthanasia and assisted suicide.

Doctors are, generally, part of a secular scientific community (though there are many Christian doctors) which has shared presuppositions and assumptions that are inconsistent with Scripture, such as naturalism, evolutionism, scientism, secular humanism and relativism, to cite a few.

Naturalism is a belief that truth is derived from nature and natural causes, not from revelation. Naturalism is a system of thought that rejects all spiritual and supernatural explanations of the world. It holds that science is the sole basis of what can be known.

Evolutionism is a biological term. It refers to the theory that all species develop from earlier forms of life.

Scientism is the use of the scientific method of acquiring knowledge. It applies to traditional sciences or other fields of inquiry, such as philosophy, psychology, sociology etc.

Scientism is the belief that science alone can explain phenomena. It is the application of scientific methods to fields unsuitable for it, such as the Bible. The attitude that predominates in much of science at present is arrogance. This has fostered dogmatism and scientism.

Secular humanism is a system of thought that is based on the values that are believed to be best in human beings. It rejects any supernatural authority. It believes in a human-based morality. This secular, cultural and intellectual movement of the Renaissance spread throughout Europe initially and then to other parts of the world, particularly America. It is a worldview that stresses human values without reference to religion or spirituality. It is a philosophy that is growing in popularity. Secular humanism is a conviction that dogmas, ideologies and traditions must be evaluated by each individual. It holds that all religious, political or social ideas must be tested, not simply accepted on faith. It is a philosophy that is committed to the use of critical reason. It is committed to factual evidence, and scientific methods of inquiry. It rejects faith in seeking solutions to human problems and answers to important human questions.

Relativism is the belief that concepts such as right and wrong, goodness and badness, or truth and falsehood are not absolute. It suggests that these change from culture to culture and situation to situation. Such pre-understandings and presuppositions are inconsistent with Scripture and from a Christian point of view; such assumptions are subject to correction by Scripture.

That is why Christians must participate in the debate, especially during official consultation processes in political constituencies where such processes are offered. Christians need to make submissions to this process because atheism is becoming more aggressive and organised and secularism is becoming more militant and coherent.

Preliminary Concerns

Before any change in the legal status of euthanasia or assisted suicide is considered, the following concerns should be addressed.

First, adequate palliative-care services must be made available. The provision of palliative care for all who are in need ought to be a mandatory precondition to the contemplation of permissive legislative change. Patients because of concerns about the availability of palliative care should never choose euthanasia and assisted suicide. Efforts to broaden the availability of palliative care and enhance the quality of such care should be intensified.

Second, suicide-prevention programmes should be maintained and strengthened where necessary. Although attempted suicide is not illegal, it is often the result of temporary depression or unhappiness. Society rightly supports efforts to prevent suicide, and physicians are expected to provide life-support measures to people who have attempted suicide. In any debate about providing assistance in suicide to relieve the suffering of persons with incurable diseases, the interests of those at risk of attempting suicide for other reasons must be safeguarded.

Third, studies of medical decision-making during dying should be undertaken. Relatively little is known about the frequency of various medical decisions made near the end of life, how these decisions are made and the satisfaction of patients, families, physicians and other caregivers with the decision-making process and outcomes. Physicians are involved in making decisions concerning whether to withhold or withdraw treatment and whether to administer sedatives and analgesics in doses that may shorten life. It is alleged that some physicians are providing euthanasia or assistance in suicide in constituencies where it is illegal. Hence, a study of medical decision-making during dying is needed to evaluate the current state of practice. This evaluation would help determine the possible need for change and identify what those changes should be. If physicians participating in such a study were offered immunity from prosecution based on information collected, as was done during the Remmelink commission in the Netherlands, the study could substantiate or refute the repeated allegations that euthanasia and assisted suicide take place.

Fourth, the public should be given adequate opportunity to comment on any proposed change in legislation. Consideration should be given to whether any proposed legislation can effectively restrict euthanasia and assisted suicide to the intended guidelines. If euthanasia or assisted suicide or both are permitted for competent, suffering, terminally ill patients, there may be legal challenges to extend these practices to others who are not competent, suffering or terminally ill. Such extension is the "slippery slope" that many fear. Courts may be asked to hear cases involving euthanasia for incompetent patients on the basis of advance directives or requests from proxy decision makers. Such cases could involve neurologically impaired patients or new-borns with severe congenital abnormalities. Psychiatrists recognise the possibility that a rational, otherwise well person may request suicide. Such a person could petition the courts for physician-assisted suicide. There must be a way to consider these possibilities in advance, so that the law is determined by the wishes of society, as expressed through parliament, rather than by court decisions.

Physicians, the public and politicians must participate responsibly in any examination of the current legal prohibition of euthanasia, assisted suicide, and arrive at a solution that respects the sanctity of life.

Care at the End of Life

Care at the end of life is an important issue. Primary care physicians help patients and their families cope with the decisions and emotions surrounding the dying process. As medical doctors they are responsible for ensuring that end of life issues honour the dignity and autonomy of individual patients. Their education and training should encompass how to best provide compassionate and effective care at the end of life.

It is important for medical professionals to support patient self-determination as far as possible without acceding to requests for euthanasia and assisted suicide. If these practices are illegal, as they ought to be, then advance directives have no status in law and are, therefore, not binding. When a patient has no advance directive and is judged by the attending physician to lack decisional capacity on this issue, every effort should be made to identify an appropriate surrogate (in compliance with state law) to address issues of care at the end of life.

Not all available treatments are beneficial in the course of a particular patient's care. After obtaining informed consent doctors can withhold or withdraw any medical intervention that the physician and patient or appropriate surrogate feel imposes a greater burden than benefit, even if the unintended result of such non-intervention or withdrawal may hasten the patient's death.

There is nothing wrong with aggressive treatment toward relieving the pain, anxiety, depression, emotional isolation, and other physical symptoms that can accompany the dying process even if the unintended result of such treatment may hasten the patient's death. All of the resources available to the medical profession and the care team should be mobilised to provide comfort to dying patients, family members and friends.

But physician involvement in assisted suicide or active euthanasia of any person regardless of age must be resisted. Physicians are entrusted with the care of people who are vulnerable in terms of physical frailty and cognitive impairment. Their involvement in assisted suicide or active euthanasia would erode the trust vital to the doctor/patient relationship.

Addressing Ignorance and Fear

Society must support professional and public education, policy development and research which enhance the delivery of compassionate and effective care at the end of life. Policy about end of life issues should not be a matter left to the discretion of care facilities and its medical directors as this leads to subjectivity, arbitrariness and even abuse. They should be obliged to conform to standardised codes of ethics that have due regard for the sanctity of life.

Assisted suicide will undermine vital patient protections and the doctor-patient relationship. There are advanced pain control technologies and medications which provide excellent alternatives to suicide and doctors need to be taught how to provide quality end-of-life care, not abandoning terminally ill patients in their most critical time of need. It is strange that "dignity" has been equated with suicide. Hospice care offers dying with dignity, fulfilling the true meaning of compassion by coming alongside the sufferer. The loving care of friends and family can bring immeasurable value to the lives of terminally ill patients.

At greatest risk are the poor, elderly, disabled, disadvantaged and others without access to good medical care, for whom the "choice to die" could become the "duty to die." Society must not allow doctors to be killers as well as healers. Doctors who participate in euthanasia and assisted suicide by either prescribing or administering controlled substances such as barbiturates or morphine or who aid and abet such practices must be subject to criminal charges with mandatory custodial sentences for those found guilty. Furthermore physicians who knowingly break the law in this regard should have their licences to practice revoked for life. This should not be a matter for medical councils to decide. Rather it should be part of a sentencing policy of the judiciary. Whereas rigid regulation might be undesirable and unworkable general principles based on the sanctity of human life need to be enshrined in law and enforced without fear of favour. Activists for euthanasia and assisted suicide resent and resist government "interference" but it is the duty of government as legislators to protect life.

However, such laws need not necessarily be retroactive, so doctors who have assisted suicides would not be prosecuted for past actions. Physician-assisted suicide is antithetical to the role of the physician as healer. Doctors must be committed to providing the best possible end-of-life care and that should be part of a universal oath taken at the time one becomes qualified to practice medicine.

The Injured Young

It is deeply saddening that the social context of contemporary culture makes assisted suicide an attractive option in certain situations. Many young people who have had spinal cord injuries or medical conditions resulting in partial paralysis have been assisted to die by physicians. There are organisations devoted to the care of people with spinal cord issues, which offer counselling and practical support. People need to be helped overcome the trauma of such injuries and encouraged to live as productive a life as possible. Physician-assisted suicide and euthanasia in such cases often affirms the depressed patients distorted view of reality and confirms such a patient's opinion that the quality of life is such that his life is meaningless.

In general, most of the people who sustain spinal cord injuries are young men. They are most often at a point in their lives when their self-image is premised upon their physicality. In fact, many are injured during activities that might be considered expressions of that physicality. All too often, these young men have not had the educational background to prepare themselves for the life ahead of them, much less the life experience to cope with such a significant event. However, they can and do learn that their life continues to be worth living if they and their families are provided with the appropriate supports.

In the UK, for example, the National Spinal Cord Injury Association (NSCIA) provides information and support services in the critical period after a person sustains a spinal cord injury while they are still in the hospital receiving acute or rehabilitation services. They provide information about life with a spinal cord injury, operate a toll-free hotline for individuals and their families and friends and provide peer support and counselling services linking people with others in their communities who have gone through an injury and successfully adapted. These are some of the core services NSCIA provides for newly injured people. Their on-going membership network provides support and access to information, advocacy and other services.

No one should go through a life-changing event such as a spinal cord injury alone. No one should feel that life with such an injury is not worth living. No one should feel compelled to resort to assisted suicide as a solution. This choice is an indictment of the health care and social support systems in our communities and in our countries. Assisted suicide is not a tenable option. Depression can be treated. Pain can be controlled or minimised in most cases. Life continues to hold promise.

Treating Depression

Terminally ill patients request suicide when they feel life is no longer enjoyable, have lost autonomy, or believe their lives to be burdensome or without dignity. Such requests are rarely the result of unbearable and untreatable pain. And although these reported symptoms are similar to those expressed by depressed patients without an underlying terminal illness, no counselling or psychiatric assessment is mandated in legislative constituencies that permit euthanasia and assisted suicide.

Psychotherapy and psychopharmacology may provide great relief for any patient suffering from depression. Physicians routinely hospitalise depressed patients who are contemplating suicide — for the purpose of treating the depression and getting the patient to a healthier mental state to deal with life. Shouldn't it be required that a thorough psychiatric assessment be done for those struggling to come to terms with their own mortality?

Spiritually Naked

Patients who have been diagnosed with a terminal illness and given a prognosis of, say, six months to live might feel like opting for euthanasia or assisted suicide when they are readily available. However, such predictions are unreliable. Some desperately ill patients somehow survive against all odds and apparently, relatively well patients die shortly after a diagnosis. Although the prediction of six months to live is often required to receive hospice care, the result of miscalculation where a patient is discharged from the hospice is a more benign outcome than ingesting lethal drugs based on flawed forecasting.

In places where euthanasia and assisted suicide are legally permitted (ostensibly because it offers a compassionate option) it is in practice incredibly isolating because one is not required to have any family members or next of kin notified. A spouse or relative struggling with the knowledge of a loved one's diagnosis could be left further dealing with a suicide. Generally there is a lack of oversight which opens the door to abuse of the sick, elderly, poor and disabled, not to mention a myriad of other concerns if the drugs get into the wrong hands.

Legislation on euthanasia and assisted suicide often presents suicide as simply one option among many as patients navigate through the choices surrounding a terminal diagnosis. Most medical doctors realise that to enable a patient's suicide is to undermine the very foundation of medicine and change the way physicians and patients understand each other's roles.

The practice of medicine involves meeting patients at their most vulnerable times. They often feel stripped of their dignity and go to the doctor spiritually naked, scared, and sometimes alone. Doctors must recognise their trepidation, embarrassment and sadness, but acknowledge their humanity and value. Doctors deal with their bodily fluids, foul smells, physical wasting, raw anguish, and yet recognise the person, not just the condition. The doctor must try to offer some treatment or care that re-establishes their dignity — perhaps in an entirely new way. Palliative care, the branch of medicine that offers care to those with chronic or terminal illnesses, seeks to treat the whole person. It attempts to heal spiritual, mental and, where possible, physical processes that cause the patient suffering. Those within palliative care teams support the whole person and often guide them toward a peaceful end at the time of natural death.

Legitimate Concerns

Society is on the threshold of ushering in a new and corrupt culture of medicine — one in which the very underpinning of medicine to "do no harm" is compromised.

Voter referendums and legislative bills on assisted suicide law have failed in many places. Why? Partly because of the concern of a broad coalition of healthcare professionals, hospice workers, disability rights advocates, minority groups, pro-life advocates, and various moral and ethical leaders who have vigorously opposed the legalisation of assisted suicides in these political jurisdictions.

What are their concerns? They have been concerned about the inability to contain assisted suicide once it starts. They are concerned too about the financial inequalities in society, fair access to medical care by the disadvantaged, the chilling effect on palliative care, and by the public documentation, which proves the so-called "safeguards" of assisted suicide law, where such laws exist, are being disregarded.

In the USA, Oregon's social experiment is failing to influence other political jurisdictions. To use a medical analogy, in the United States assisted suicide remains a "local infection" confined to Oregon while its harmful effects are becoming more widely known. Perhaps the presence of assisted suicide in Oregon is providing an "immunologic response" which is keeping this harmful infection from spreading. Learning from the Oregon experience, leaders across the world are recognising that it is better to put efforts into promoting palliative and hospice care rather than to give doctors the legal right to directly and intentionally kill patients. We need to affirm the ethic that all human life has inherent value and that doctor-assisted suicide undermines trust in the patient-physician relationship. It alters the role of the physician in society, from the traditional one of healer to executioner. It endangers the value that society places on life, specifically for those who are most vulnerable.

Advice from the General

Regarding euthanasia, C. Everett Koop, M.D., the former Surgeon General of the United States says:

...we must be wary of those who are too willing to end the lives of the elderly and the ill. If we ever decide that a poor quality of life justifies ending that life, we have taken a step down a slippery slope that places all of us in danger. There is a difference between allowing nature to take its course and actively assisting death. The call for euthanasia surfaces in our society periodically, as it is doing now under the guise of "death with dignity" or assisted suicide. Euthanasia is a concept, it seems to me, that is in direct conflict with a religious and ethical tradition in which the human race is presented with "a blessing and a curse, life and death," and we are instructed '...therefore, to choose life." I believe 'euthanasia' lies outside the commonly held life-centered values of the West and cannot be allowed without incurring great social and personal tragedy.

This is not merely an intellectual conundrum. This issue involves actual human beings at risk...

While the terror of state-sponsored euthanasia may never grip America as it once did Germany, it is possible that the terror of the euthanasia ethic - tolerated by medicine and an indifferent public and practiced by a few physicians - may grip many invisible and vulnerable Americans. Over fifty years ago, German doctors and courts collaborated to identify millions of people who were labelled 'devoid of value'. Some Americans are labeled the same today: members of a racial or ethnic 'underclass', a sidewalk screamer...an illegal alien...a nursing home resident with Alzheimer's disease ... an abandoned migrant worker...or anyone too old or weak or poor to help himself or herself. For two millennia, the Hippocratic tradition has stood for the 'sanctity' of human life. We can alleviate the unbearable in life better than ever before. We can do that and not eliminate life itself. As I have said many times, medicine cannot be both our healer and our killer.[6]

It is misleading to refer to euthanasia as medical or physician aid in dying. Physicians, nurses, psychologists, social workers, therapists, spiritual care counsellors, pharmacists and others who work with the dying patient already offer aid in dying. When pain becomes an argument for ending life, it is the pain that must be killed, not the patient.

---

[6] C. Everett Koop, M.D. *KOOP: The Memoirs of America's Family Doctor*, Random House, 1991.

Qualified to Comment

I have decided to write about euthanasia and physician-assisted suicide out of a sense of deep concern about the situation in the Netherlands and the fact that the debate is underway in the UK. What qualifies me to write about this issue? I am not a medical doctor, I am not a legal professional and I am neither Dutch nor British.[7] But this issue is not just a medical, legal and exclusively Dutch or British issue. I am, however, a concerned European citizen. As an experienced Christian writer I have developed a keen interest in contemporary social issues. I have ministered to the dying and the bereaved in my *professional* experience as a pastor. In addition, my experience as a lecturer in Intercultural Studies and Practical Ministry at Tyndale Theological Seminary in Badhoevedorp, the Netherlands, has not only enhanced my research skills but has caused me to see the issue from a particular perspective, from within the Dutch landscape. But it is my *personal* experience of depression that impels me to comment.

In 2004, I attempted to commit suicide and very nearly succeeded. I had been suffering from depression related to particularly difficult circumstances in my life and my thinking became seriously distorted. Initially I began to think about death. Then I began to wish for it. Then I began to plan it and rehearse it in my mind and ultimately this morbid ideation led to action to end my life. It is because I know what it is to suffer psychologically and because I have stood on the precipice of despair and not only looked into it but leapt into it that I feel competent to comment. My heart yearns to reach out to those who think life is not worth living.

---

[7] I'm Irish.

I had written suicide notes to each of my three children and my wife and I was determined to die. Ten years on and I am so pleased that I failed in that ambition because I am living a happy and fulfilled life with a supportive and loving family.

Furthermore, other personal circumstances contribute to the shaping of certain presuppositions in my understanding. My belief in the sanctity of human life is rooted in my religious views but it is also a very personal matter. I come in the middle of a family of seven children. I have three brothers and three sisters. The eldest, Michael, was Down's syndrome and the second youngest, Margaret, also has Down's syndrome.[8] Michael died on 22 June 2014, aged 63 – the oldest person with Down's in the Republic of Ireland.

To say that life was not easy for my parents is an understatement. It was difficult too for all the siblings. I think the pain of parenting a Down's syndrome child is well captured in the song "Scorn Not His Simplicity" by Irish musician and songwriter, Phil Coulter.

Scorn Not His Simplicity

See the child
With the golden hair
Yet eyes that show the emptiness inside
Do we know
Can we understand just how he feels
Or have we really tried?

---

[8] Down's syndrome is a genetic abnormality caused by the inheritance of an extra copy of the chromosome 21 in the body. The condition is a major cause of genetic disability since the additional genetic material makes unnecessary changes to the body composition. The condition cannot be prevented, but it can be detected when a woman is pregnant.

See him now
As he stands alone
And watches children play at children's games
Simple child
He looks almost like the others
Yet they know he's not the same.

Scorn not his simplicity
But rather try to love him all the more
Scorn not his simplicity
Oh no
Oh no

See him stare
Not recognising that kind face
That only yesterday he loved
The loving face
Of a mother who can't understand what she's been guilty
of

How she cried tears of happiness
The day the doctor told her it's a boy
Now she cries tears of helplessness
And thinks of all the things he can't enjoy

Scorn not his simplicity
But rather try to love him all the more
Scorn not his simplicity
Oh no
Oh no

Only he knows how to face the future hopefully
Surrounded by despair
He won't ask for your pity or your sympathy
But surely you should care

Scorn not his simplicity
But rather try to love him all the more

Scorn not his simplicity
Oh no
Oh no
Oh no. [9]

When I was a teenager, I wondered if it would have been better for our family if Michael and Margaret had had not been born or if it would have been better if they were euthanized. I never spoke of this to my parents, siblings or anybody in my extended family. I did share it once with a friend who was very understanding. However, I never spoke of it again. I am not ashamed that I had such thoughts. They were part of a process of thinking through the issue. My thoughts at that stage of my teenage life never actually developed into what could be called a desire to see their lives terminated. Nevertheless, I suppose it could be a shock for family and friends to read about it now. However, I also suspect that they too harboured such secret contemplations and that our silence on the matter has been shrouded in guilt.

There is no doubt that our lives would have been easier without Michael and Margaret but I am convinced our lives would not have been better. It is not easy to convey the psychological impact that their condition had on my parents. I am in awe of them for their untiring devotion and uncomplaining spirits. Their characters were refined in the crucible of affliction. They loved well and their unselfish lives

---

[9] It is performed on his albums *Classic Tranquility* and *The Songs I Love So Well*. The song has also been performed by several Irish musicians, including Sinéad O'Connor on *Universal Mother*, Paddy Reilly and others but, in my opinion the definitive performance is by the late Luke Kelly of the Dubliners. Phil Coulter's eldest son was born with Down's syndrome. He first played the song to Luke Kelly. Because of the personal nature of the song, Luke Kelly felt it should not be sung except for special occasions, and not on every performance. It appears on The Dubliners 1970 *Revolution* album.

bore testimony to the nobility of their broken hearts. They are deceased now but they went to their graves knowing that two of their children would need on-going support, care and love.

In one sense, Michael and Margaret were an affliction but in another way they were a blessing. Their existence brought much sorrow and suffering. All members of the family were wounded and we all bear the psychological scars. However, their existence also brought great joy and laughter to us as a family. My older sister Betty cared for Michael for over 16 years after the death of my parents. During this time, she also cared for Margaret, developed breast-cancer and had a double mastectomy. To add to the suffering of that household Betty's husband, John became gravely ill and spent about 18 months in hospital, frequently in intensive care. My admiration for Betty's unselfish devotion to the care of our brother and sister cannot be adequately expressed in words. She deserves to be honoured.

My extended family, particularly my mother's sister, Theresa, and her family were very supportive.[10] The community was also supportive. I am not saying that all suffering is ennobling. Some suffering is degrading. But I am saying that Michael and Margaret have enriched my life and the lives of many others. I could tell many stories about how Michael, in particular, made us laugh.

I sympathise and empathise with those whose lives are impacted by debilitating circumstances. However, I fear that the introduction of euthanasia will be applied involuntarily to

---

[10] Particularly the O' Halloran family - and notably Terry O' Halloran - deserves special mention for their love and support for Michael. Inspired by her strong faith Terry served Betty as a crucial support in the most practical ways. I admire her immensely and thank her for all she did.

babies with Down's syndrome and perhaps even to older people with Down's syndrome. I do not think my fears are unreasonable. As the condition can be detected when a woman is pregnant, many women decide to abort their babies if they have Down's syndrome. I think it is a relatively short step from that to euthanizing babies.

CHAPTER 1 "You shall not Kill"

What relevance, if any, does the sixth Commandment have in the twenty-first century? Following the death of Tony Nicklinson (in August 2012), who was suffering from "locked-in syndrome", the relevance of the sixth commandment is coming under scrutiny. In spite of his terrible illness he led a campaign (assisted by his family, friends and the media, especially Channel 4 News) to have the UK law changed in order to allow a medical doctor to assist him to die. In a written statement to judges of the High Court he described his life as "miserable, demeaning and intolerable." Mr Nicklinson communicated by blinking at an alphabet board and was fed by tube and completely unable to move, while his mental faculties remained intact. Although it is a very sad case, it must be said that Mr Nicklinson could have travelled to Switzerland at any time to fulfil his wish. However, his agenda was not simply to be allowed to die but to have the law changed to accommodate euthanasia in the UK.

It is important to apply the principles of the commandment to particular cases, as this sort of issue is likely to become increasingly pertinent in the near future. Thus, it would be helpful to explore the relevance of this commandment in contemporary culture, particularly as it relates to euthanasia and assisted suicide.[11]

---

[11] This chapter, taken together with the "Appendix A" offers a more comprehensive analysis of the sixth commandment. Here we are dealing

Respect for the sanctity of life is enshrined in this commandment. Some versions of the Bible say, "you shall not kill" but *murder* conveys the true meaning better than *kill*. This commandment is not a ban on all killing but it does, clearly, disallow homicide. People were allowed to kill animals for food and for sacrifice and the death penalty was not merely commended - it was commanded. Thus Exodus states:

Exodus 21:12-14

[12] "Whoever strikes a man so that he dies shall be put to death. [13] But if he did not lie in wait for him, but God let him fall into his hand, then I will appoint for you a place to which he may flee. [14] But if a man willfully attacks another to kill him by cunning, you shall take him from my altar, that he may die.

The taking of a person's life is a very serious matter. These verses reveal that different punishments were administered to those who took a human life and this depended on the circumstances. Violent action, which resulted in a person's death, was deemed to be different to premeditated murder and this was reflected in the respective penalties imposed.

Euthanasia is a euphemism for murder. Many people in the world: cultured, educated people do not know what a human being is. Many say we are related to animals and that we have evolved from a lower species of animal. These people are not fully (spiritually) aware of what it is to be human. As this commandment is examined, the first question to be asked is "What is it that is distinctive about a human

---

only with the commandment inasmuch as it pertains to the relevant issues (euthanasia and assisted suicide) under discussion.

being?" The answer is that people have been made in the image of God. People have souls:

Then God said, "Let us make man in our image, after our likeness. And let them have dominion over the fish of the sea and over the birds of the heavens and over the livestock and over all the earth and over every creeping thing that creeps on the earth." So God created man in his own image, in the image of God he created him; male and female he created them. And God blessed them. And God said to them, "Be fruitful and multiply and fill the earth and subdue it and have dominion over the fish of the sea and over the birds of the heavens and over every living thing that moves on the earth."—Genesis 1:26-28.

This is not written of any of the other animals that were brought into existence. This is the distinctive feature of mankind. That was said before the fall of man recorded in Genesis 3. When we come to the other side of the Fall and the Flood we see God entering into covenant with man and laying down certain stipulations, "Whoever sheds the blood of man, by man shall his blood be shed, for God made man in his own image." (Genesis 9:6). Here we are given the reason why we are not to murder. When a person murders somebody they strike at the very image of God. Some animal rights activists will put human life at risk to protect animals but this is unbiblical, however legitimate they think their cause may be. All life belongs to God and is important to God but humanity is God's special creation. He is the giver of life and he has the right to take it. That prerogative belongs to him alone.

This commandment reinforces the distinctiveness of mankind and the value of human life. Society seems to be obsessed with murder and this is reflected in the fact that it is a major theme in many films, such as psychological thrillers, true crime stories, detective programmes and T.V. series. It is the most popular genre of fiction. It is a moot point as to whether this desensitises people to the notion of homicide. But in reality murder is prohibited because it is abhorrent to God. We live in a wicked world where murder is all too common. This commandment speaks covers issues such as: abortion, euthanasia, mercy killing and suicide.[12]

Suicide

The word "suicide" comes the Latin *suicidium* (from *sui caedere*, to kill oneself). Suicide was, in the recent past, a criminal offence and even though it has been decriminalised some people still consider it to be a selfish and dishonourable act.[13] However, most people today are aware that suicide is a mental health issue. It is associated with psychological factors such as difficulty coping with loneliness, depression, shame, pain, stress, or other undesirable situations. A person's perspective becomes distorted and when that person sees no other way out they might opt for suicide. Such people need help and hope.

Usually suicide leaves others who are intimately affected by the death; either as a spouse, parent, significant other, sibling, or child of the deceased person. The suicide of a child, for example, may leave not only his/her immediate family to

---

[12] See "Appendix" for more comprehensive treatment of the commandment as it pertains to contemporary culture.

[13] Incidentally it is worthy of note that when certain actions are decriminalised they tend to become legitimised and seen as a human right. The decriminalisation of homosexuality ultimately leads to same-sex marriage and the decriminalisation of suicide leads ultimately to demands for the right to terminate one's own life. This is not a homophobic statement. I am not advocating a return to the criminalisation of these things but merely observing where the process begins and ends.

make sense of the act, but also his/her extended family, school community and, indeed, the entire community, struggling to comprehend what has happened.

As is true with any death, family and friends of a suicide victim feel grief associated with loss. However, suicide deaths leave behind a unique set of issues for the survivors. They are often overwhelmed with psychological trauma and feel guilty and confused. It can be especially difficult for survivors because many of their questions as to the victim's final decision are left unanswered, even if a suicide note is left behind. Moreover, survivors often feel that they should have intervened in some way to prevent the suicide, even if the suicide comes as a surprise and there are no obvious warning signs.

Suicide is generally an act of despair and people with suicidal thoughts need sympathy and support. Suicide could be described as self–murder and as such it is a violation of this commandment. However, the person who commits suicide is often severely depressed or distressed. In that condition their judgement is impaired and the bereaved family and friends need comfort and pastoral care. Is suicide a sin? Yes. People need to be told that it is morally wrong. That standard needs to be upheld. However, this is not something that should be stressed with grieving survivors. They need kindness and Christian compassion at such a tragic time. May God help us to minister to those who are affected by such a terrible event!

Assisted Suicide

Regarding "assisted suicide," the current legal position in Britain is that such activity is illegal. The law states: "A person who aids, abets, counsels or procures the suicide of another, or an attempt by another to commit suicide, shall be liable on conviction on indictment to imprisonment for a term not exceeding fourteen years."[14]

This law is applicable when a substantial part of the aiding, abetting, procuring or counselling of the suicide occurs in England or Wales. The suicide itself can be committed in any country.

However, this may soon be altered. The Director of Public Prosecutions (DPP) in Britain announced that relatives of people who kill themselves will not face prosecution as long as they act out of compassion and assist only a clear wish to commit suicide.[15] This means that relatives of people who kill themselves will not face prosecution as long as they do not maliciously encourage them and assist only a "clear, settled and informed wish" to die. He outlined guidance to make it easier for those helping someone end their life to know if they might be open to prosecution. The D.P.P. said:

> There are no guarantees against prosecution and it is my job to ensure that the most vulnerable people are protected while at the same time giving enough information to those people like Mrs Purdy who want to be able to make informed decisions about what actions they may choose to take. Assisting suicide has been a criminal offence for nearly 50 years and my interim policy does nothing to change that. There is no immunity from prosecution in these guidelines. We've simply listed the factors that are relevant in a decision whether to prosecute and whether not to prosecute. What is important is to ensure that those who fluctuate in and out of depression or fluctuate in their view

---

[14] Section 2 (1) Suicide Act 1961.

[15] Reported on *Channel 4 News*, 23 September, 2009.

about suicide are properly protected. It has to be a clear and settled wish over a period of time and that's what we'll be looking for in the evidence. The policy is intended to be clear. It's in plain English. If people want further advice they should seek that advice from a lawyer or somebody else who can assist.[16]

The law lords, Britain's highest court, asked the D.P.P. to clarify the guidelines surrounding assisted suicide following the case of an individual with multiple sclerosis. This lady asked for clarification on whether or not her husband would face prosecution if he helped her to travel to a clinic in Switzerland to take her own life. The law lords unanimously ruled that this woman had the right to argue that the rules on assisted suicide were unclear.

Launching his interim policy on prosecuting cases of assisted suicide the D.P.P. called for public participation in a public consultation process on the factors he has identified which will be taken into account when considering whether prosecutions will be brought for this offence.

The public interest factors *in favour of prosecution* identified in the interim policy are as follows:

1. The victim was under 18 years of age.

2. The victim's capacity to reach an informed decision was adversely affected by a recognised mental illness or learning difficulty.

3. The victim did not have a clear, settled and informed wish to commit suicide; for example, the victim's history suggests that his or her wish to commit suicide was temporary or subject to change.

---

[16] *Channel 4 News*, 23 September, 2009.

4. The victim did not indicate unequivocally to the suspect that he or she wished to commit suicide.

5. The victim did not ask personally on his or her own initiative for the assistance of the suspect.

6. The victim did not have a terminal illness; or a severe and incurable physical disability; or a severe degenerative physical condition from which there was no possibility of recovery.

7. The suspect was not wholly motivated by compassion; for example, the suspect was motivated by the prospect that they or a person closely connected to them stood to gain in some way from the death of the victim.

8. The suspect persuaded, pressured or maliciously encouraged the victim to commit suicide, or exercised improper influence in the victim's decision to do so and did not take reasonable steps to ensure that any other person did not do so.

The public interest factors *against a prosecution* include that:

1. The victim had a clear, settled and informed wish to commit suicide.

2. The victim indicated unequivocally to the suspect that he or she wished to commit suicide.

3. The victim asked personally on his or her own initiative for the assistance of the suspect.

4. The victim had a terminal illness, a severe and incurable physical disability, or a severe degenerative physical condition from which there was no possibility of recovery.

5. The suspect was wholly motivated by compassion.

6. The suspect was the spouse, partner or a close relative or a close personal friend of the victim, within the context of a long-term and supportive relationship.

7. The actions of the suspect, although sufficient to come within the definition of the offence, were of only minor assistance or influence, or the assistance which the suspect provided was as a consequence of their usual lawful employment.

These guidelines effectively indicate terms and conditions for the possible introduction of legalisation on assisted suicide. The current legal position is that the taking of life by another person is murder or manslaughter. These are among the most serious criminal offences and it seems inappropriate to launch a public consultation process about such a matter with a predetermined direction already having a definite pro-assisted suicide thrust. Should policy (legal or moral) be governed or even guided by considering as many views as possible or should it be determined by the revealed mind of God? Obviously, in a democracy people ought to be consulted but for the believer God's Word must be the final arbiter.

It is clear that this new code is a departure from the existing law, in spite of soundings to the contrary from the D.P.P. It sets out a substantial number of factors both for and against prosecution in all types of cases. It assumes that people, under certain circumstances, have the right to assist others in taking their own lives. This is where there is a clear departure from the existing law and more importantly a clear departure from the absolute moral position of God's law. Public opinion can be variable from time to time and culture to culture. This will inevitably go the same route as abortion legislation.

Abortion was initially permitted in limited and clearly defined circumstances, primarily for therapeutic reasons such as a necessary life-saving intervention for the mother. But ultimately it led to abortion on demand. The interim policy on assisted suicide paves the way for euthanasia by conceding the principled position, "you shall not kill."

One must question what is actually in the public interest here. There is a difference between what the public is interested in and what is in the public interest. But this distinction is not often made. There is historical precedent (as in the case of abortion cited above) which suggests that such departures from absolute positions to relative positions act as a catalyst for further change and ushers in a new order.

Assisted suicide, though presented as an act of compassion, is actually a violation of the sanctity of life. Ultimately, it will contribute to a depreciation of human life. It certainly goes a long way toward bridging the gap between suicide and euthanasia and to deny this is either disingenuous or naïve. These guidelines not only indicate current thinking on this issue but they also move toward the legitimisation of assisted suicide. Is it inevitable that existing legislation will be amended to accommodate assisted suicide?

The dilemma about assisted suicide emerges partly from the medical ability to sustain life beyond the point where, in the past, patients would have been allowed to die. We all want our loved ones to die with dignity and we all hope for a good death ourselves. Certainly, there are times when a patient's life should not be prolonged by unnatural interventions. This is a complex and emotive issue often exacerbated by authoritarian regimes in medical institutions. People feel that they should have autonomy and in certain instances this is appropriate. If a person is diagnosed with terminal cancer they should have the right to refuse treatments which may prolong the duration of life but adversely affect the quality of that life. It is not wrong to want to avoid spending your last few months of life in a hospital bed on chemo or radiation therapy but that is not the same as asking somebody to assist you to take your own life.

Euthanasia

Medical professionals face many difficult ethical issues. One of the issues facing them, and society in general, is that of euthanasia. Some people (usually atheistic) argue that laws should accommodate "mercy killing". They contend that, in certain circumstances, the bringing about of a gentle death in the case of incurable and painful disease is a humane and appropriate response.

This is an emotive issue. None of us want to witness our loved ones suffer. We feel helpless and we suffer (emotionally) in their pain. When that person has a terminal illness and there is loss of mobility, dignity and consciousness we may think a simple injection which brings an end to their life is the solution. But this is very dangerous thinking and raises many ethical and legal issues including the consent of the patient and the role of the doctor. Medical professionals still exercise their judgement about whether or not a person, in certain circumstances, should be resuscitated.

It was revealed in a newspaper article that "46% of elderly patients who had the words "do not resuscitate" on their charts were not consulted and in most cases these fateful words were written by relatively inexperienced junior doctors."[17]

If the patient has given prior consent to have his life terminated there are still moral and social issues to be addressed. If euthanasia is legalised or accommodated by not prosecuting relatives, friends and medical professionals who assist in this process there will be undesirable (and perhaps, unforeseen) outcomes. For example, some patients may feel pressurised to relieve their families or the state of the burden (emotional and financial) of keeping them alive.

There are many pragmatic arguments against euthanasia, such as the fact that pain can now be effectively managed and medicated so that physical suffering is virtually eliminated and improvements in this regard are being made all the time. It may be perfectly legitimate in certain circumstances to allow somebody to die. It is acceptable in certain circumstances not to attempt resuscitation. But there is a difference between that and killing people. It is the principled argument against it that is the most compelling. The sanctity of life must be protected.

In a society where economics is the paramount consideration there is a danger that ultimately even clinical decisions will be primarily determined by financial management policies and professionals. The elderly, the chronically sick and the intellectually and physically disabled would become vulnerable. It is easy to say that these groups could be protected in law but laws change ultimately by the will of the people. As already stated there was a time when abortion on demand would never have been contemplated

---

[17] Kate Holmquist, The Irish Times, 19 September, 2009. I am not sure that doctors write these actual words, perhaps an abbreviated form is "DNR"?

by society but now it is for many a form of post-sex contraception.

Abortion

When considering the issues of euthanasia and assisted suicide it is important to bear in mind that the 1966 UK Abortion Act allowed for abortion in limited circumstances, such as medical reasons. It envisaged that therapeutic abortion would really be a result or side effect of the medical treatment of the mother. However, people have driven a coach and two horses through that piece of legislation and now abortion on demand is the reality and the norm, whatever the small print might say.[18] Only a tiny proportion of the abortions performed are for legitimate "medical" reasons. The vast majority are for social reasons and come into the category of late birth control.

Media Bias

The media, in particular *Channel 4 News*, has an agenda that it has been driving forward for several years. It would be naïve to suppose that this news channel merely reports news. It pursues issues, some very positive, such as the rights of the disabled, notably championing the Paralympics. Nevertheless, in spite of the fact that it gives the appearance of impartiality (by hosting people with opposing/conservative views) it has a liberal bias. Often the questions posed to those on the liberal side, such as the author Brian Jacques (who has Alzheimer's

---

[18] I am not suggesting that women don't experience emotional trauma in coming to a decision to terminate a pregnancy. I acknowledge that in cases of rape and incest many women have agonised about such a choice. I believe that where there are medical complications in a pregnancy, which would threaten the health and life of the mother, abortion can be morally justified.

disease and wants to be allowed to terminate his own life rather than enter an advanced stage of dementia) are supportive whereas the questions posed to the other side are hostile. Generally, it is thought that intellectualism and liberalism are compatible whereas conservative views are deemed unintelligent, injudicious, ridiculous and laughable.

Some of the people selected for interview on religious matters (such as atheism) have been powerful on the liberal side and weak on the conservative side. It is likely that this is intentional. In some debates with Richard Dawkins, his opponents have been fuddy-duddies who actually agree with much of what he says. Why not invite some formidable figure to present the religious view?

In the heart-breaking case of Tony Nicklinson (following his death) they interviewed his wife and in conclusion said that she was hoping that somebody in a similar situation to her late husband would come forward to champion the cause for which he fought. She is being exploited in a wider cause and is merely a puppet. The puppeteers will continue pulling the strings leading society in a dance beyond the boundaries of morality.

CHAPTER 2 Background to Euthanasia in the Netherlands

Right-to-die advocates often point to Holland as the model for how well physician-assisted, voluntary euthanasia for terminally-ill, competent patients can work without abuse. However, the facts indicate otherwise. Dutch Penal Code Articles 293 and 294 made both euthanasia and assisted suicide illegal. However, as the result of various court cases, doctors who directly killed patients or helped patients kill themselves were not prosecuted as long as they followed certain guidelines. Physicians were expected to report every euthanasia/assisted-suicide death to the local prosecutor and there was a tacit understanding that the patient's death request should be enduring. That means that a death request ought to be carefully considered and requested on more than one occasion by the patient. Then the Rotterdam court in 1981 established the following guidelines for euthanasia:

1. The patient must be experiencing unbearable pain.

2. The patient must be conscious.

3. The death request must be voluntary.

4. The patient must have been given alternatives to euthanasia and time to consider these alternatives.

5. There must be no other reasonable solutions to the problem.

6. The patient's death cannot inflict unnecessary suffering on others.

7. There must be more than one person involved in the euthanasia decision.

8. Only a doctor can euthanize a patient.

9. Great care must be taken in actually making the death decision.[19]

Since 1981, the Dutch courts and Royal Dutch Medical Association (KNMG) have interpreted these guidelines in ever-broadening terms. One example is the interpretation of the "unbearable pain" requirement reflected in the Hague Court of Appeal's 1986 decision. The court ruled that the pain guideline was not limited to physical pain, and that "psychic suffering" or "the potential disfigurement of personality" could also be grounds for euthanasia.[20]

The main argument in favour of euthanasia in Holland has always been the need for more patient autonomy — that patients have the right to make their own end-of-life decisions. Yet, over the past twenty years, Dutch euthanasia practice has ultimately given doctors, not patients, more and more power. The question of whether a patient should live or die is often decided exclusively by a doctor or a team of physicians.[21]

The Dutch define euthanasia in a very limited way: "Euthanasia is understood as an action which aims at taking the life of another at the latter's expressed request. It concerns

---

[19] Carlos Gomez, *Regulating Death*, New York: Free Press, 1991, p.32.

[20] Ibid, p.39.

[21] H. Jochemsen, trans., "Report of the Royal Dutch Society of Medicine on 'Life-Terminating Actions with Incompetent Patients, Part 1: Severely Handicapped Newborns,'" *Issues in Law & Medicine*, vol. 7, no.3, 1991, p. 366.

an action of which death is the purpose and the result."[22] This definition applies only to voluntary euthanasia and excludes what the rest of the world refers to as non-voluntary or involuntary euthanasia, the killing of a patient without the patient's knowledge or consent. The Dutch call this "life-terminating treatment."

Some physicians use this distinction between "euthanasia" and "life-terminating treatment" to avoid having a patient's death classified as "euthanasia" thus freeing doctors from following the established euthanasia guidelines and reporting the death to local authorities. One such example was discussed during the December 1990 Institute for Bioethics conference in Maastricht, Holland. A physician from The Netherlands Cancer Institute told of approximately thirty cases a year where doctors ended patients' lives after the patients intentionally had been put into a coma by means of a morphine injection. The Cancer Institute physician then stated that these deaths were not considered "euthanasia" because they were not voluntary, and that to have discussed the plan to end these patients' lives with the patients would have been "rude" since they all knew they had incurable conditions.[23]

The Remmelink Report

On September 10, 1991, the results of the first official government study of the practice of Dutch euthanasia were released.[24] The two-volume report (popularly referred to as

---

[22] From KNMG Euthanasia Guidelines as quoted in *Regulating Death*, p. 40.

[23] Alexander Morgan Capron, "Euthanasia in the Netherlands: American Observations," *Hastings Center Report*, March, April 1992, p. 31.

[24] *Medical Decisions about the End of Life, I. Report of the Committee to Study the Medical Practice Concerning Euthanasia, II. The Study for the*

the Remmelink Report) documents the prevalence of involuntary euthanasia in Holland as well as the fact that, to a large degree, doctors have taken over end-of-life decision-making regarding euthanasia.[25] The data indicates that, despite long-standing, court-approved euthanasia guidelines developed to protect patients, abuse has become an accepted norm. According to the Remmelink Report, in 1990, 2,300 people died as the result of doctors killing them upon request (active, voluntary euthanasia).[26] 400 people died as a result of doctors providing them with the means to kill themselves (physician-assisted suicide).[27] 1,040 people (an average of 3 per day) died from involuntary euthanasia, meaning that doctors actively killed these patients without the patients' knowledge or consent.[28] 14% of these patients were fully competent.[29] 72% had never given any indication that they would want their lives terminated.[30] In 8% of the cases, doctors performed involuntary euthanasia despite the fact that they believed alternative options was still possible.[31] In addition, 8,100 patients died as a result of doctors deliberately giving them overdoses of pain medication, not for the primary purpose of controlling pain, but to hasten the patient's death.[32] In 61% of these cases (4,941 patients), the

---

Committee on Medical Practice Concerning Euthanasia (2 vols.), The Hague, (September 19, 1991). Hereafter cited as Report I and Report II, respectively.

[25] After Professor J. Remmelink, M.J., attorney general of the High Council of the Netherlands, who headed the study committee.

[26] Report I, p. 13.

[27] Ibid.

[28] Op. cit., p. 15.

[29] Report II, p.49, table 6.4.

[30] Op. cit., p.50, table 6.6.

[31] Ibid, table 6.5.

[32] Op. cit., p. 58, table 7.2.

intentional overdose was given without the patient's consent.[33]

According to the Remmelink Report, Dutch physicians deliberately and intentionally ended the lives of 11,840 people by lethal overdoses or injections–a figure which accounts for 9.1% of the annual overall death rate of 130,000 per year. The majority of all euthanasia deaths in Holland are involuntary deaths.

The Remmelink Report figures cited here do not include thousands of other cases, also reported in the study, in which life-sustaining treatment was withheld or withdrawn without the patient's consent and with the intention of causing the patient's death.[34] Nor do the figures include cases of involuntary euthanasia performed on disabled new-borns, children with life-threatening conditions, or psychiatric patients.[35]

The most frequently cited reasons given for ending the lives of patients without their knowledge or consent were: "low quality of life"; "no prospect for improvement"; and "the family couldn't take it anymore".[36] In 45% of cases involving hospitalised patients who were involuntarily euthanized the patients' families had no knowledge that doctors deliberately terminated their loved ones' lives.[37]

According to the 1990 census, the population of Holland was approximately 15 million. That is only a quarter of the population of the UK and half the population of California. To get some idea of how the Remmelink Report statistics would apply to the USA, those figures would have to be

---

[33] Ibid.
[34] Ibid.
[35] Report I, pp. 17-18.
[36] Report II, p. 52, table 6.7.
[37] Ibid, table 6.8.

multiplied 16.6 times (based on the 1990 USA census population of approximately 250 million).

Falsified Death Certificates

In the overwhelming majority of Dutch euthanasia cases, doctors–in order to avoid additional paperwork and scrutiny from local authorities–deliberately falsify patients' death certificates, stating that the deaths occurred from natural causes.[38] In reference to Dutch euthanasia guidelines and the requirement that physicians report all euthanasia and assisted-suicide deaths to local prosecutors, a government health inspector told the *New York Times*, "In the end the system depends on the integrity of the physician, of what and how he reports. If the family doctor does not report a case of voluntary euthanasia or an assisted suicide, there is nothing to control."[39]

Inadequate Pain Control and Comfort Care

In 1988, the British Medical Association released the findings of a study on Dutch euthanasia conducted at the request of British right-to-die advocates. The study found that, in spite of the fact that medical care is provided to everyone in Holland, palliative care (comfort care) programmes, with adequate pain control techniques and knowledge, were poorly developed.[40] Where euthanasia is an accepted medical solution to patients' pain and suffering,

---

[38] I. J. Keown, "The Law and Practice of Euthanasia in the Netherlands," *The Law Quarterly Review*, January 1992, pp. 67-68.

[39] Marlise Simons, "Dutch Move to Enact Law Making Euthanasia Easier," *New York Times*, 9 February, 1993, p.A1.

[40] *Euthanasia: Report of the Working Party to Review the British Medical Association's Guidance on Euthanasia*, British Medical Association, May 5, 1988, no. 195, p. 49.

there is little incentive to develop programmes which provide modern, available, and effective pain control for patients. As of mid-1990, only two hospice programmes were in operation in all of Holland, and the services they provided were very limited.[41]

Broadening Interpretations of Euthanasia Guidelines

In July 1992, the Dutch Paediatric Association announced that it was issuing formal guidelines for killing severely handicapped new-borns. Doctor Zier Versluys, chairman of the association's Working Group on Neonatal Ethics, said that "Both for the parents and the children, an early death is better than life."[42] Doctor Versluys also indicated that euthanasia is an integral part of good medical practice in relation to newborn babies. Doctors would judge if a baby's "quality of life" is such that the baby should be killed.

A statement released by the Dutch Justice Ministry (15th February 1993) proposed extending the court-approved, euthanasia guidelines to formally include "active medical intervention to cut short life without an express request." Liesbeth Rensman, a spokesperson for the Ministry, said that this would be the first step toward the official sanctioning of euthanasia for those who cannot ask for it, particularly psychiatric patients and handicapped new-borns.[43]

---

[41] Rita L. Marker, *Deadly Compassion: The Death of Ann Humphry and the Truth About Euthanasia*, New York; William Morrow and Company, 1993, p. 157.

[42] Abner Katzman, "Dutch debate mercy killing of babies," *Contra Costa Times*, 30 July 1992, p. 3B.

[43] "Critics fear euthanasia soon needn't be requested," *Vancouver Sun*, 17 February, 1993, p. A.l0. Also, "Dutch may broaden rules to permit involuntary euthanasia," *Contra Costa Times*, 17 February, 1993. p. 4B.

A landmark Dutch court decision (21st April 1993) affirmed euthanasia for psychiatric reasons. The court found that psychiatrist Dr Boudewijn Chabot was medically justified and followed established euthanasia guidelines in helping his physically healthy, but depressed, patient commit suicide. The patient, 50-year-old Hilly Bosscher, said she wanted to die after the deaths of her two children and the subsequent breakup of her marriage.[44] It is not surprising that this woman wanted to die. It seems like a natural reaction to such awful tragedy in her life. But such a distressed woman should have been helped to live.

Policy and Practice

The effects of euthanasia policy and practice have been felt in all segments of Dutch society. Some Dutch doctors provide "self-help programmes" for adolescents to end their lives.[45] General practitioners wishing to admit elderly patients to hospitals have sometimes been advised to give the patients lethal injections instead.[46] Cost containment is one of the main aims of Dutch health care policy.[47] Euthanasia training has been part of both medical and nursing school curricula.[48] Euthanasia has been administered to people with diabetes,

---

[44] *New York Times*, 5 April, 1993, p.A3, and *Washington Times*, 22 April, 1993, p.A2.

[45] "It's Almost Over — More Letters on Debbie," Letter to the editor by G.B. Humphrey, M.D., Ph.D., University Hospital, Groningen, the Netherlands, *Journal of the American Medical Association*, vol. 260, no. 6, 12 August 1988, p. 788.

[46] "Involuntary Euthanasia in Holland", *Wall Street Journal*, 29 September, 1987, p.3.

[47] "Restructuring Health Care", *The Lancet*, 28 January, 1989, p.209.

[48] "The Member's Aid Service of the Dutch Association for Voluntary Euthanasia," *Euthanasia Review*, vol. 1, no. 3, Fall 1986, p.153.

rheumatism, multiple sclerosis, AIDS, bronchitis, and accident victims.[49]

In 1990, the Dutch Patients' Association, a disability rights organisation, developed wallet-size cards which state that if the signer is admitted to a hospital "no treatment be administered with the intention to terminate life." Many in Holland see the card as a necessity to help prevent involuntary euthanasia being performed on those who do not want their lives ended, especially those whose lives are considered low in quality.[50]

In 1993, the Dutch senior citizens' group, the Protestant Christian Elderly Society, surveyed 2,066 seniors on general health care issues. The Survey did not specifically address the euthanasia issue in any way, yet 10% of the elderly respondents clearly indicated that, because of the Dutch euthanasia policy, they were afraid that their lives could be terminated without their request. According to the Elderly Society director, Hans Homans, "They are afraid that at a certain moment, on the basis of age, a treatment will be considered no longer economically viable, and an early end to their lives will be made."[51]

The Irony of History

During World War II, Holland was the only occupied country whose doctors refused to participate in the German euthanasia programme. Dutch physicians openly defied an order to treat only those patients who had a good chance of full recovery. They recognised that to comply with the order would have been the first step away from their duty to care

---

[49] "Suicide on Prescription," *Sunday Observer*, 30 April, 1989, p. 22.
[50] Rita L. Marker, *Deadly Compassion*, p. 156.
[51] "Elderly Dutch afraid of euthanasia policy," *Canberra Times* (Australia), 11 June, 1993.

for all patients. The German officer who gave that order was later executed for war crimes. Remarkably, during the entire German occupation of Holland, Dutch doctors never recommended or participated in one euthanasia death.[52] Commenting on this fact in his essay "The Humane Holocaust," highly respected British journalist Malcolm Muggeridge wrote that it took only a few decades "to transform a war crime into an act of compassion."[53] Misguided mercy that often exists in a moral vacuum is at the core of this issue and one wonders if "handiphobia" (i.e. negative views about handicapped people) is a cause of euthanasia.

With regard to misguided mercy John Piper has written of "The Failure of Christless Tenderness" and it seems apt to cite it here:

The grotesque is part of what this fallen age is. Seeing it and seeing God with clear, uncompromising eyes of faith keeps us from making gulags or gas chambers. When sentimentalism separates the grotesque from the sovereign goodness of God, we are on our way to Auschwitz. It is a great irony that in rejecting God, in defense of a less grotesque humanity, we become hideous as we cleanse the world of imperfections.

The tender-hearted souls who cannot bear to look on the deformed, and thus impute their distaste to God, so as to discredit him, sever the only sure root that can keep them from the "final solution" of mercifully ridding the world of the grotesque.

---

[52] Leo Alexander, "Medical Science Under Dictatorship," *New England Journal of Medicine*, vol.241, 14 July, 1949, p.45.
[53] Nancy Gibbs, "Love and Let Die," *Time* Magazine, 19 March, 1990, p.67.

The Burden over Posed Compassion

Flannery O'Connor wrote about the grotesque. And she believed in God — a God who was good and had not lost control of his world. Part of what governed her obsession with the grotesque was this conviction: There is a false tenderness in the world — a tenderness cut off from Christ — that poses as compassion and leads to concentration camps.

Mary Ann was a girl with a grotesque, cancerous tumor on her face. She died from it at the age of twelve. By all accounts, she was a radiantly cheerful girl, whose short life was worth living. Flannery O'Connor...revealed her burden.

"One of the tendencies of our age is to use the suffering of children to discredit the goodness of God, and once you have discredited his goodness, you are done with him...Busy cutting down human imperfection, they are making headway also on the raw material of good."

"Ivan Karamazov cannot believe, as long as one child is in torment; Camus' hero cannot accept the divinity of Christ, because of the massacre of the innocents. In this popular pity, we mark our gain in sensibility and our loss in vision. If other ages felt less, they saw more, even though they saw with the blind, prophetical, unsentimental eye of acceptance, which is to say, of faith. In the absence of this faith now, we govern by tenderness."

"It is a tenderness which, long since cut off from the person of Christ, is wrapped in theory. When tenderness is detached from the source of tenderness, its logical outcome is terror. It ends in forced labor camps and in the fumes of the gas chamber"[54]

These words are explosive with wisdom. If you try to cut down the grotesque, you may sacrifice the trees on which much good grows. A gain in sensibility may be a loss of vision, and without that vision, the gain may be ghastly. The "unsentimental eye" of faith in God's goodness in the face of horrors is paradoxically the tenderest eye. Tenderness, cut off from Christ, can justify the camps, or we would say today, cutting children in pieces.

Dwell in the Whole Counsel of God

Who can discern his errors? (Psalm 19:12). "The heart is deceitful above all things, and desperately sick" (Jeremiah 17:9). One generation's tenderness is another's terror. They grow from the same root of Christlessness — Truthlessness.

Amid such unexpected turns in history as we have seen, the safest place on earth for us to dwell is the whole counsel of God — all of the Bible, with all its shocking parts, humbly grasped, shaping a kind of people who are inexplicable in the fierceness of their tender defense of the helpless and grotesque.[55]

Implications of the Dutch Euthanasia Experience

Right-to-die advocates often argue that euthanasia and assisted suicide are "choice issues." The Dutch experience clearly indicates that, where voluntary euthanasia and assisted suicide are accepted practice, a significant number of patients

---

[54] "Introduction to a Memoir of Mary Ann", *Mystery and Manners*, 1957, 226–227.
[55] http://www.desiringgod.org/blog/posts/the-failure-of-christless-tenderness Posted 6 August 2013 Accessed 22 August, 2013.

end up having no choice at all. Euthanasia does not remain a "right" only for the terminally ill, competent adult who requests it, no matter how many safeguards are established. It is inevitably applied to those who are chronically ill, disabled, elderly, mentally ill, mentally retarded, and depressed, the rationale being that such individuals should have the same "right" to end their suffering as anyone else, even if they do not or cannot voluntarily request death.

Euthanasia, by its very nature, is an abuse and the ultimate abandonment of patients. In actual practice, euthanasia only gives doctors greater power and a license to kill. Once the power to kill is bestowed on physicians, the inherent nature of the doctor/patient relationship is adversely affected. A patient can no longer be sure what role the doctor will play, healer or killer. Unlike Holland, where medical care is automatically provided for everyone, in the USA millions of people cannot afford medical treatment. If euthanasia and assisted-suicide were to become accepted in the USA, death would be the only medical option many could afford.

Even with health care reform in the USA, many people would still not have long-standing relationships with their doctors. Large numbers of Americans would belong to health maintenance organisations (HMOs) and managed care programmes, and they often would not even know the physicians who end up treating them. Given those circumstances, doctors would be ill equipped to recognise if a patient's euthanasia request was the result of depression or the sometimes-subtle pressures placed on the patient to "get out of the way." Also, given the current push for health care cost containment in the USA medical groups and facilities may be tempted to view patients in terms of their treatment costs instead of their innate value as human beings. For some, the bottom line would be that dead patients cost less than live ones. Giving doctors the legal power to kill their patients is dangerous public policy. Patients should never be viewed as merely customers in a health-care business. What is needed is customised care not customer care. Amoral clinicians, rapacious lawyers and avaricious accountants must not ultimately decide end of life issues.

The legal debate concerning euthanasia in the Netherlands took off with the "Postma case" in 1973, concerning a physician who had facilitated the death of her mother following repeated explicit requests for euthanasia. While the physician was convicted, the court's judgement set out criteria when a doctor would not be required to keep a patient alive contrary to their will. This set of criteria was formalised in the course of a number of court cases during the 1980s.

Termination of Life on Request and Assisted Suicide (Review Procedures) Act took effect on April 1, 2002. It legalises euthanasia and physician assisted suicide. Els Borst, the D66 minister of Health, proposed the law.[56] The procedures codified in the law had been a convention of the Dutch medical community for many years.

Current Law

On April 10, 2001, a Dutch law permitting both euthanasia and assisted suicide was approved and (as stated above) came into effect on April 1, 2002. In summary that law states that the physician must have "terminated a life or assisted suicide with due care."[57] This requirement – that the procedure be carried out in a medically appropriate

---

[56] D66 is a political party in the Netherlands.
[57] Chapter II, Article 2, 1 f.

79

fashion – transforms the crimes of euthanasia and assisted suicide into medical treatments.

Specifically it allows euthanasia for incompetent patients. Persons 16 years old and older can make an advance "written statement containing a request for termination of life" which the physician may carry out.[58] The written statement need not be made in conjunction with any particular medical condition. It could be a written statement made years before, based upon views that may have changed. The physician could administer euthanasia based on the prior written statement.

Teenagers 16 to 18 years old may request and receive euthanasia or assisted suicide. A parent or guardian must "have been involved in the decision process" but need not agree or approve.[59] Children 12 to 16 years old may request and receive euthanasia or assisted suicide. A parent or guardian must "agree with the termination of life or the assisted suicide."[60]

A person may qualify for euthanasia or assisted suicide if the doctor "holds the conviction that the patient's suffering is lasting and unbearable."[61] There is no requirement that the suffering be physical or that the patient be terminally ill.

Oversight is by Non-Judicial Committees

All oversight of euthanasia and assisted suicide will be done by a "Regional Review Committee for Termination of Life on Request and Assisted Suicide" after the death of the

---

[58] Chapter II, Article 2, 2.
[59] Chapter II, Article 2, 3.
[60] Chapter II, Article 2, 4.
[61] Chapter II, Article 2, 1b.

patient.[62] Each regional committee will be made up of at least one legal specialist, one physician and one expert on ethical or philosophical issues.[63] An expert in "philosophical issues" is one who has expertise regarding the "discussion on the prerequisites for a meaningful life."[64] One wonders who these "experts on ethical and philosophical issues" might be. If a person is eligible to sit on such a committee and selected or elected to do so that person must approve of euthanasia and assisted suicide in principle or he/she could not function in such a role. So such "experts" cannot be opposed to these practices. Surely this skews what ought to be a judicial process. However, this is how it has to be in a system, which is processing euthanasia and assisted suicide because, otherwise, it would be unworkable.

Change in the Burden of Proof

Under the prior practice of euthanasia in Holland, the burden of proof was on the physician to justify the termination of life. The change in the law shifts the burden of proof to the prosecutor who will be required to show that the termination of life did not meet the requirements of due care. The prosecutor will not receive information about any euthanasia death unless a Regional Committee forwards it.[65]

Residency not Required

Euthanasia tourism exists in the Netherlands. Although public relations statements (in the Netherlands) about the law have claimed that only Dutch residents would be able to receive euthanasia or assisted suicide, the reality is that law

---

[62] Chapter III.
[63] Chapter III, Article 3, 2.
[64] Chapter III, Article 3, 2, footnote 1.
[65] Chapter III, Articles 9 and 10.

does not prohibit doctors from administering euthanasia to non-residents.

Mention the Netherlands or Holland to anybody and they immediately think of drugs and sex. This is unfortunate because the Netherlands is a wonderful place of art and culture, particularly Amsterdam, The Hague, Maastricht and Utrecht.[66] But the Netherlands has established certain notoriety because of its liberal laws. And drug tourism is a reality in the Netherlands, which even has a marijuana museum. Recently there have been moves to introduce resident only policies in relation to the availability and use of drugs. There is growing concern that medical tourism for euthanasia and assisted suicide will become increasingly popular.[67] Medical tourism is a reality in the world today. People already travel to foreign countries for dental, medical, and cosmetic treatments that are more readily available, of higher quality and cheaper.

The Dutch government wants to restrict medical tourism in relation to euthanasia and assisted suicide. But in relation to recent proposals to restrict the availability of marijuana to residents only there has been vehement opposition from liberal parties, local officials, civic movements and worries over the impact such measures will have on local and national economies.

For many young Europeans their first parent-free trip to Amsterdam is a rite of passage and not for the unique architecture, beautiful canals, and rich museums, but rather to

---

[66] I am sure there are many other artistic hotspots but this is just a mention of the main cultural centres.

[67] Medical tourism is a reality in many countries for surgery and dental treatment. This is often for economic reasons but sometimes based on the belief (right or wrong) that medical care is better and preferable in another country.

explore the internationally-renowned coffee-shops where they can buy marijuana in small amounts and smoke it legally.

However, this is big business. Of the four to five million international visitors to Amsterdam each year 23% say they visit a Dutch coffee-shop. The federal government wants it to stop and has implemented various measures to ensure it will. First, in 2012 in southern border towns including Maastricht they prohibited the sale of pot to all foreigners except for Germans and Belgians ostensibly, to relieve traffic congestion. Then the prohibition was extended to other regions and all visitors. Amsterdam had been excluded because the city government is against the curbs and the coffee-shops have been able to exert enough pressure to hold them off.

Citing, among other reasons, the criminal drug industry allegedly developed around the coffee shops, the government has begun the first phase of a programme to restrict coffee-shop operations, hoping to end drug tourism.

In January 2014 as I waited with my wife in the long queue to gain access to the Anne Frank Museum, I met a young woman (in her late twenties) from Rio de Janero, Brazil. We engaged in conversation and she asked, rather nonchalantly, if I planned to visit the red-light district. She did not seem to think this was an unusual or inappropriate question at all. For her (as for many others) this is just another tourist attraction. I explained that many of the women were drug addicts who were controlled by pimps and that they were slaves in the sex trade. I explained that I thought it was humiliating and degrading for these women to be forced to sell themselves for a fix and that I certainly would not be visiting the red-light district. She seemed genuinely surprised by what I told her and said she would cross it off her list of things to do while in Amsterdam.

The mayor of Amsterdam, Eberhard van der Laan has won court permission to close down more than a third of the marijuana cafes in Rossebuurt, the city's red-light district. Amsterdam District Court ruled in April, 2014 that he "has freedom to carry out policies he considers desirable to protect public order."[68] Eberhard van der Laan persuaded the court that the coffee shops generate criminality. He plans to close 26 of the 76 shops in business, to follow from the forced closure of 192 of the 482 legal brothels in the district. The tourist authorities welcomed the plan as they desire to move visitor attention away from drug tourism.

Officially, only Dutch residents should receive medical assistance to commit suicide. However, as noted the law does not prohibit doctors from administering euthanasia to non-residents. The Netherlands was the first country to legalise euthanasia and its legislation on the right to die is considered the most liberal in the world, although it applies only officially to cases of "hopeless and unbearable" suffering it has been extended to those who are just tired of living.

The Netherlands is not the only destination for assisted suicide. First and foremost is Zurich, Switzerland, where hundreds of tourists, mostly British, make the journey to end their lives.

It's not the existence of assisted-suicide tourism that is behind the latest controversy but, rather, the implicit danger that it could spin out of control just like the coffee shops. Two initiatives pushed by the organisation "Right to Die" guarantee an increase in dark tourism. One makes euthanasia

---

[68] Fionn Davenport, "Closing Time for Amsterdam Coffee Shops", *Travel Desk*, *The Irish Times Magazine*, 3 May 2014, p. 35.

widely available with mobile teams to assist patients to die at home and the other is the proposed legislation to give the right to die to everybody over seventy years old.

Conservative members of the government and various religious organisations fear that such measures could trigger a wave of euthanasia tourism. Right or not, the country's longstanding reputation as a haven for live-and-let-live is becoming a die-and-let-die culture.

CHAPTER 3 Society at Death's Door

R ecent developments indicate that many Dutch doctors say that the anguish of parents is another reason to euthanize disabled babies. The Belgian parliament recently reached a consensus on expanding controversial euthanasia policies to include access for gravely ill children. The Royal Dutch Medical Association (KNMG), which represents doctors in the Netherlands, has stated that distress felt by parents of a dying newborn is a justification for killing their child.

In a new policy document, "Medical decisions about the lives of new-borns with severe abnormalities" the KNMG explained why it is acceptable, and sometimes even necessary, to euthanize children.[69] In the Netherlands, giving lethal injections to severely disabled babies or starving them is no longer headline news, as newborn euthanasia is clearly allowed under the 2004 Groningen Protocol.

The Groningen Protocol is a text created in September 2004 by Eduard Verhagen, the medical director of the department of paediatrics at the University Medical Centre Groningen (UMCG) in Groningen, the Netherlands. It contains directives with criteria under which physicians can perform "active ending of life on infants" (child euthanasia) without fear of legal prosecution.

The interesting development lies in the statement that the parents' suffering may be a reason to kill the new-born. Amongst other conditions, the policy states that a lethal

---

[69] In Dutch only.

injection of muscle relaxant is ethically possible when "The period of gasping and dying persists and the inevitable death is prolonged, in spite of good preparation, and it causes severe suffering for the parents." This is a radical development inasmuch as a human being may be killed without expressing a desire to die because his/her continued existence is emotionally distressing for others. Severely disabled babies, brain-damaged teenagers and the demented elderly are becoming increasingly vulnerable. It is becoming a case of "Doctor put him out of *our* misery."

Dr Verhagen, one of the authors of the KNMG report and the architect of the Gronignen Protocol, explained to *Volkskrant*, a leading Dutch newspaper, why parental anguish is relevant: "These children are grey and cold, they get blue lips and suddenly every few minutes they take extremely deep breaths. That's very nasty to see, and it can go on for hours and sometimes days." The experience is extremely stressful for parents. The sight of a child shuddering in its last moments is undoubtedly distressing. However, even Dr Verhagen admits that the child may not actually be suffering. He argues that doctors should spare parents the anguish of seeing their child die in distress. No right-minded person wants children to suffer unnecessarily but trying to present the alternative (killing the pain rather than the child) is like arguing against the universally loved concept of motherhood. It is a highly charged emotive issue.

The criteria for euthanizing new-borns are as follows.[70] If the child is suffering, if it cannot express its own wishes, if death is inevitable and if the dying process is prolonged, then the child may be euthanized and spare the parents further severe suffering. Of the 175,000 babies born every year in

---

[70] See page 54 of the report.

The Netherlands, the KNMG suggests that about 650 might be cases which would be worthy of euthanasia.

Dr Verhagen is probably the best-known exponent of euthanasia for children in the Netherlands. The *Journal of Medical Ethics* published his defence of the Groningen Protocol. He dismissed fears that the Netherlands is sliding down a slippery slope. "Over the five years since its publication the gloomy predictions have failed to materialize", he said. The number of cases of neonatal euthanasia has not increased. Instead, antenatal screening improved and the severely disabled babies were aborted instead. "This resulted in increased terminations of pregnancy and fewer instances of euthanasia," he wrote triumphantly!

In the Netherlands, the criteria for euthanasia are being continuously expanded and the process of liberalisation has shifted from terminally ill adults, to adults who have lost their interest in living, to suffering children, and now to children whose parents are suffering. One could logically conclude that a day is approaching when the suffering of adult children will be sufficient reason to euthanize their frail and aged parents.

The Groningen Protocol was introduced in 2005 in The Netherlands. Its development was triggered by the case of a baby girl with excruciatingly painful and progressive skin disease whose parents asked doctors to end her suffering. The request was refused on the grounds that the doctors concerned could be prosecuted for murder. The young patient died three months later.

But protocol author, Dr Eduard Verhagen, has said that evidence from two national surveys of end of life care in 1995 and 2001 indicate that doctors were taking decisions to end a child's life for humanitarian reasons before 2005, but were not being open about it.

In 1% of deaths among children under the age of 12 months during this period, drugs were given with the explicit intention of hastening death, leading the author to conclude that between 15 and 20 children every year had their lives ended in this way in the Netherlands. Yet only three such cases were officially reported.

The protocol stipulates that five criteria must be met before euthanasia for new-borns can even be considered: diagnosis and prognosis beyond doubt; presence of hopeless and unbearable suffering; a second independent medical opinion to confirm the first; the consent of both parents; and compliance with strict medical standards. But the protocol's publication provoked a storm of controversy, with critics suggesting it would open the floodgates for euthanasia of new-borns.

So the author reviewed all reported cases of infant euthanasia between 2001 and 2010. In 95% of cases, treatment was withheld or withdrawn. In 60% of cases this was because the child had an incurable condition from which they were soon going to die. In the remainder, the child's quality of life prompted the decision.

Neonatal euthanasia in some instances is becoming a preferable option to abortion. Some parents prefer the option of euthanasia for very sick babies to termination of pregnancy, because the level of certainty around diagnosis and prognosis is much clearer after birth, and they can discuss all the treatment options available, including palliative care. If all the stakeholders conclude that the prognosis is very grim, the baby's condition is judged as one with sustained and intolerable suffering, and the parents request euthanasia it is seen as a legitimate and permissible alternative to second trimester termination.

However, there is a moral difference is between withholding food/water and standard treatment such as increasing dosages of morphine or the withdrawal of treatment and euthanasia. Withholding treatment with the intention of hastening death is not uncommon in neonatal intensive care. The active withdrawal of life-prolonging medical care (an intentional act that kills, even if not necessarily with the intention to kill) is a standard part of medical practice in relation to people who experience severe disability and suffering, including new-borns. The euthanizing of new-borns is infanticide euphemistically re-described.

Dispatching the Demented

The Dutch government is pressing doctors to be more aggressive with euthanasia for Alzheimer's patients. Recently senior figures in Dutch medicine and politics met to decide whether advanced euthanasia directives can, in practice, replace verbal requests if patients with dementia are no longer able to express their wishes. Doctors in the Netherlands have expressed difficulties with this grey area, arguing that some communication is essential if they are to understand properly their patients' wishes.

Former health minister Els Borst, who piloted the euthanasia law through parliament, has said that, "A professional body cannot choose its own interpretation of the law." What if the patient no longer wants to die? What if the patient isn't really suffering? The law says killing can be done only when that is required to end suffering. Once a society broadly accepts euthanasia, the killable categories become more elastic and ultimately introduce a culture of death.

The Dutch doctors' organisation (KNMG) recently met with Health Minister Edith Schippers to discuss the possibility of limiting the scope of the law on euthanasia, which came into force in 2002.[71] A large proportion of doctors believe that euthanasia should not be used in cases where patients suffering from serious dementia are no longer able to communicate, even if they have previously signed a request for euthanasia. Instead, they want the practice restricted to cases where patients can confirm — verbally or otherwise — they want to put an end to their lives.

However, the medical profession remains divided on the issue, with some doctors still in favour of the full application of the law. As a General Practitioner (GP) cited by *Volkskrant* explains, "In respecting his or her will, we pay homage to a patient who was once alive, and not to a human being who no longer knows if he or she exists."

Britain

Kevin Fitzpatrick, a researcher with the group Not Dead Yet has claimed that relaxing the law in Britain would threaten old and disabled people, as it would allow moral judgements that their lives were not worth living. He said it is "nonsensical" to say that we all have a right to die, when what is really being sought is the right to a premature death that is not sought by all in society.[72]

A debate has begun and is continuing in Britain where there is an increasingly high-profile campaign to decriminalise assisted suicide. The current status quo is that individuals are unlikely to be prosecuted for helping terminally ill loved ones die in most cases. In recent times a series of public figures including writers Ian McEwan and Terry Pratchett have

---

[71] On 16 May, 2013.

[72] In a head to head article entitled "Should the law on assisted dying be changed?" published in the *British Medical Journal* (online) BMJ 2011;342:d2355, 21 April, 2011,
http://www.bmj.com/content/342/bmj.d2355

spoken out in favour of the law being relaxed still further but charities and groups supporting disabled people and the elderly fear that any change in the law would leave them feeling under pressure to end their lives.

Many people feel that allowing assisted suicide would pressurise disabled people to kill themselves. Fitzpatrick said, "Disabled people, like others, and often with more reason, need to feel safe. Thus eroding what may already be a shaky sense of safety in medical care poses a further threat to disabled people's wellbeing, continuing care, and life itself."[73] He cited the experience of Baroness Campbell of Surbiton, the disabled founder of Not Dead Yet, who was once told by doctors that they "presumed" she would not want resuscitation if she experienced complications during treatment.[74] Very scared, she stayed awake in hospital for more than 48 hours. Fitzpatrick said, "The doctors' judgement, based on the idea of a "life not worth living" is a moral judgement not of facts (medical or otherwise). He went on to say, "A law permitting euthanasia would reinforce this position, further clearing the ground to take away lives based on a moral judgement rather than medical fact. The threat will extend to the lives of older, disabled people too."[75] He mentioned the comments of Lord McColl made in the House of Lords that in the Netherlands, where euthanasia has been officially legalised and regulated since 2002, doctors found the cases increasingly easy to carry out

---

[73] BMJ 2011; 342: d1883
http://www.bmj.com/content/342/bmj.d1883, 21 April, 2011.
[74] Baroness Campbell, born with spinal muscular atrophy, was being treated for life threatening pneumonia when two doctors told her they presumed that if she experienced respiratory failure, she wouldn't want to be resuscitated: "You wouldn't want to live on a ventilator." No ventilation and no resuscitation meant she would die.
[75] BMJ 2011; 342: d1883
http://www.bmj.com/content/342/bmj.d1883, 21 April, 2011.

while "many elderly people in the Netherlands are so fearful of euthanasia that they carry cards around with them saying that they do not want it." There is growing concern that patient safety might not be at the heart of good clinical governance as it ought to be.

This was a reference to the Dutch Patients' Association (NPV), which has 70,000 members of whom at least 6,000 have "living will declarations" stating that they do not want euthanasia if they are taken into hospital or a nursing home. Other Dutch people, however, make written declarations of their "will to die". Mr Fitzpatrick concluded:

> These discussions are complex involving deep moral questions that cannot and must not be treated as though they were merely matters of fact with clear and obvious answers that everyone must share, as though logic dictated it. The lives of many disabled people depend on resisting attempts to introduce a law legalising the intentional act of killing.[76]

Fears that Britain might introduce a euthanasia law have been mounting since Law Lords ordered Keir Starmer, the Director of Public Prosecutions, to clarify when a person should be prosecuted for assisting suicide. His guidance said prosecution was likely if the "victim" was under the age of 18, had a mental illness or was in good physical health. Assisting in more than one case or being paid for assistance would also lead to prosecution. Although it does not guarantee anyone immunity, it says a criminal action is unlikely if the victim had a grave illness or disability, was determined to kill themselves and was a close friend or relative of a helper, who was motivated by compassion.

---

[76] Ibid.

But once the concept is allowed in law the criteria are subject to review and revision. It is invariably introduced with "high standards", "adequate safeguards" or "strict guidelines" but these lines are continuously redrawn in an ever more liberal sense. Besides, people's motives are difficult to discern.

The Dutch Model

The Right to Die (NL) (and the Exit International) agenda comes out of a moral vacuum, impelled by an atheistic worldview.[77] As such it is consistent with that view. But it comes from a world of shifting sands where there is no solid foundation. Old people are being fed a diet of views that make them feel, unloved, unwanted, redundant, and not beautiful. A generation ago old people were respected for the contribution they had made to society and for their wisdom. In a pragmatic world where the sanctity of life is an outmoded principled position, they are worthless in the sense that they do not have a function and many cannot care for themselves. So their value is equated with their function and when they cannot function, they have no value. When old people need minding and can no longer fend for themselves, they are deemed to be burden. This is the spectre that lurks in the shadows of an atheistic worldview. I am not saying that atheists have no morals but I am questioning the basis and solidity of the foundations of such a position. It is ultimately subjective, relativistic and pragmatic rather than principled and absolute.

The Right to Die (NL) - NVVE - assists people with chronic psychiatric problems, with Alzheimer disease or other forms of dementia and people who feel they have "completed" their life. These categories of people often do

---

[77] Exit International will be examined later.

not meet the requirements of hospices, which specialise in terminal care. However, euthanasia is also available in Dutch hospices. The NVVE would like to see the "life's end" clinic made part of an ordinary hospital or nursing home.

The steady growth in euthanasia deaths in the Netherlands is partly due to the fact that the taboo surrounding euthanasia is fading. People are being gradually desensitised to the idea. It is simply becoming part of mainstream medicine. However, the reasons for so-called "mercy killings" have little to do with mercy. It is based on misguided compassion and rooted in individualism rather than a proper understanding of what is ultimately good for society. One reason for the increasing numbers is that doctors are more likely to report it.

Many people feel that legalised euthanasia has led to deterioration in the quality of care for terminally ill patients in Holland. Many ask to die out of fear because of an absence of effective pain relief. The introduction of the law on euthanasia and assisted suicide has societal side effects because it inevitably affects services for the elderly. Dr Els Borst, the former Health Minister and Deputy Prime Minister who guided the law through the Dutch parliament, has said that it was introduced "far too early." She admitted that medical care for the terminally ill had declined since the law came into effect. She said more should have been done legally to protect people who wanted to die natural deaths. She said "In the Netherlands, we first listened to the political and societal demand in favour of euthanasia. Obviously, this was not in the proper order." The former hospital doctor made her remarks in an interview with researcher Dr Anne-Marie The, for a book on the history of euthanasia called *Redeemer Under God*. Dr The, who has studied euthanasia for fifteen years, said that palliative care was so inadequate in Holland that patients "often ask for euthanasia out of fear" of dying in agony because care and pain relief is so poor. She added that a crisis had developed and that "to think that we have neatly arranged everything by adopting the euthanasia law is an illusion."

Phyllis Bowman of Right to Life, a British group opposed to euthanasia, said she had witnessed pro-euthanasia campaigners picket hospices in Holland: "People were marching round the building shouting and roaring and were screaming that the hospice was denying people their right to die" she said. She said it was so bad that Amsterdam, which has a population of 780,000 people, is now served by just two tiny hospices. According to Bowman, "pro-euthanasia campaigners set out to smash the hospice movement. People can no longer get palliative care when they need it - they just get an injection."

Dr Peter Saunders, from the Care Not Killing Alliance, an umbrella group of more than 50 disabled, medical and religious charities, said "If you introduce guidelines that help people to avoid prosecution then you will get a huge escalation of cases."

The Dutch experience with euthanasia and assisted suicide should be taken into account by legislators in other parts of the world because possible changes in legalisation will have serious ramifications and undesirable (and perhaps unforeseen) negative consequences for society. There are sufficient grounds to warrant investigation of the "slippery-slope" and "thin-end-of-the-wedge" views.

Discussion about legalising physician-assisted suicide and euthanasia should lead to more informed conversations between health-care providers and patients about end-of-life care. When a patient starts talking about being ready to die, this should be a signal for proper medical intervention focused on quality of life issues and rather than referring such vulnerable people to the doctors of death they should be offered support (not the same thing as doing what people want you to do) and referred for counselling. The whole issue raises serious questions about end-of-life care. Doctors should not have the right to prescribe poison or administer lethal injections.

CHAPTER 4 Brave New World

In a previous generation society had a greater appreciation for the sanctity of human life. There was a shared understanding that people were created in the image of God. However, the transcendent values of a religious perspective have been replaced, largely, with a secular and atheistic worldview. Absolute moral principles have metamorphosed into relativistic and subjective codes that are leading contemporary culture into a dystopian nightmare. A generation ago, murder was rare, abortion was illegal and euthanasia and physician-assisted suicide was unthinkable. Now murder is frequent, abortion is "normal" and euthanasia and physician-assisted suicide is legal in some places.

Increasing Numbers

On 11 July, 2012, *The Lancet* published a study concerning the practice of euthanasia and end-of-life practices in the Netherlands. *The Lancet* study indicated that in 2010, 23% of all euthanasia deaths were not reported. There were 3136 *reported* euthanasia deaths in 2010 but there were *actually* 3859 euthanasia deaths and 192 assisted suicide deaths that year. Since 23% of all euthanasia deaths are not reported in the Netherlands we can estimate that in 2011, the number of actual euthanasia deaths in the Netherlands was more likely (3695 + 23%) 4544. Assisted suicide deaths are a separate category that is not counted within the official euthanasia statistics in the Netherlands. There were 192 assisted suicide deaths in the Netherlands in 2010. The number of euthanasia deaths increased by 18% in 2011.

Therefore, it is likely that there were (192 + 18%) 226 assisted suicide deaths in 2011. Therefore the total number of assisted deaths in the Netherlands in 2011 is more likely (4544 + 226) 4770.

The number of reported euthanasia deaths in the Netherlands increased by 13% in 2009 and 19% in 2010. There were 1923 reported euthanasia deaths in 2006. There were 2120 reported euthanasia deaths in 2007. There were 2331 reported euthanasia deaths in 2008. There were 2636 reported euthanasia deaths in 2009. There were 3136 reported euthanasia deaths in 2010. There were 3695 reported euthanasia deaths in 2011.

Death on Wheels

There are mobile euthanasia teams operating in the Netherlands, which meet a demand for euthanasia from people with chronic depression (mental pain), people with disabilities, people with dementia/Alzheimer disease, loneliness, and those whose request for euthanasia is declined by their physician. In 2010, 45% of all euthanasia requests resulted in death by euthanasia. Notice that one does not have to be terminally ill to avail of these "services".

The elderly, the sick, the mentally ill, babies, young children, teenagers are being euthanized and many without their consent if the doctors of death deem the quality of their lives to be unworthy of treatment. Many elderly are now carrying cards to say they do not want to be euthanized because one has to almost opt out of what is becoming the normal practice. It seems that other countries want to follow the same path. Society is going Dutch, which means that everybody will pay the price.

In 1989 Dr Petra de Jong, a Dutch pulmonologist was asked for help by a terminally ill patient, a man with a large cancerous tumour in his trachea.[78] He wanted to end his life. She gave the man pentobarbital, a powerful barbiturate — but not enough. It took him nine hours to die. "I realise now that I did things wrong" Dr de Jong, 58, said in an interview, adding, "Today you can Google it, but we didn't know."[79] The man was the first of sixteen patients whom Dr de Jong, now the head of the euthanasia advocacy group Right to Die-NL, has helped to achieve what she calls "a dignified death."[80]

Founded in 1973, Right to Die-NL has been at the forefront of the movement to make euthanasia widely available in the Netherlands, even as the practice remains highly controversial elsewhere. Polls find that an overwhelming majority of the Dutch believe euthanasia should be available to suffering patients who want it, and thousands formally request euthanasia every year.

Right to Die-NL, which claims 124,000 members, made worldwide headlines in early March, 2013 with the news that it was creating mobile euthanasia teams to help patients die at home. These are now fully functional. The organisation has also courted controversy with its call for legislation to make euthanasia available to anyone over age 70, sick or not. Paul Root Wolpe, director of the Centre for Ethics at Emory University in Atlanta has said, "Internationally, the Dutch have pushed the conversation on both the wisdom of allowing people to choose how and when they die when

---

[78]Pulmonology is the branch of medicine that deals with the structure, physiology, and diseases of the lungs.

[79]David Jolly, "Push for the Right to Die Grows in the Netherlands", *New York Times*, 3 April, 2012.

[80] Ibid.

they're in great suffering, and on the nature of compassion in dying."[81]

Under the Netherlands' 2002 Termination of Life on Request and Assisted Suicide Act, doctors may grant patients' requests to die without fear of prosecution as long as they observe certain guidelines. However, these guidelines are being largely ignored. Technically, an informed patient who is undergoing suffering that is both lasting and unbearable must make the request voluntarily. Doctors must also obtain the written affirmation of a second, independent physician that the case meets the requirements and report all such deaths to the authorities for review. If the Dutch experiences teach anything, it is that legal requirements become guidelines that in turn are not observed. Once the principle is conceded such pragmatic "controls" can be easily modified.

Dr de Jong said Dutch physicians typically euthanize patients by injecting a barbiturate to induce sleep, followed by a powerful muscle relaxant like curare. For assisted suicide, the doctor prescribes a drug to prevent vomiting followed by a lethal dose of barbiturates. Dr de Jong said Dutch physicians typically euthanize patients by injecting a barbiturate to induce sleep, followed by a powerful muscle relaxant like curare.[82] It is more accurate to talk about "curare like" muscle relaxants. Curare is no longer used as synthetic

---

[81] Ibid.
[82] Curare is a powerful muscle relaxant which is typically administered in euthanasia. It causes respiratory paralysis but does not directly stop the heart. Curare is a common name for various arrow poisons originating from South America. It was used as a paralyzing poison by South American indigenous people. The prey was shot by arrows or blowgun darts dipped in curare, leading to asphyxiation owing to the inability of the victim's respiratory muscles to contract. The word curare is derived from *wurari*, from the Carib language of the Macusi Indians of Guyana.

agents are now available. For assisted suicide, the doctor prescribes a drug to prevent vomiting followed by a lethal dose of barbiturates.

Almost 80% of all such deaths take place in patients' homes, according to the Royal Dutch Medical Association. In 2010, the latest year for which data are available, there were 3,136 reported cases of "termination on request". Serious illnesses such as late-stage cancer typically lie behind a vast majority. Euthanasia is responsible for about 2% of all deaths annually in the Netherlands, according to Eric van Wijlick, a policy adviser for the association.

Pro-euthanasia people want to argue that the general practitioners who serve as the backbone of the country's universal health care system, doctors who often have enjoyed long relationships with their patients and know their feelings well, typically carry out euthanasia. Nevertheless, one of the reasons for introducing the mobile units is to step in where the local GP has refused euthanasia or assisted suicide. Mr van Wijlick said the euthanasia law was possible because of "the moderate and open climate we have in the Netherlands, with respect for other points of view," and acknowledged that it would be difficult to carry out elsewhere, because everyone in the Netherlands has access to health care, an income and housing. "There are no economic reasons to ask for euthanasia," he said, something that might not be true in the United States, with its for-profit health care system.[83]

The mobile teams were needed, Dr de Jong said, because many general practitioners, either for moral reasons or perhaps because of uncertainty about the law, refused to help suffering patients to die after it had become too late to find

---

[83] Ibid.

another doctor. The mobile teams will work to help them do so, she said.

Say a hypothetical 72-year-old man with metastasising prostate cancer and poor prospects is told by his doctor that he does not qualify for euthanasia. The man could contact the Right to Die-NL's new "life-ending clinic," and if he appeared to meet the criteria, a doctor and a nurse would go to his home to make an assessment. If all the conditions were met (and these are frequently ignored) he would be euthanized, ideally with his family beside him. Dr de Jong emphasised that a patient could never be euthanized on the initial visit, because the law requires that a second physician be consulted. There is a well-known network of such doctors, so getting an agreeable second opinion is not difficult. In reality it can happen very quickly, within twenty-four hours and there is no requirement to even inform other family members. Chilling!

Dr de Jong's group has been courting controversy by seeking to extend help in dying to everyone age 70 and over, even if they are not sick and by offering mobile euthanasia teams to assist people whose doctors refuse to provide them life-ending treatment. Clearly the professed respect for the intimate relationship between family physician and patient is merely lip-service in a public relations campaign.

For an outsider there is something striking about the Dutch attitude to euthanasia, as well as to marijuana and prostitution, all of which are legal, but regulated. Those in favour of the Dutch liberal attitude would contend that policies of tolerating these practices grew from experience showing that making them illegal caused even worse problems. Crime and disease in the case of drugs and prostitution and unrelieved suffering and deeply troubling cases of supposed mercy killing in the case of euthanasia and assisted suicide. However, such views need to be challenged.

The red-light district in Amsterdam is near the railway station and I, like many other people have inadvertently strolled into it at night and seen naked women sitting in shop windows. This commodification of women is deeply disturbing. It is in your face, hard to avoid seeing. But I have also been in the area very early in the morning to catch a train and those prostitutes, who are mostly heroin addicts, can be seen waiting in the square for their drug-fix to help them feel normal. They are sex slaves in one of Europe's most "advanced" societies in an industry that exploits women. The idea that this is somehow more benign or benevolent than illegal and unregulated activity of this nature is nonsense. All that the Netherlands has done is legalised pimps and effectively legitimised a reprehensible business, which controls, exploits and abuses women.

Incidentally, as prostitution is legal in the Netherlands, does this mean that an unemployed woman in receipt of social welfare payments (job seeker's allowance), on the basis that she is actively seeking employment, could be directed by the relevant government department to make herself available for such work? In spite of the fact that one has to be registered as a prostitute there have been issues relating to this question.

Dr de Jong argues that by insisting on "unbearable suffering," the law fails old people who have decided that their lives are complete. These people, whom she described as "suffering from life," may well try to take their own lives anyway, she said. "Suicide is not illegal, you can always do that," she said. "But you need a way. Old people are less mobile and there are fewer good ways. In addition, some of the ways we know are really awful."[84]

For Dr de Jong the questions are deeply personal. Her parents took their own lives. They died together in 2010. She explains - "they had gathered medication for insurance against when they didn't want to live anymore, and they didn't want to depend on their G.P."[85] Her father was suffering from cancer and her mother "didn't want to be alone" she said, after a long life together. "They died in each other's arms together in their bed. So, suddenly my private life and my work here came together. That was a bit strange."[86]

Rick Santorum received quite a bit of publicity when he claimed Dutch physicians euthanize elderly patients against their will.[87] He is remembered in the Netherlands for saying that elderly Dutch people wear bracelets reading "Do not euthanize me." Santorum claimed (at an appearance at a conservative rally in Columbia, Missouri on 3 February, 2012) that in the Netherlands physicians euthanize elderly Dutch patients against their will to hold down medical costs: "Half the people who are euthanized in the Netherlands -- and it's 10% of all deaths for the Netherlands -- half of those people are euthanized involuntarily at hospitals, because they

---

[84] David Jolly, *International Herald Tribune: The Global Edition of the New York Times*, "Inside a Story about Helping the Elderly to Die", 3 April, 2012.

[85] Ibid.

[86] Ibid.

[87] Rick Santorum (born May 10, 1958) is an American attorney and Republican Party politician. He was born in Virginia but lived most of his life in Pennsylvania. He served as a United States Senator representing Pennsylvania from 1995 to 2007. He ran as a candidate for the 2012 Republican Party presidential nomination, finishing second to the eventual Republican nominee Mitt Romney.

are older and sick."[88] Santorum's claims sparked indignant reactions and a political row in the media in the Netherlands. According to the CIA *World Factbook* approximately 140,000 people die in the Netherlands annually. According to the Netherlands Ministry of Health, the intentional ending of life with a doctor's help accounts for about 3,000 of those deaths. That is 2.5%, which is lower than Santorum's figures.

The Santorum claim that elderly people in the Netherlands wear bracelets reading, "Do not euthanize me" is a claim denied by de Jong. It seems that Santorum got his statistics wrong. But it also seems that he has a valid point to make.[89]

The *New England Journal of Medicine* has published percentages of doctor-assisted death at a patient's request in the Netherlands, and they range from 1.7% and 2.6% of all deaths in the country. It also placed the percentage of patients dying in palliative care at 7%. Palliative and hospice care are common end-of-life treatment alternatives in many countries, including the U.S.A. It is not clear if Santorum was including palliative and hospice care when he said 10% of all deaths in the Netherlands are the result of euthanasia.

Those seeking medical help to alleviate their suffering by ending their lives have to take a long road to get it, according to the Dutch health ministry, and the majority of patient requests (two-thirds) are denied.[90] However, as we have

---

[88] Ben Brumfield, "Dutch euthanasia clinic offers mobile service", CNN, 9 March, 2012.

[89] See earlier in this book, which indicates that there is concern among the elderly. One might argue that such fear is unjustified but it is nonetheless real and not entirely unwarranted.

[90] One can assume it will continue to move in the direction it has been going, with accelerated momentum, especially now that mobile units are offering euthanasia to patients whose doctors refuse to assist in their deaths. Another factor, which will soon tip the balance to a majority

seen, the numbers of those being euthanized is steadily increasing. "Right to Die" advocates say that the patient must first convince his doctor that his suffering is unbearable but that is a rather subjective process. And the notion that his ailment must be incurable is, in practice, interpreted quite liberally.

Dr de Jong said, "The criteria are that there must be a reoccurring voluntary request."[91] She says, "There must be an unbearable and hopeless suffering, no alternatives anymore, and there must also be a second opinion doctor, who says "yes, this doctor is fulfilling the criteria." And then the euthanasia or assisted suicide can be done."[92] But in reality there are many doctors who believe in the Right to Die agenda and willingly subscribe to the view that if you want to die that's your business and so they willingly facilitate the process.

Doctors sometimes give false medical certificates to employers when a patient has a medical (or emotional) issue where there might be some stigma attached. Such certificates are bogus and a doctor could, technically, lose his/her licence for this. For example, they might issue certificates to people suffering from depression that certify them as suffering from something else, such as glandular fever. I'm sure any doctor who would admit to such a practice would justify it on the grounds that the patient has a right to privacy etc.

Sometimes the patient dies while waiting for the euthanasia to be approved and this skews the statistics in

---

of applicants receiving euthanasia, is the Right to Die-NL's aspiration to extend the service to people over the age of 70 irrespective of whether or not they are ill.

[91] Ben Brumfield "Dutch euthanasia clinic offers mobile service", CNN, 9 March, 2012.

[92] Ibid.

favour of those who say that a minority of applicants are granted their request.

A doctor who assists in terminating life is obliged to report it as a death by unnatural causes to the coroner's office, where it faces review by a legal expert, a doctor and an ethics expert. If they do not like what they see, the case is forwarded to the Public Prosecution Service. For this reason (together with more personal qualms), many doctors will not administer that lethal dose.

However, the End of Life Clinic (founded by the advocacy group Right to Die - NL) for which de Jong is also the spokeswoman has no such qualms of conscience. She has said, "People are dependent on their doctors, and when you have a doctor who doesn't want to do it, sometimes you have no one to turn to."[93] She continued:

> The biggest doctors' organisation in the Netherlands says that every doctor has the moral obligation to refer to another doctor, when he doesn't want to do it. But there are also doctors who don't want to refer to another doctor. Therefore this clinic can be a possibility for those people.[94]

Here is a flagrant disregard for the legal criteria and a determined agenda-driven approach to delivering death. After the patient has filed a request, "a doctor and a nurse will look whether they can fulfil the criteria," de Jong said.[95] Right to Die NL encourages its 130,000 members (the largest of its kind in the world) to make a living will, which includes end of life plans, ahead of time.

---

[93] Ibid.
[94] Ibid.
[95] Ibid.

There is no legal obligation to contact the patient's relatives for a series of conversations. There is no legal obligation to refer the person for counselling or psychotherapy. There is no obligation to explore and treat depression. There is, therefore, in practice no attempt to persuade the person toward a more healthy perspective. Yes, the desire to die is a sick perspective. It is not natural or normal and ought not to be validated by doctors, lawyers or society at large. The desire to die runs counter to the basic human instinct to live.

There are also new-borns, children and teenagers who are euthanized allegedly in accordance with strict legal protocols and parental involvement, which include that "suffering must be unbearable and with no prospect of improvement." Teenagers over 16 years of age are allowed to make the request without parental approval but require their consultation.

People with psychiatric illness also request and receive help ending their lives. Some say this practice is discouraged but it seems there is some advocacy for the practice of dispatching the demented. Doctor assisted end-of-life practices involving children or psychiatric patients, raises questions about consent and dare I say it, "right" and "wrong". It seems that pragmatism determines decisions rather than absolute values.

A 2010 review revealed terminal cancer at the root of the overwhelming majority of cases. However humane the intention, euthanasia and assisted suicide raise serious ethical questions for any civilised society.

The End of Life Clinic's mobile team is active. It does not have any kind of special vehicle like an ambulance. The doctors and nurses simply drive their own cars. It seems society is moving from meals-on-wheels to death-on-wheels.

It seems that even doctors, who perform euthanasia and assisted suicide struggle, at least initially, with the process. The clinic focuses not only the patient but also on ensuring the doctor feels comfortable in the process. As such, they are assisting in the training and support of doctors of death.

CHAPTER 5 The Pied Piper of Hamelin

Euthanasia has been legal in the Netherlands since 2001 and was widely practiced for thirty years before that. However, the "Right to Die" organisation's mobile euthanasia service is a worrying development. These death squads are comprised of ordinary doctors and nurses. The Dutch government is not doing enough to enforce the strict medical codes of practice that is meant to accompany the procedure. Teams are travelling around the country assisting patients whose own doctors refuse to help them to die. There is something inappropriate about such a unit offering such profound intervention to patients they do not know. These units consist of a doctor, a nurse and all the medical equipment required for carrying out euthanasia. Patients can choose injections administered by the medical team, or they may drink a lethal concoction of life-ending drugs. The Dutch right-to-die organisation (NVVE) with its office in Amsterdam is funding the scheme.

The group's spokesperson, Dr Walburg de Jong is on record as saying, "They will first give the patient an injection, which will put them into a deep sleep, then a second injection follows, which will stop their breathing and heartbeat."[96]

One of the creators of the *Levenseinde* (Life-End) units, Jan Suyver, a retired judge, says he was inspired to take

---

[96] Anna Holligan, "Dutch offered 'euthanasia on wheels'", BBC News, The Hague, 2 March, 2012.

action after seeing many people who met the criteria for euthanasia but were not accommodated by their own doctors. Suyver contends that as euthanasia is legal under Dutch law it is an entitlement. Therefore if someone wants this and they meet all the requirements they have a legal right to it. That is why he was involved in setting up the mobile units. Every year there are about 3,000 procedures carried out, accounting for about 2% of deaths annually.

Belgium also legalised euthanasia in 2002, and assisted suicide has been allowed in Switzerland since the 1940s. In the UK there have been discussions about changing the law for many years, and a recent report published by the Commission on Assisted Dying, funded by campaigners who want to see a change in the law, recommended the legalisation on euthanasia in the UK be changed to facilitate these practices.

Bert Dorenbos who represents the Dutch Cry for Life campaign group thinks mobile units push the limits of the legislation too far:

> It's a crazy idea. It's an excuse for pro-euthanasia people to push their agenda. I think it's a PR campaign more than caring for patients who are suffering. "Come to our clinic and we will help you die." They make it sound so easy and simple and it should not be that way.[97]

What makes this scheme even more controversial is that the Royal Dutch Medical Association has raised concerns that the remote nature of the mobile units will not allow the doctors to develop a strong enough relationship with the patient to be able to decide if they are eligible for euthanasia. The patient needs someone to talk to, not just a legal

---

[97] Ibid.

assessment. It is more than just assessing whether criteria for euthanasia has been met. A normal doctor might be able to offer other solutions; better pain relief perhaps, the euthanasia doctor does not do that.

The mobile units deal with over 1,000 cases a year and are free of charge to Dutch citizens. Initially the organisation covered the costs but then entered discussions with insurance companies on agreements that allow the mobile euthanasia unit service to be available through Dutch medical insurance. This is a serious cause for concern because the bottom line for insurance companies, including medical insurers, is profitability. In a system where economics takes precedence over ethics decisions about end of life care can be determined by financial controllers. The mobile euthanasia units are easily accessed as people (sick or not) or their relatives can submit their applications via telephone or email and if the patient's request fulfils a number of criteria, the team is then dispatched.

The team makes contact with the doctor who refused to help the patient to die and ask what his or her reasons were. Frequently the reasons given are religious or ethical. If the team is satisfied that the patient's motives are genuine, they will contact another doctor with whom they will start the euthanasia process.

The Royal Dutch Medical Association (KNMG) supports euthanasia in principle if there is no alternative, but has distanced itself from the NVVE initiative, arguing that giving it the name Life End will foster the idea that it is for those who are simply "weary of life" rather than those who are sick. The teams are limited to one house visit a week to minimise the psychological impact on them. "Mercy killings" of this nature are based on a warped understanding of the meaning of autonomy and a lack of understanding of the true nature of mercy.

Legalising euthanasia and assisted suicide undermines the sanctity of life and the Federation of Dutch Physicians fears the teams may end the lives of people who could be treated. A spokesman said: "In the worst cases, people could die who perhaps could have received some other help".[98] In Britain, Phyllis Bowman of Right to Life said she was "absolutely appalled" by the development.[99] The units, which are backed by the Dutch government are supposed to conform to the 2002 law that made Holland the first country in the world to allow euthanasia since Nazi Germany.

The former Archbishop of Canterbury, Dr Rowan Williams, said in a General Synod debate (February 2012) that it would be a "disaster" if assisted suicide was legalised in Britain.[100] However, one senses that his appeal will fall on deaf ears and that ultimately this is the road the rest of Europe is headed down. Liberalism is like the Pied Piper of Hamelin playing a hypnotic tune while many are dancing their way merrily into the captivity of such an agenda.[101]

---

[98] Simon Caldwell, *The Guardian*, 1 March, 2012.

[99] Ibid.

[100] Ibid.

[101] The Pied Piper of Hamelin is the subject of a legend concerning the departure or death of a great number of children from the town of Hamelin in Germany, in the Middle-Ages. The earliest references describe a piper, dressed in multi-coloured clothing, leading the children away from the town never to return. In the 16th century the story was expanded into a full narrative, in which the piper is a rat-catcher hired by the town to lure rats away with his magic pipe. When the citizenry refuses to pay for this service, he retaliates by turning his magic on their children, leading them away as he had the rats. This version of the story spread as a fairy tale. This version has also appeared in the writings of, amongst others, Johann Wolfgang von Goethe, the Brothers Grimm and Robert Browning.

Rowan Williams said: "To change the law on this subject is, I believe, to change something vital in our sense of the value of life itself."[102]

In the past, most euthanasia cases have involved cancer patients who ran out of treatment options. Now people in the early stages of dementia and those suffering from chronic psychiatric problems can also be eligible under present legislation. Although the NVVE says it will, if possible, co-operate with family doctors it is in reality interfering with the family doctor/patient relationship.

The Mail Online reported that a senile sixty-four year old Dutch woman was euthanized even though she was no longer able to express her wish to die.[103] The unnamed woman was a long-term supporter of the controversial practice and had made a written statement when she was still well, saying how she wished to die. But the pensioner, who died in March, 2011 had been unable to reiterate her instructions as the disease progressed. Constance de Vries, who acts as a second opinion doctor for such cases said the case had serious implications for Dutch euthanasia law as it means patients who are no longer able to make their wishes clear can still be helped to die.[104]

A report released in 2011 revealed a total of 21 patients with early-stage dementia, including Alzheimer disease, died by lethal injection in Holland in 2010. This was the first time dementia sufferers were included in the country's euthanasia statistics.

---

[102] Simon Caldwell, The Guardian, 1 March, 2012
[103] Sarah Nelson, "Senile 64-year-old Dutch woman is euthanized even though she was no longer able to express her wish to die", Daily Mail, 10 November, 2011.
[104] Ibid.

None of the cases is thought to have involved any illegal act on the part of health professionals, and each time the patient was considered capable of giving their consent. However, the figures are alarming as the pool of patients who qualify for euthanasia in the Netherlands is expanding. The figures, which were formally released later in the summer, were leaked on NOS, the state television news channel.

The NOS report included video footage of a sixty-three year old Alzheimer's sufferer Guusje de Koning, explaining to her children why she wanted to die at the hands of her doctor. She said she had witnessed her own father's slow decline and death through the illness, adding: "I don't want that. I don't want to suffer." Euthanasia advocates are using her story to promote the idea that euthanasia for dementia sufferers is a suitable way to avoid suffering and expensive healthcare and nursing home costs.

However, the practice of assisted suicide for dementia patients remains controversial. While some 95% of Holland's population support the country's euthanasia laws, only 33% of Dutch doctors agree with offering lethal injections to dementia sufferers.

Those who defend euthanasia and assisted suicide say that it can only be applied under very strict conditions, under medical supervision, and at the request of the patient. But a position paper published by the Dutch Physicians Association (KNMG) says unbearable and lasting suffering should not be the only criteria physicians consider when a patient requests euthanasia. The KNMG says the new guidelines clarify the responsibilities, possibilities and limitations that physicians have within the regulations of the 2002 euthanasia law.[105]

---

[105] 'Termination of Life on Request and Assisted Suicide [Review Procedures] Act' or 'Euthanasia Act' for short.

Until now, factors such as income or a patient's social life played almost no role when physicians were considering a euthanasia request. However, the new guidelines will certainly change that. After almost a year of discussions, the KNMG has published a paper, which says a combination of social factors and diseases and ailments that are not terminal may also qualify as unbearable and lasting suffering under the Euthanasia Act.

Vulnerable

At the moment, there are approximately one million elderly people in the Netherlands with multi-morbidity (two or more long-term diseases or ailments) and that number is expected to rise to 1.5 million in the course of the coming decade. According to the new guidelines, vulnerability (or fragility) refers to health problems, and the ensuing limitations, as well as a concurrent decline in other areas of life such as financial resources, social network and social skills.

As people age, many suffer from a complex array of gradually worsening problems, which can include poor eyesight, deafness, fatigue, difficulty in walking and incontinence as well as loss of dignity, status, financial resources, an ever-shrinking social network and loss of social skills. Although this accumulation of ailments and diseases is not life threatening as such, it does have a negative impact on the quality of life and make the elderly vulnerable or fragile.

Loneliness

Under the Euthanasia Act, a request for euthanasia may be honoured only if a patient is undergoing unbearable and lasting suffering. The KNMG now says that, if non-medical factors such as income or loneliness are to be taken into consideration, other specialists must be consulted when a patient has requested euthanasia. But weighing up non-medical factors is far from simple. It is quite possible that the same constellation of factors would be experienced as unbearable and lasting suffering by one patient but quite tolerable by another. This makes it extremely difficult. If euthanasia is allowed for "patients" who are not suffering from a terminal disease, that is, for non-medical reasons, that could include the onset of dementia or chronic psychological problems. Some people would consider these conditions constitute unbearable and lasting suffering. Many people suffer from depression. The thought of dying might be the only thing that gives them any relief. In this condition the emotional pain is sometimes unbearable. The only thing that prevents them from suicide is the impact this would have on their families, and perhaps their faith. One other significant deterrent is the unavailability of an easy-to-access euthanasia or assisted suicide service. If these services are available, many depressed people will use them. However, if given a chance and offered appropriate help and hope most people will emerge from the dark tunnel of despair into the brighter realisation that life is worth living.

Dutch Doctors Support Euthanasia

An on-line poll in July 2011 surveyed general practitioners in the Netherlands and found that Dutch doctors support it, though sometimes reluctantly.[106] Here is what the poll of 800 doctors found. The vast majority (87%) were willing in principle to participate in legal euthanasia. About 68% said that they had participated in euthanasia in the last

---

[106]http://opinie.eenvandaag.nl/uploads/doc/huisartsen-euthanasie.pdf
One accepts that on-line polls may be unreliable but it is an interesting snapshot.

five years. Of these, 29% did it once; 25% twice; 33% 3 to 5 times; and 11% more than 5 times.

Euthanasia is certainly on the agenda. In half of the doctors' practices, euthanasia is a topic, which is increasingly discussed. About 65% had felt pressure from patients or relatives to perform euthanasia and about half of them said that there was pressure to do it quickly. About a third of them felt that the pressure had increased over the last five years.

There was a limit for most of the doctors. About 74% said that they would not be willing to euthanize patients simply because they feared unbearable suffering. About 65% were not willing if patients are simply tired of living – although 20% were willing.

Most doctors are satisfied with the current state of euthanasia regulation in the Netherlands – about 76%. And in response to the statement "euthanasia has no place in a general practice" 89% disagreed.

In the Netherlands, terminal sedation is said to be displacing euthanasia to some extent. Several questions dealt with what the poll termed "palliative sedation." About 90% had used this at some stage in the past five years. However, most doctors said that "palliative sedation" seldom led to the death of their patients.

National Survey

A national survey conducted by three university hospitals shows that just 33% of Dutch doctors are willing to use euthanasia in cases of early dementia. The poll was carried out by the university hospitals of Utrecht, Groningen and

Rotterdam.[107] People with dementia are only able to give their consent to euthanasia in the early stages of the disease. In the later stages, patients are too disoriented to make informed decisions.[108]

American Research

Between 1994 and 1998, support among America's cancer specialists for physician-assisted suicide declined more than 50% and support for euthanasia plummeted by almost 75%, according to a survey published in the *Annals of Internal Medicine*.

The study—conducted in 1998 by researchers from Maryland, Colorado, Massachusetts, New York, Texas, and Tennessee—surveyed 3,299 members of the American Society of Clinical Oncology (ASCO) regarding their attitudes and practices with respect to assisted suicide and euthanasia.

Researchers, led by Dr Ezekiel Emanuel from the National Institutes of Health, found that only 22.5% supported "physician-assisted suicide for a terminally ill patient with prostate cancer who had unremitting pain despite optimal pain management," while 6.5% favoured euthanasia for such a patient. Moreover, fewer than 16% (15.6%) expressed a willingness to engage in assisted suicide, and only 2% said they would be willing to euthanize the patient.

When the findings were compared to a similar study conducted by Dr Emanuel in 1994, researchers discovered

---

[107] Report from a television programme.

[108] The number of people with dementia who have resorted to euthanasia has risen from 3 in 2006 to 21 in 2010. The overall number of cases of euthanasia has also risen: in 2006 the body responsible for the judicial review of euthanasia cases was informed of 1,900 cases, compared with 2,700 in 2010.

that support for euthanasia and physician-assisted suicide has decreased substantially. Using the same prototypical case of the terminally ill patients with unremitting pain they found that support for assisted suicide dropped by half, from 45.5% in 1994 to 22.5% in the current study. Euthanasia support fell by nearly 75%, from 22.7% in 1994 to only 6.5% in the new survey.

Equally significant are the findings that doctors who had received better training in end-of-life care were less likely to engage in assisted suicide or euthanasia, and that physicians who were unable to obtain adequate care for their cancer patients were more likely to favour both practices.[109] These study results emphasise the need for physician education of optimal pain and palliative care practices. Physicians who are better informed about end-of-life issues feel less need to use euthanasia and physician-assisted suicide.

Terminally Ill Seldom Consider Euthanasia or Assisted Suicide

While 60% of terminally ill patients in a study indicated support for euthanasia and assisted suicide in a hypothetical case, only 10% said that they had seriously considered the induced-death practices for themselves. The study presents the first research to actually track over a period of time terminally ill patients' attitudes and desires regarding euthanasia and assisted suicide.[110]

---

[109] E. J. Emanuel et al., "Attitudes and Practices of U.S. Oncologists regarding Euthanasia and Physician-Assisted Suicide," *Annals of Internal Medicine*, 1 October, 2000, pp. 527-532.
[110] Published in the 15 November, 2000 issue of the *Journal of the American Medical Association* (JAMA) as one of a series of articles and commentaries on end-of-life care.

Between March 1996 and July 1997, researchers surveyed 988 terminally ill patients and 893 patient-designated primary caregivers. The data revealed that psychological factors, such as depression and the patients' sense that they were no longer appreciated, were the most significant factors associated with patients' considering and planning euthanasia or assisted suicide deaths. Those who reported that they had more pain or required substantial care were also more likely to consider having their lives ended, and their caregivers were more likely to support a decision for euthanasia or assisted suicide. In contrast, the majority (89.6%) of terminally ill patients who did not personally consider either practice were less likely to have depressive symptoms and more likely to feel appreciated, be 65 or over, African American, and religious.

Researchers also noted, "While a majority (60.2%) of those surveyed find euthanasia acceptable for terminally ill patients with unremitting pain, less than a third support it when the patient desires it because of fear of being a burden on the family." Furthermore, the study's authors observed that there appears to be "a tension between attitudes and practices, between the reason people find euthanasia and Physician Assisted Suicide (PAS) acceptable—predominantly pain—and the main factor motivating interest in euthanasia or PAS—patient depression."

In addition, researchers found that the patients' personal considerations of euthanasia and assisted suicide were significantly unstable. More than 50% of the patients who initially expressed interest in ending their lives later changed their minds, and some of those who had not considered these induced-death practices at the initial interview began to do so. "Depressive symptoms and dyspnea (shortness of breath) were associated with this instability," researchers wrote. "This suggests that when physicians are confronted by a patient's request for euthanasia or PAS, they should attend to the possibility of depression and other psychological stressors" they concluded.[111]

Regarding the researchers' recommendation that physicians should take steps to determine if patients who request euthanasia or assisted suicide are depressed or are under other "psychological stressors," it is interesting to note that during the first two years under Oregon's permissive assisted-suicide law, less than 35% (15 out of 43) of the patients who received lethal prescriptions were referred for a psychiatric or psychological consultation.[112]

The mental assessment rate is even lower in the Netherlands where only 3% of all those euthanized or assisted in suicide receive professional mental health evaluations. According to Dr Linda Ganzini, director of geriatric psychiatry at the Veteran's Affairs Medical Center in Portland, Origen, "Studies of dying cancer patients reveal that between 59%-100% of patients wanting hastened death have major depressive disorders." "Depressed people," she explained, "often focus on the worst possible outcomes and are impaired by apathy, pessimism, and low self-esteem." Ganzini wrote, "The experience of palliative care psychiatrists is that depression treatment is effective in terminally ill patients."[113]

---

[111] E. J. Emanuel, D. L. Fairclough, and L. L. Emanuel, "Attitudes and Desires Related to Euthanasia and Physician-Assisted Suicide Among Terminally Ill Patients and Their Caregivers," *JAMA*, 15 November, 2001, pp. 2460-2468.
[112] Oregon Health Division, "Oregon's Death with Dignity Act: The Second Year's Experience," Table 2, 23 February, 2000.
[113] L. Ganzini, "Commentary: Assessment of Clinical Depression in Patients Who Request Physician-Assisted Death," *Journal of Pain and Symptom Management*, June 2000, pp. 474-478.

CHAPTER 6 Dancing with Death

I n his book *Seduced by Death*, Herbert Hendin reported that one reason the Dutch people have not turned against their euthanasia law is that doctors and the media in Holland do not candidly report about the many abuses and violations of the law that occur with regard to their country's euthanasia policy.

A news report on Radio Netherlands, to commemorate the fifth anniversary of formal legalisation, gives a good example. It contained no discussion of the approximately 1,000 patients per year who, without requesting euthanasia, are nonetheless killed by Dutch doctors. It contained no discussion of the Dutch Supreme Court permitting the depressed to be assisted in suicide. It contained no substantive dissent at all.

It did, however, contain quotations from Dr Bert Keizer, author of the book *Dancing with Mr D* in which he describes his euthanasia work as a nursing home doctor. He said, for instance, "People who ask for euthanasia are not put under pressure; they are under the burden of suffering."

Hendin and others have demonstrated otherwise. And there are all sorts of ways to pressure patients into killing themselves—some of which Keizer himself notes in his book. For example, there is Van de Berg, a Parkinson's patient who asks for euthanasia. However, before Keizer can kill him, Van de Berg receives a letter from his religious brother telling him that it would be a sin to commit suicide and would violate the way they were raised as children by their parents. The man hesitates. Keizer is not amused:

And now this letter, which to my surprise, he takes seriously. I don't know what to do with such a wavering death wish. It's getting on my nerves. Does he want to die or doesn't he? I hope I don't have to go over the whole business again...Suddenly, I have an idea: "You know what we'll do? We"ll ask Hendrik Terborgh, our vicar. Would you agree to that?" He cries and types "yes". Next day Hendrik tells me that it's all right. He refers to his meeting with Van de Berg. "Well, he knows what has to be done. He knows what he wants now"...It goes well. He has good veins. [114]

Keizer does not tell us what the vicar told Van de Berg, but I think it is a good guess that he did not engage in suicide prevention or validate the brother's religious concerns. Also, note that Keizer is far more concerned about the bureaucratic matters than with the well-being of his own patient. One can imagine how depressing it would feel to have such a doctor, how alone and abandoned it would seem.

Here is another form of pressure: Not telling a patient about the ability to control pain, or even waiting for a final diagnosis before agreeing to kill a patient. Keizer is asked to euthanize Teus, a man whom he thinks—but does not know—has lung cancer. He discusses the case with his colleague who asks if the patient is really suffering badly. The reply: "Is it for us to answer that question? All I know is that he wants to die more or less upright and that he doesn't want to crawl to his grave the way a dog crawls howling to the sidewalk after he's been hit by a car." [115]

Patients with cancer do not have to die in this manner. Proper medical care would prevent it. However, this is never mentioned to the patient. Nor, from what we read, does

---

[114] Dr. Bert Keizer, *Dancing with Mr. D*, Nan A. Talese / Doubleday; 1st edition, February 17, 1997, p.94.
[115] Op. cit., p 37.

Keizer even know about the powers of morphine to control cancer pain. He does not even discuss hospice with Teus or his family—which is outrageous negligence. Instead, as he describes when Keizer gets ready to euthanize Teus, he will countenance no doubts:

I tell Jaarsma and De Goover (Keizer's colleagues) that Teus is going to die that evening. Jaarsma seems sore but raises no objection. De Goover looks sharply at me, trying to work out how scared I am. If anyone so much as whispers "cortisone" or "uncertain diagnosis" I'll hit him.[116]

An interesting question is raised in the book when Keizer is asked by a colleague whether he should love his patients. His response is that although there are upsetting situations he does not love them.

Normalisation

The ultimate attempt to normalise euthanasia in the Netherlands and make it seem an ordinary part of everyday life was the showing in 1994 on Dutch television of *Death on Request*.[117] This was a film of a patient being put to death by euthanasia. Maarten Nederhurst, who created the film, found an agreeable patient and doctor by contacting the Dutch Voluntary Euthanasia Society.

The patient, Cees van Wendel, had been diagnosed as having motor neuron disease in June 1993.[118] He expressed his wish for euthanasia a month later. Severe muscular weakness confined him to a wheel chair; his speech was

---

[116] Op. cit., p.39.

[117] "Death on Request", Ikon Television Network, 1994.

[118] Motor neuron disease is a debilitating disease characterised by rapidly progressive weakness, muscle atrophy and muscle spasticity, difficulty speaking (dysarthria), difficulty swallowing (dysphagia), and difficulty breathing (dyspnea).

barely audible. Almost 700,000 people saw the first showing of the film in the Netherlands. Subsequently, the right to show the film has been acquired by countries throughout the world. *Prime Time Live* excerpted and showed a representative segment to American viewers with a voiceover in English. Sam Donaldson introduced the programme saying that it took no sides on the issue but added "It is a story of courage and love."[119] In contextualising the programme as such, a keynote was struck for acceptance of euthanasia. The doctor, Wilfred van Oijen, is the film's most significant person and the patient is not nearly as conspicuous.

The film opens with a chilly scene in winter and trees are bare of leaves. It is cold, wet, inhospitable - not a bad time to die. In an undershirt in his bathroom, the doctor combs his hair getting ready for just another day. His encounters will include treating a child of about ten months, a pregnant woman and a baby, and bringing death to Cees. The purpose of the film is to include euthanasia both as part of his daily burden as a doctor and as the natural course of events.

In the two house calls van Oijen makes to Cees, of most interest is the tension between the films professed message - that all want release from illness, the patient most of all - and the message conveyed by what is actually filmed. The relationship depicted is between van Oijen and Antoinette, who has called the doctor and clearly wants her husband to die.

The wife appears repulsed by her husband's illness, never touching him during their conversation and never permitting Cees to answer any questions the doctor asks directly. She "translates" for him, although Cees is at this point in his illness intelligible, able to communicate verbally, but slowly, and

---

[119] "Death on Request," *Prime Time Live*, December 8, 1994.

able to type out messages on his computer. The doctor asks him if he wants euthanasia, but his wife replies.

When Cees begins to cry, the doctor moves sympathetically toward him to touch his arm, but his wife tells the doctor to move away and says it is better to let him cry alone. During his weeping she continues to talk to the doctor. The doctor at no time asks to speak to Cees alone; neither does he ask if anything would make it easier for him to communicate or if additional help in his care would make him want to live.

Virtually the entire film is set up to avoid confronting any of the patient's feelings or how the relationship with his wife affects his agreeing to die. Cees is never seen alone. Van Oijen is obliged to obtain a second opinion from a consultant. The consultant, who appears well known to the doctor, also makes no attempt to communicate with Cees alone, and he too permits the wife to answer all the questions put to Cees. When the consultant asks the *pro forma* question if Cees is sure he wants to go ahead, Antoinette answers for him. The consultant seems uncomfortable, asks a few more questions, and leaves. The consultation takes practically no time at all. The pharmacist who supplies the lethal medication (one shot to put Cees to sleep and another to help him die) seems only another player in this carefully choreographed event.

Antoinette visits the doctor to ask where "we stand." She wants the euthanasia over with. Cees has set several dates, but keeps moving them back. Now he has settled on his birthday, and they arrange for van Oijen to do it at eight o'clock after Cees celebrates by drinking a glass of port. Cees makes a joke that sleeping is a little death but this time his sleep will be a lot of death. Van Oijen tries to laugh warmly. Antoinette keeps her distance from the two and remarks that the day has gone slowly and it seemed eight o'clock would never come.

Antoinette helps Cees into bed in preparation for van Oijen to administer the first shot. Van Oijen smiles, gives the injection, and explains the medication will take a while to put Cees into a deep sleep. No one says goodbye. Only after the shot has put Cees to sleep does Antoinette murmur something to her husband. She then moves into the other room with the doctor to permit Cees to sink into a deeper sleep. After a few minutes, they return. When the doctor wants to place Cees in a more comfortable position, she withdraws again. After the second shot is administered, Antoinette and van Oijen sit next to the bed, both holding the arm that has received the injections. Antoinette asks if this was good, presumably wanting to know if it was "good" to kill Cees. Van Oijen reassures her. They leave Cees alone very quickly. On the way into the next room, Antoinette takes a note Cees wrote to her about their relationship and what it meant to him and reads it to the doctor. She seems to want to convey to him that they in fact once had a relationship.

From the beginning, the loneliness and isolation of the husband haunts the film. He is treated from the start as an object and his death seems inevitable. One leaves the film feeling that death with dignity requires more than effective management. It requires being accorded personhood even though one's speech is slurred or one needs to point to letters on a board or communicate through writing on one's computer. Throughout the film, Cees's wife denies him such personhood, as does the doctor, who never questions her control over all of the patient's communications and even the doctor's communication with Cees. The doctor and wife took away Cees's personhood before motor neuron disease had claimed it.

A Good Death for Louise

An article in the *New York Times Magazine* in 1993 (and featured on the cover) also used a case study to try to prove the value of assisted suicide to an American audience.[120] The article described the assisted suicide of Louise, a Seattle woman whose death was arranged by her doctor and the Reverend Ralph Mero, head of Compassion in Dying, a group that champions legalising assisted suicide. Members of the group counsel the terminally ill, offer advice on lethal doses, convince cautious doctors to become involved, and are present during the death. Mero and his followers do not provide the means for suicide (the patients obtain such help from their doctors) and claim not to encourage the patients to seek suicide.

Mero arranged for a *Times* reporter to interview Louise in the last weeks of her life, offering Louise's death as an illustration of the beneficial effects of the organisation's work. Yet the account serves equally to illustrate how assisted suicide made both life and death miserable for Louise.

Louise, who was referred to Mero by her doctor, had been ill with an unnamed, degenerative neurological disease. The reporter tells us "Louise had mentioned suicide periodically during her six years of illness, but the subject came into sudden focus in May during a sombre visit to her doctor's office." As Louise recounted it, "I really wasn't having any different symptom; I just knew something had changed. I looked the doctor right in the eye and said, 'I'm starting to die.' And she said, 'I've had the same impression for a couple of days.'"

---

[120] Lisa Belkin, "There's No Simple Suicide," *New York Times Magazine*, 14 November, 1993.

130

An MRI scan confirmed that the frontal lobes of Louise's brain had begun to deteriorate, a sign that led her doctor to warn Louise that her life would most likely be measured in months, perhaps weeks. Louise said her doctor explained that:

She didn't want to scare me... she just wanted to be honest. She told me that once the disease becomes active, it progresses very fast, that I would become mentally incapacitated and wouldn't be myself, couldn't care for myself anymore. She would have to look into hospice care, or the hospital, or some other facility where I would stay until I died.

We are told that Louise did not hesitate with her answer. "I can't do that... I don't want that." The reporter continues, "Her doctor, Louise thought, looked both sad and relieved. 'I know, I know,' the doctor said. 'But it has to come from you.'" Louise makes sure that they are both talking about suicide and says, "That's what I'd like to do, go for as long as I can and then end it."

What has happened between Louise and her doctor? The doctor's quick affirmation that Louise is starting to die, even before the MRI scan confirms her decline, is disturbing. She prefaces a grim description of Louise's prognosis with assurance that she does not want to scare her. The doctor's relief when Louise indicates that she is choosing suicide gives us some feeling about her attitudes toward patients in Louise's condition.

As the account continues, the doctor indicates that she would be willing to help, had recently helped another patient whom Louise knew, and said she would prescribe enough barbiturates to kill Louise. To avoid legal trouble, she would not be there when Louise committed suicide. They exchanged several hugs and Louise went home. The doctor called

Compassion in Dying for advice. The reporter quotes the doctor as saying about contacting Mero, "I was ecstatic to find someone who's doing what he's doing...I loved the fact that there were guidelines."

On the phone, Mero advises the doctor on the medication to prescribe and then visits Louise, suggesting that he is prepared to help Louise die before knowing or even meeting her or in any way determining whether she meets any guidelines. When he does meet Louise, she asks him at once if he will help her with her suicide and be there when she does it and she is almost tearfully grateful when he says "yes".

He repeats many times that it has to be her choice. Louise affirms that it is, saying that all she wants "these next few weeks is to live as peacefully as possible." Louise seems concerned with being close to others during her final time and with spending what is left of her life in an environment of loving leave-taking.

The doctor is concerned that Louise's judgement might soon become impaired: "The question is, at what point is her will going to be affected, and, if suicide is what she wants, does she have the right to do it when she still has the will?" The doctor, like Mero, says she does not want to influence the patient, but worries that Louise might not act in time. "If she loses her mind and doesn't do this, she's going into the hospital. But the last thing I want to do is pressure her to do this."

Yet the closeness before dying that Louise seemed to want is lost in the flurry of activity and planning for her death as each of those involved with her dying pursues his or her own requirements. At a subsequent meeting of Mero and Louise, with Louise's mother and her doctor also present, Mero gives Louise a checklist in which he reviews steps to be taken during the suicide from the food to be eaten to how the doctor would call the medical examiner.

The doctor indicates she will be out of town for the next week, but that she has told her partner of Louise's plans. "You don't have to wait for me to get back," she tells Louise, hinting, the reporter tells us, that it might be a good idea not to wait. The doctor was more direct when alone with Louise's mother, telling her that she was afraid Louise might not be coherent enough to act if she waited past the coming weekend.

The doctor and Mero discuss how pointed they can be with Louise, wanting her to make an informed decision without frightening her into acting sooner than she was ready. They hoped, "she would read between the lines." Mero assures the reporter that he always wants to err on the side of caution. Nonetheless, a few days after the meeting, Mero called the reporter in New York, asking her to come to Seattle as soon as possible. He knew she was planning to come the following week, but he warned her not to wait that long.

The reporter leaves immediately for Seattle and finds Louise in a debilitated condition. She is in pain, getting weaker, and speaks of wanting to end her life while she can still be in control. She says she is almost ready, but not quite. She needs about a week, mainly to relax and be with her mother.

The reporter blurted out, "Your doctor feels that if you don't act by this weekend you may not be able to." Her words are met with a "wrenching silence" and Louise, looking sharply at her mother, indicates that she hadn't been told that. Her mother says gently that is what the doctor had told her. Louise looks terrified and her mother tells her it's OK to be afraid. "I'm not afraid. I just feel as if everyone is ganging up on me, pressuring me," Louise said, "I just want some time."

Louise's mother was growing less certain that Louise would actually take her own life. When she tried to ask her directly, Louise replied, "I feel like it's all we ever talk about." A friend who had agreed to be with Louise during the suicide is also uncomfortable with Louise's ambivalence but is inclined to attribute her irritability and uncertainty to her mental decline. When Louise indicates that she would wait for Mero to return from a trip and ask his opinion on her holding on for a few days, the friend indicates that this was a bad idea since someone like Mero who did not know her well might miss the change in her mood.

Like many people in extreme situations, Louise has expressed two conflicting wishes - to live and to die - and found support only for the latter. The anxiety of her doctor, Mero, her mother, and her friend that Louise might change her mind or lose her "will" may originate in their desire to honour Louise's wishes, or even in their own view of what kind of life is worth living, but eventually overrides the emotions Louise is clearly feeling and comes to affect what happens more than Louise's will. Although those around her act in the name of supporting Louise's autonomy, Louise begins to lose her own death.

Despite predictions, Louise makes it through the weekend. Over the next days, she speaks with Mero by phone, but he tells the reporter he kept the conversations short because he was uncomfortable with her growing dependence on his opinion. Nevertheless, after a few such conversations, the contents of which are not revealed, Louise indicated she was ready; that evening Mero came and the assisted suicide was performed.

A detailed description of the death scene reveals that Louise did not die immediately but lingered for seven hours. Had she not died from the pills, Mero subsequently implied to the reporter, he would have used a plastic bag to suffocate her, although this violates the Compassion in Dying guidelines.

Everyone - Mero, the friend, the mother, the doctor, and the reporter - became part of a network pressuring Louise to stick to her decision and to do so in a timely manner. The death was influenced by their anxiety that she might want to live. Mero and the doctor influence the feelings of the mother and the friend so that the issue is not their warm leave-taking and the affection they have had for Louise, but whether they can get her to die according to the time requirements of Mero, the doctor (who probably cannot stay away indefinitely), the reporter (who has her own deadlines), and the disease, which turns out to be on a more flexible schedule than previously thought.

Louise is explicit that the doctor, mother, friend, and reporter have become instruments of pressure in moving her along. Mero appears to act more subtly and indirectly through his effect on the others involved with Louise.

Without a death, there is, of course, no story, and Mero and the reporter have a stake in the story. The doctor develops a time frame for Louise; her own past troubling experiences with a patient who was a friend seems to colour the doctor's need to have things over with quickly and in her absence if possible. Louise is clearly frustrated by not having someone to talk to who has no stake in persuading her.

Individually and collectively, those involved engender a terror in Louise with which she must struggle alone, while they reassure each other that they are gratifying her last wishes. The end of her life does not seem like death with dignity; nor is there much compassion conveyed in the way Louise was helped to die.

Although the mother, friend, and physician may have acted out of good intentions in assisting the suicide, none appears to have honoured Louise's need for a "peaceful" parting. None seems to have been able to accept the difficult emotions involved in loving someone who is dying and knowing there is little one can do but convey love and respect for the life that has been lived. The effort to deal with the discomfort of Louise's situation seems to drive the others to "do something" to eliminate the situation.

Watching someone die can be intolerably painful for those who care for the person. Their wish to have it over with quickly is understandable. Their feelings can become a form of pressure on the patient and must be separated from what the patient actually wants. The patient who wants to live until the end but senses his family cannot tolerate watching him die is familiar to those who care for the terminally ill. Once those close to the patient decide to assist in the suicide, their desire to have it over with can make the pressure put on the patient many times greater. The mood of those assisting is reflected in Macbeth's famous line, "If it were done when 'tis done, then 'twere well it were done quickly."[121]

Short of actually murdering her, it is hard to see how her doctor, Mero, her mother, her friend, and the reporter could have done more to rush her toward death. Case vignettes limited to one or two paragraphs describing the patient's medical symptoms, and leaving out the social context in which euthanasia is being considered, obscure such complex

---

[121] William Shakespeare, *Macbeth* (1.7.1-2). Macbeth says this to himself, meaning that if everything could be over with as soon as Duncan is killed, then it would be best for Macbeth to kill him quickly.

and often-subtle pressures on patients' "autonomous" decisions to seek death.

Empowerment for Whom?

Our culture supports the feelings that we should not tolerate situations we cannot control. "Death," Arnold Toynbee has said, "is un-American." The physician who feels a sense of failure and helplessness in the face of incurable disease, or the relative, who cannot bear the emotions of loss and separation, finds in assisted suicide and euthanasia an illusion of mastery over the disease and the accompanying feelings of helplessness. Determining when death will occur becomes a way of dealing with frustration.

In the selling of assisted suicide and euthanasia words like "empowerment" and "dignity" are associated only with the choice for dying. However, who is being empowered? The more one knows about individual cases, the more apparent it becomes that needs other than those of the patient often prevail. "Empowerment" flows toward the relatives, the doctor who offers a speedy way out if he cannot offer a cure, or the activists who have found in death a cause that gives meaning to their lives. The patient, who may have said she wants to die in the hope of receiving emotional reassurance that all around her want her to live, may find that like Louise she has set in motion a process whose momentum she cannot control. If death with dignity is to be a fact and not a selling slogan, surely what is required is a loving parting that acknowledges the value of the life lived and affirms its continuing meaning.

Euthanasia advocates try to use the individual case to demonstrate that there are some cases of rational or justifiable assisted suicide or euthanasia. If they can demonstrate that there are *some* such cases, they believe that would justify legalising euthanasia. Euthanasia advocates are arguing that if there are ten cases where euthanasia might be appropriate, we should legalise a practice that is likely to kill thousands inappropriately.

The appeal of assisted suicide and euthanasia is a symptom of our failure to develop a better response to death and the fear of intolerable pain or artificial prolongation of life. Work of a wider scope needs to be done now. There is a great deal of evidence that doctors are not sufficiently trained in relieving pain and other symptoms in the terminally ill. The principles of hospice care and development of effective interventions to alleviate suffering are well established and although in many parts of the UK it is well developed, the widespread provision of this resource is in its infancy. The public has not yet been educated as to the choices they have in refusing or terminating treatment nor has the medical profession learned how best to avoid setting in motion the technology that only prolongs a painful process of dying. And we have not devoted enough time in medical schools or hospitals to educating future physicians about coming to terms with the painful truth that there will be patients they will not be able to save but whose needs they must address.

How we deal with illness, age, and decline says a great deal about who and what we are, both as individuals and as a society. We should not buy into the view of those who are engulfed by fear of death or by suicidal despair that death is the preferred solution to the problems of illness, age, and depression. To do so would be encouraging the worst tendencies of depressed patients, most of whom can be helped to overcome their condition. By rushing to "normalise" euthanasia as a medical option along with accepting or refusing treatment, we are inevitably laying the groundwork for a culture that will not only turn euthanasia into a "cure" for depression but may prove to exert a coercion to die on patients when they are most vulnerable. Death ought to be hard to sell.[122]

[122] See Herbert Hendin, M.D., professor of psychiatry at New York Medical College and the executive director of The American Suicide Foundation, New York. I am indebted to the argument of his article which originally appeared in the Hastings Center Report, vol. 25, no. 3, May-June 1995.

CHAPTER 7 Sick Society

The Groningen Protocol (as mentioned earlier) was the proposal of doctors in the Netherlands for the establishment of an independent committee charged with selecting babies and other severely handicapped or disabled people for euthanasia. Under the Groningen protocol, if doctors at the hospital think a child is suffering unbearably from a terminal condition, they have the authority to end the child's life. The protocol is used primarily for new-borns, but it covers any child up to age twelve. It is ostensibly about infants born with such severe disabilities that doctors can see they have extreme pain and no hope for life. It sounds merciful and humanitarian and may well be motivated by compassion but it must be stated clearly that such "compassion" is seriously misguided.

In highly charged polemical debate, the Groningen Protocol has been compared to the Wannsee Conference.[123] The Wannsee Conference was a meeting of senior officials of the Nazi German regime, held in the Berlin suburb of Wannsee on 20 January, 1942. The purpose of the conference, called by the director of the SS, was to ensure the cooperation of administrative leaders of various government departments in the implementation of the final solution to the Jewish question, whereby most of the Jews of German-occupied Europe would be deported to Poland and exterminated.

---

[123] In some parliamentary discussions in the Hague.

Undoubtedly, pro-euthanasia activists and others find such a comparison deeply offensive. The Nazi programme was about non-voluntary euthanasia (murder) which was not motivated by compassion. Nevertheless, there are some parallels, which will be explored later. Opponents of euthanasia and assisted suicide should not be gagged by such hypersensitivity.

The Hippocratic Oath

In the Netherlands, 31% of paediatricians have killed infants and a fifth of these killings were performed without the consent of parents. The arrogance of those in the medical profession who behave like this just beggars belief. In Ireland in the recent past, it was discovered that hospitals were harvesting organs from deceased patients without the knowledge or consent of their next of kin.

The Hippocratic Oath has been historically taken by physicians and other healthcare professionals swearing to practice medicine honestly. It states:

> I will apply dietetic measures for the benefit of the sick according to my ability and judgement; I will keep them from harm and injustice. I will neither give a deadly drug to anybody if asked for it, nor will I make a suggestion to this effect. Similarly I will not give to a woman an abortive remedy. In purity and holiness I will guard my life and my art...Whatever houses I may visit, I will come for the benefit of the sick, remaining free of all intentional injustice, of all mischief...[124]

---

[124] Stephen H. Miles, *The Hippocratic Oath and the Ethics of Medicine*, Oxford University Press, 2003.

Doctors who engage in euthanasia and assisted suicide might like to emphasise the phrasing concerning their discretion about what is of "benefit" to the sick, in their "judgement". However, the oath clearly states, "I will neither give a deadly drug to anybody if asked for it, nor will I make a suggestion to this effect." No amount of hermeneutical gymnastics can evade the original intended meaning of this. But one cannot be too surprised about the willingness of doctors to breach the terms of this solemn vow given that many have long ago compromised on other clauses of the oath, such as, "I will not give to a woman an abortive remedy".

The Oath has been modified many times, in several different countries. One of the most significant revisions is the Declaration of Geneva, first drafted in 1948 by the World Medical Association, which in turn has since been revised several times. While there is currently no legal obligation for medical students to swear an oath upon graduating, 98% of American medical students swear some form of oath, while only 50% of British medical students do.

However, the vast majority of oaths or declarations sworn have been heavily modified and modernised. For example, the oath's prohibition on abortion predates modern laws.

The Declaration of Geneva (Physician's Oath) was adopted by the General Assembly of the World Medical Association (WMA) at Geneva in 1948, amended in 1968, 1983, 1994 and editorially revised in 2005 and 2006. It is a declaration of a physician's dedication to the humanitarian goals of medicine, a declaration that was especially important in view of the medical crimes which had just been committed in Nazi Germany. The Declaration of Geneva was intended as a revision of the Hippocratic Oath to a formulation of that oath's moral truths that could be comprehended and acknowledged in a modern way.

During the post-World War II era and immediately after its foundation, the WMA showed concern over the state of medical ethics in general, taking the responsibility for setting ethical guidelines for the world's physicians. The details of the Nazi Doctors' Trial at Nuremberg and the revelations about what the Imperial Japanese Army had done at Unit 731 in China during the war clearly demonstrated the need for reform, and for a re-affirmed set of guidelines regarding both human rights and the rights of patients.

In 1946, a study committee had been appointed to prepare a "Charter of Medicine" which could be adopted as an oath or promise that every doctor in the world would make upon receiving his medical degree or diploma. It took two years of intensive study of the oaths and promises submitted by member associations to draft a modernised wording of the ancient oath of Hippocrates which was sent for consideration to the WMA's second general assembly in Geneva in 1948. The medical vow was adopted and the assembly agreed to name it the "Declaration of Geneva." This document was adopted by the World Medical Association only three months before the United Nations General Assembly adopted the Universal Declaration of Human Rights (1948) which provides for the security of the person.

The Declaration of Geneva, as currently published by the WMA says that at the time of being admitted as a member of the medical profession the following statement should be read:

I solemnly pledge to consecrate my life to the service of humanity;

I will give to my teachers the respect and gratitude that is their due;

I will practice my profession with conscience and dignity;

The health of my patient will be my first consideration;

I will respect the secrets that are confided in me, even after the patient has died;

I will maintain by all the means in my power, the honour and the noble traditions of the medical profession;

My colleagues will be my sisters and brothers;

I will not permit considerations of age, disease or disability, creed, ethnic origin, gender, nationality, political affiliation, race, sexual orientation, social standing or any other factor to intervene between my duty and my patient;

I will maintain the utmost respect for human life;

I will not use my medical knowledge to violate human rights and civil liberties, even under threat;

I make these promises solemnly, freely and upon my honour.[125]

Statements like "I will practice my profession with conscience and dignity" might seem a bit vague and subjective in the postmodern world but when they were coined they had a universally accepted meaning and that meaning is far from the way it is interpreted today.

---

[125] Stephen H. Miles, *The Hippocratic Oath and the Ethics of Medicine*, Oxford University Press, 2003.

The original oath read, "My colleagues will be my brothers" later changed to "sisters and brothers" to reflect gender balance. Age, disability, gender, and sexual orientation have been added as factors that must not interfere with a doctor's duty to a patient. It should be noted that "age" is mentioned because being old now is deemed to be a bad thing in society where once the wisdom of grey hairs was respected. Other rephrasing of existing elements has occurred. Secrets are to remain confidential "even after the patient has died." The violation of "human rights and civil liberties" replaces "the laws of humanity" as a forbidden use of medical knowledge.

The original declaration stated that a doctor would respect human life "from the time of conception" and the 1994 revision stated "from its beginning." which was removed altogether in the editorial revisions in the English version.[126] "The health" in general of a patient is now the doctor's first consideration compared to the "health and life" as stated in the original declaration. This was apparently changed to free the medical profession from extending life at all cost. It is clear that values have changed and previously accepted universal moral principles have been qualified, modified and/or deleted altogether.

Changing Criteria

Dutch euthanasia advocates initially said that patient killing would be limited to the competent, terminally ill who repeatedly ask for it. But then doctors began euthanizing patients who clearly were not terminally ill. Then they assured the public that medical killing would be limited to

---

[126] But is still found in other language versions that have not followed the editorial changes such as the German *Handbuch der ärztlichen Ethik.*

competent people with incurable illnesses (though not necessarily dying as such) or disabilities. Then doctors began killing patients who were depressed but not physically ill. Then they said only competent depressed people whose desire to commit suicide is "rational" will have their deaths facilitated. Then doctors began killing incompetent people, such as those with Alzheimer's. Then they said non-voluntary killing will be limited to patients who would have asked for it if they were competent. Now they euthanize children.

In the Netherlands, Groningen University Hospital has decided its doctors will euthanize children under the age of twelve, if doctors believe their suffering is intolerable or if they have an incurable illness. But what does that mean? In many cases, as occurs now with adults, it will become an excuse not to provide proper pain control for children who are dying of potentially agonising maladies such as cancer, and doing away with them instead. As for those deemed "incurable", this term is frequently a euphemism for killing babies and children who are seriously disabled.

For anyone paying attention to the continuing collapse of medical ethics in the Netherlands, this is not at all shocking. Dutch doctors have been surreptitiously engaging in eugenic euthanasia of disabled babies for years, although it technically is illegal, since infants cannot consent to be killed. Indeed, a disturbing 1997 study published in the British medical journal, *The Lancet*, revealed how deeply paediatric euthanasia has already metastasised into Dutch neonatal medical practice. According to the report, doctors were killing approximately 8% of all infants who died each year in the Netherlands. That amounts to approximately 80-90 per year. Of these, one-third would have lived more than a month, at least 10-15 of these killings involved infants who did not require life-sustaining treatment to stay alive. The study found that a shocking 45% of neo-natologists and 31%

146

of paediatricians who responded to questionnaires had killed infants.

It took the Dutch almost thirty years for their medical practices to fall to the point that Dutch doctors are able to engage in the kind of euthanasia activities that got some German doctors hanged after Nuremberg. For those who object to this assertion by claiming that German doctors killed disabled babies during World War II without consent of parents, so too do many Dutch doctors. Approximately 21% of the infant euthanasia deaths occurred without request or consent of parents. Moreover, since when did parents attain the moral right to have their children killed?

Euthanasia consciousness is catching. The Netherlands' neighbour Belgium decided to jump – lemming-like - off the same cliff as the Dutch. They have caught up with the Dutch in their free-fall into the moral abyss. The very first Belgian euthanasia of a person with multiple sclerosis violated the law; and just as occurs routinely in the Netherlands, the doctor involved faced no consequences. Belgium also practices neo-paediatric euthanasia. They justify permitting children to ask for their own mercy killing on the basis that young people have as much right to choose euthanasia as anyone else. Yet, the same children who are supposedly mature enough to decide to die would be ineligible to obtain a driver's license.

Why does accepting euthanasia as a remedy for suffering in very limited circumstances inevitably lead to never-ending expansion of the killing license? Blame the radically altered mind-set that results when killing is redefined from a moral wrong into a beneficent and legal act. If killing is right for, say the adult cancer patient, why shouldn't it be just as right for the disabled quadriplegic, the suicidal mother whose children have been killed in an accident, or the infant born with profound mental retardation? At that point, laws and regulations erected to protect the vulnerable against abuse come to be seen as obstructions that must be surmounted. From there, it is only a hop, skip, and jump to deciding that killing is the preferable option.

Physician Sentiment

A survey in the United States of more than 10,000 physicians concluded that approximately 16% of physicians would consider halting life-sustaining therapy because the family demands it, even if they believed that it was premature. Approximately 55% would not, and for the remaining 29%, it would depend on circumstances.[127] This study also stated that approximately 46% of physicians agree that physician-assisted suicide should be allowed in some cases; 41% do not, and the remaining 13% think it depends.[128]

In the United Kingdom, the pro assisted-dying group Dignity in Dying cite conflicting research on attitudes by doctors to assisted dying: with a 2009 Palliative Medicine-published survey showing 64% support (to 34% oppose) for assisted dying in cases where a patient has an incurable and painful disease, while 49% of doctors in a study published in the British Medical Council's *Medical Ethics* oppose changing the law on assisted dying to 39% in favour.[129]

Dr Peter Saunders, Chief Executive of the Christian Medical Fellowship (CMF) has commented on "Why the

---

[127] Leslie Kane "Exclusive Ethics Survey Results: Doctors Struggle With Tougher-Than-Ever Dilemmas", Medscape Medical Ethics, 11 November 2010.

[128] Op. cit.

[129] Dignity in Dying, Opinion on assisted dying.

Royal College of General Practitioners (RCGP) should stand firm on opposing a change in the law to allow assisted suicide."[130] Writing in July, 2013 at a time when the RCGP was conducting a consultation about the College's collective position on "assisted dying", asking, "What should the College's position be on assisted dying – in favour, opposed or neutral?", he points out that the College's current position on the issue is that, with good palliative care, a change in legislation is not required. He advocates that this ought to remain unchanged.

In 2012 the RCGP Council Chair, Clare Gerada, made it known that she personally favoured a move to a neutral position and proposed to the RCGP Council that they consult RCGP members on the matter. The consultation comes just after the introduction of an 'Assisted Dying Bill' into the House of Lords by Lord Falconer on 15 May and just before a similar bill is introduced into the Scottish Parliament by Margo Macdonald MSP. Saunders says, "Taking a neutral position would mean that the RCGP would take a position that the legality of assisted dying is a matter for Parliament, on behalf of society, to decide, and is not an issue that the College should seek to influence." The consultation process concluded 9 October 2013.

Dr Peter Saunders points out that the RCGP adopted its current strong opposition to a change in the law in 2005

---

[130] Posted by Dr Peter Saunders CMF Chief Executive on CMF Blogs on 9 July, 2013 and accessed 26 October, 2013 http://www.cmfblog.org.uk/2013/07/09/why-the-rcgp-should-stand-firm-on-opposing-a-change-in-the-law-to-allow-assisted-suicide/ Dr Saunders was formerly a general surgeon. He also serves on the boards of the International Christian Medical and Dental Association and Coalition for Marriage and is campaign director for the Care Not Killing Alliance.

after substantial discussion and consultation with its Faculties and Members as follows:

The RCGP believes that, with current improvement in palliative care, good clinical care can be provided within the existing legislation and that patients can die with dignity. A change in legislation is not required.[131]

It restated this position in 2011 saying, "nothing has occurred since 2005 to alter or change the ethical issues around assisted dying." Saunders then offers eight reasons why RCGP members will strongly support the College's current policy of opposition:

1. The majority of doctors are opposed to a change in the law. Opinion polls show an average of 65% doctors opposing the legalisation of assisted suicide and/or euthanasia with the remainder undecided or in favour. Palliative Medicine Physicians are 95% opposed and the Royal College of Physicians and British Geriatrics Society are officially opposed.

2. Assisted suicide and euthanasia are contrary to all historic codes of medical ethics, including the Hippocratic Oath, the Declaration of Geneva, the International Code of Medical Ethics and the Statement of Marbella. Neutrality would be a quantum change for the profession and against the international tide.

3. Neutrality on this particular issue would give it a status that no other issue enjoys. Doctors, quite understandably, are strongly opinionated and also have a responsibility to lead. The RCGP is a

---

[131] Ibid.

democratic body which takes clear positions on a whole variety of health and health-related issues. Why should assisted suicide and euthanasia enjoy a position which no other issue shares, especially when doctors will actually be the ones carrying it out?

4. Dropping medical opposition to the legalisation of assisted suicide and euthanasia at a time of economic recession could be highly dangerous. Many families and the NHS itself are under huge financial strain and the pressure vulnerable people might face to end their lives so as not to be a financial (or emotional) burden on others is potentially immense.

5. Were the RCGP to drop its opposition, and as a consequence a law were to be passed, it would also leave the medical profession hugely divided at a time when, perhaps, more than any other time in British history, we need to be united as advocates for our patients and for the highest priorities in a struggling health service.

6. Going neutral would leave the RCGP gagged with no collective voice. The British Medical Association (BMA) rejected an attempt to move it neutral at its 2012 annual representative meeting saying that neutrality was the worst of all positions. This was based on bitter experience. When the BMA took a neutral position for a year in 2005/2006 we saw huge pressure to change the law by way of the Joffe Bill. Throughout that crucial debate, which had the potential of changing the shape of medicine in this country, the BMA was

forced to remain silent and took no part in the debate.

7. Going neutral would instead play into the hands of a campaign led by a small pressure group with a strong political agenda. Healthcare Professionals for Assisted Dying (HPAD), which is affiliated to the pressure group 'Dignity in Dying' (formerly the Voluntary Euthanasia Society) has only 520 supporters, representing fewer than 0.25% of Britain's 240,000 doctors. But in 2012 they flooded the BMA ARM with no less than nine motions calling for the association to go neutral in an attempt to silence medical opposition ahead of new bills being introduced to parliament in 2013.

8. The RCGP has been historically opposed to a change in the law on assisted suicide and euthanasia for good reasons. These reasons have not changed.[132]

Adopting a policy of neutrality on euthanasia and physician-assisted suicide would be inappropriate and potentially hazardous to public health. Saunders points out that "it would also be playing into the hands of a small unrepresentative pressure group and giving an advantage to only one side of the debate."[133] At a time when society is morally sick doctors need to take an ethical stand that upholds the sanctity of life and dignity in dying.

---

[132] Ibid.

[133] Ibid.

Outcome of the Consultation Process

On 21 February 2014 the Royal College of General Practitioners (RCGP) announced its continued opposition to change in law on assisted dying. So it remains opposed to any change in the law on assisted dying. This decision is the outcome of one of the most comprehensive consultations of its members.

More than 1,700 members responded to the consultation, which was open from 22 May 2013 until 9 October 2013. College members responded either as individuals, or through one of the RCGP Devolved Councils, one of the RCGP Faculties (local branches), or via a College committee or group. The consultation was conducted through a range of methods, including debates at local meetings, online polls and individual correspondence.

Seventy seven per cent of RCGP members who submitted individual responses to the consultation expressed the opinion that the College should remain opposed to a change in the law to permit assisted dying. In addition, of the 28 RCGP bodies that took part in the consultation, 20 reported a majority view against a change in the law.

Although a minority of respondents put forward cases to shift the College's collective position to "neutral" or "in favour" of a change in law on assisted dying, most respondents were against a change in the law for a range of reasons, including that a change in the legislation would:

- be detrimental to the doctor-patient relationship

- put the most vulnerable groups in society at risk

- be impossible to implement without eliminating the possibility that patients may be in some way coerced into the decision to die

- shift the focus away from investing in palliative care and treatments for terminal illnesses

- instigate a "slippery slope" whereby it would only be a matter of time before assisted dying was extended to those who could not consent due to reasons of incapacity and the severely disabled.

In addition, some respondents thought that the possibility of a wrong decision being made was too high to take the risk.

The GP-patient relationship, with GPs often attending patients in the final days and hours of their lives, means that GPs would be one of the professional groups most affected by any change in the law on assisted dying.

The decision to consult with members on this issue was made at the RCGP's governing Council meeting in February 2013 to acknowledge that some members' views might have changed and to take into account that many new members had joined the College since 2005, when the position was last debated.

The RCGP is the largest membership organisation in the UK solely for GPs, with over 49,000 members, making it the most representative voice in the UK for GPs.[134] The consultation included all of the College's Faculties, Devolved

---

[134] One cannot help but notice that the total number of respondents in this extensive consultation process amounts to approximately 3.5%. of GPs. Whereas one may be pleased about the outcome and the overwhelming majority to remain "opposed" it raises concerns about how the issue is perceived among GPs. I suspect many did not participate because they are overwhelmed with paperwork. I spoke to the RCGP press office about this on 14 March, 2014 and they assured me that in relation to other polls and consultation processes that the number of respondents was quite good.

Councils and relevant College committees, including the RCGP Patient Participation Group.

Dr Maureen Baker, Chair of the RCGP, said:

This was one of the most comprehensive consultations the College has ever undertaken and the quality of the responses on this extremely important issue has been very high. GPs will continue, as they have always done, to provide excellent care to patients in the final days and hours of their lives.[135]

---

[135] See RCGP official website.

CHAPTER 8 Politics of Death

On 14 April 2001, the daily newspaper, *NRC Handelsblad*, published an interview with Dutch health minister Els Borst in which Borst discussed the passage of Holland's law legalising euthanasia and assisted suicide. In the article, Borst also declared that she is not against "Drion's pill." Drion's pill is named after Hulb Drion, the former vice-president of the Dutch High Court. In 1991, Drion proposed that a suicide pill be made available to elderly people free of charge upon request.

Borst and the D66 political party are immensely proud of their achievement in seeing euthanasia and assisted suicide legislation through parliament and they glory in their triumph.[136]

"Democrats 66" is a progressive and social-liberal political party in the Netherlands. D66 was formed in 1966 by a group of politically unaligned, young intellectuals, led by journalist Hans van Mierlo. The party's main objective was to democratise the political system; it proposed to create an American style presidential system. In the 1967 general election, the party won 7 of the 150 seats in the House of Representatives; no new party had ever gained that many seats before. The electoral history of the party is characterised by large fluctuations. At one point they had 24 seats. Following the September 2012 parliamentary elections they had 12. The party was in government from 1973-1977, 1981-

---

[136] Dutch: Democraten 66, D66; official name: *Politieke Partij Democraten 66*.

1982, 1994-2002 and 2003-2006. Over time the party began to emphasise other issues in addition to democratic reform, creating a social-liberal programme.

Currently the party is represented by twelve seats in the House of Representatives, five in the Senate and three in the European Parliament.[137] The party leader, and chair of the parliamentary party in the House of Representatives, is Alexander Pechtold. The party is in opposition against the Rutte cabinet. The party has a small number of elected local and provincial politicians, but supplies a relative large share of the mayors, which are appointed. The party's voters are concentrated in larger cities, especially those with a university degree.

The organisation of D66 is based on principles of direct democracy. Important decisions are made by referendum. D66 is a member of Liberal International and the Alliance of Liberals and Democrats for Europe Party.

Elida Wessel-Tuinstra took the initiative in submitting the first euthanasia law proposal in 1984 on behalf of the D66 party. Roger van Boxtel, likewise D66, also presented an initiative bill during the *paars* (purple) I cabinet.

Purple is a common term in politics for governments or other political entities consisting of parties that have red and blue as their political colours. "Purple" (Dutch: *paars*) is the nickname of a government coalition of social democrats and liberals together, excluding Christian democrats. It is derived from the combination of the colour of the social democrats (red) and liberals (blue).

In the Netherlands, the two cabinets of Prime Minister Wim Kok (Kok I and Kok II, 1994–2002) were composed of social democrats (the Labour Party, PvdA), conservative

---

[137] At the time of writing, October, 2013.

liberals (People's Party for Freedom and Democracy, VVD) and progressive liberals (Democrats 66).

The party is smugly satisfied that they have done society a great service in introducing euthanasia and physician-assisted suicide. They are proud to be identified with it. It is seen as a success in the liberal versus conservative agenda in the Netherlands. In other words it is perceived by many as progressive legislation and a triumph for liberalism. Moral matters are usually contextualized in polemical terms in political debate.

Over a decade ago, Els Borst was vice-chairman of the Health Council and she was a member of the Remmelink commission, which investigated euthanasia practices in the Netherlands. Due to the findings of this commission (which concluded in 1991) that the active ending of life was not reported in at least a thousand cases per year, the cabinet, after years of postponement, could no longer avoid the issue: whoever wanted to persuade doctors to report, had to be able to exclude them from prosecution with a euthanasia law.

The discussion about life and death never ends and we all have a duty to participate in that conversation. The euthanasia and assisted suicide law in the Netherlands will be continuously monitored and modified. We ought to engage in critical analysis of the practice and support proposals for change with research and reasoned argument. Such an approach can potentially persuade legislators to introduce significant amendments and reforms as a first step in the eventual repeal of such a law. One should not abandon the hope that such laws can be repealed as this is precisely what happened in Australia's Northern Territory, which at one time permitted assisted suicide.[138]

The debate has been contextualised in terms of personal autonomy. The rhetoric of the Christian Unity party in the Senate drew comparisons with Nazi practices and (as stated earlier) this was deeply resented. But the desire to gag anybody who speaks of these comparisons is far from democratic or liberal or tolerant. The crucial initial debate may have been lost in the Netherlands but it is only beginning in other countries.

Most Western democracies have suicide prevention programmes but the Netherlands has assisted suicide programmes. Rather than offering support to live they offer support to die.

Els Borst has been a member of the Netherlands Association for Voluntary Euthanasia for years. Her own involvement with euthanasia began in 1983 when she was medical director of the Utrecht Academic Hospital. It is widely believed that euthanasia was practiced there before any legal protocol was in place. She went to the public prosecutor stating her desire to set up a protocol for euthanasia.

There is a difference between the act of ending life at the moment that vital functions begin to fail, on the one hand, and euthanasia and assisted suicide on the other. The discontinuation of treatment for terminally ill patients is common practice, with or without the consent of patients, and is considered to be normal in medical care. "Do not resuscitate" policy fits into this category.[139] That is different to

---

[138] This will be discussed later.

[139] Where it is practiced properly "do not resuscitate" policy only applies to the use of cardiac massage ventilation and defibrillation if a

interventions when a patient has difficulty breathing and/or his heart or kidney function deteriorates. Such medical interventions are frequently used to assist dying people over the threshold. That too is considered normal medical practice. There is no judicial alternative between murder and euthanasia. Doctors who give "aid-in-dying" still continually risk prosecution if the patient has been unable to request it properly. Consequently, such activity goes unreported. This is an area where legal and ethical clarity is needed.

Subjectivity

In 1994, the High Court in the Netherlands determined that suffering includes psychic suffering.[140] More recently the Haarlem High Court reached a more far-reaching judgement in the case against P. Sutorius, who assisted ex-senator E. Brongersma (aged 86) in suicide, because he was tired of life. The bench ruled that it was justified. The court said that the intolerability of suffering is subjective and that only the patient can judge its severity.

Being bored with life is now deemed to be sufficient reason for euthanasia or assisted suicide. One certainly feels sorry for people who wake in the morning regretting they had not died in their sleep. But there are many positive ways

---

terminally ill patient, or very frail patient, collapses. This is because it is extremely unlikely such actions would ever revive the patient. It is much more likely to do them harm, such as break their ribs, and it can be quite undignified out of a hospital environment, where the patient has to be dragged out of bed onto the floor or other surface firm enough to give cardiac massage, to no avail. It doesn't prevent the patient having other treatments such as antibiotics for infections. The discontinuation of treatment when organ failure sets in and the patient would not survive for long even if artificial means were used to keep them alive is used and is not in the same category as euthanasia and assisted suicide.

[140] In the case of a depressed patient of psychiatrist B. Chabot.

of assisting such people without helping them to die. When the will to live is replaced with the wish to die that is a sickness that can and should be treated. That is the medical issue that really needs to be addressed. It is not just a medical and judicial issue it is also a spiritual issue and that too ought to be discussed.

The Reaper and the Dog

As the Grim Reaper began to move stealthily through the Dutch landscape, the watchdog for human rights began to bark. The "Concluding Observations of the Human Rights Committee" that considered the issue of euthanasia is an interesting commentary on the legitimate fears of objective observers.[141] Its remarks concerning the issues of euthanasia and assisted suicide are of particular relevance.

The Committee acknowledged that the new Act concerning review procedures on the termination of life on request and assisted suicide (due to come into force on 1 January 2002) was "the result of extensive public debate addressing a very complex legal and ethical issue."[142] It also recognised that the new law "seeks to provide legal certainty and clarity in a situation which has evolved from case law and medical practice over a number of years."[143]

The Committee expressed serious concerns about the Netherland's plans to relax legal protections regarding actions "deliberately intended to put an end to human life."[144]

---

[141]   CCPR/CO/72/NET   (Concluding   Observations/Comments) Netherlands, 27 August, 2001.
[142] Op. cit.
[143] Op. cit.
[144] Op. cit.

Noting that the new Act contained a number of conditions under which a doctor would not be punishable when he or she terminated the life of a person the Committee expressed its concern that such a system might "fail to detect and prevent situations where undue pressure could lead to these criteria being circumvented."[145] The Committee was also concerned that "with the passage of time, such a practice may lead to routinization and insensitivity to the strict application of the requirements in a way not anticipated."[146]

Even a cursory glance at this report reveals the depth of disquiet felt by the Committee about these issues. It referred to the fact that, "under the present legal system more than 2,000 cases of euthanasia and assisted suicide (or a combination of both) were reported to the review committee in the year 2000 and that the review committee came to a negative assessment only in three cases."[147] The Committee did not disguise its suspicion that the large numbers involved indicated that the then present system was not being used only in extreme cases. It raised doubts that all the substantive conditions were being scrupulously maintained. The Committee's language is unrestrained and reflects the level of concern it felt, particularly in relation to minors:

> The Committee is seriously concerned that the new law is also applicable to minors who have reached the age of 12 years. The Committee notes that the law provides for the consent of parents or guardians of juveniles up to 16 years of age, while for those between 16 and 18 the parents' or guardian's consent may be replaced by the will of the minor,

---

[145] Op. cit.
[146] Op.cit.
[147] Op. cit.

provided that the minor can appropriately assess his or her interests in the matter. The Committee considers it difficult to reconcile a reasoned decision to terminate life with the evolving and maturing capacities of minors. In view of the irreversibility of euthanasia and assisted suicide, the Committee wishes to underline its conviction that minors are in particular need of protection.[148]

There were many flaws identified in the new Act. Of particular concern was the monitoring task of the review committee was not able to prevent the termination of life when the statutory conditions were not fulfilled. It could only comment on post euthanasia and post assisted suicide events.

Thus the Committee recommended that The Netherlands should re-examine its law on euthanasia and assisted suicide in the light of their observations. It strongly recommended (using the word "must") that the Netherlands ensure that "the procedures employed offer adequate safeguards against abuse or misuse, including undue influence by third parties."[149]

The application of the law to minors caused the Committee to stress the importance of strengthening control mechanisms *prior to* carrying out euthanasia or assisted suicide rather than merely reviewing afterwards.

The Committee requested detailed information as to what criteria would be applied to determine the existence of a "voluntary and well-considered request" for euthanasia or assisted suicide. It also requested clarity concerning what criteria would be used to assess what constituted "unbearable suffering" and a more comprehensive definition of what

---

[148] Op. cit.
[149] Op. cit.

exactly was meant by "no other reasonable alternative" The Committee then advised the Dutch government to strictly monitor the application of the new law.

The Committee went on to say that it was "gravely concerned at reports that new-born handicapped infants have had their lives ended by medical personnel" and instructed the Dutch government to "...scrupulously investigate any such allegations of violations of the right to life (article 6 of the Covenant) which fall outside the law on euthanasia and inform the Committee on the number of such cases and on the results of court proceedings arising out of them."

Vacuum and Vortex

The euthanasia and assisted suicide law would have been unthinkable fifty years ago. It was cultivated in a moral vacuum and its force is like a vortex pulling society under the dark waters of despair. The law was introduced after years of intense debate. But for nearly thirty years prior to that euthanasia was practiced under certain circumstances. It was tolerated even though it was not formally sanctioned by the Dutch authorities and courts.

The debate about how to deal with the end of life is one, which will become increasingly relevant in other nations. The Dutch example has been scrutinised closely by campaigners on both sides of the debate. Other countries have also wrestled with the ethical and practical dilemmas posed by advances in medical technology and an ageing population, which have meant that the vast majority of people in the Western world now die in hospital.

Although the passage of the bill into law had long been expected, it was an emotional and controversial occasion, with thousands of opponents protesting outside the Dutch parliament and passionate speeches from both sides within. In the weeks immediately after the passing of the law senators received some 60,000 letters and e-mails, most from opponents of the measure. There is a lesson here for Britain, the USA and other countries. Opposition must be mustered, coordinated, focused, based on research and articulately presented. Christians should not be mere respondents to an agenda driven by those who see euthanasia and assisted suicide as progressive.

Although opposition in the Netherlands was impassioned, opinion polls consistently showed that about 90% of Dutch voters were in favour of the bill. The parliament's lower house passed it by a large 104-40 majority. The law essentially codified guidelines instituted in 1993, under which Dutch doctors had been exempt from prosecution if they followed certain rules.

In an aside comment, here it should be stated that death (and birth) has been professionalised. One issue of recent concern in the UK is the change in organ donation policy and practice in Wales. Up until recently, one had to opt in to the organ donation system but now one has to opt out. In other words every Welsh citizen is an organ donor. One can certainly understand the good intentions behind the change as one definitely sympathises with the recipients of organs and their families. Although it is possible for a person to opt out of the system now that might change in time and one might find that their body is owned by the state. If the state owns your corpse it could also begin to see itself as the owner or keeper of your life, especially in relation to end of life issues, ostensibly on the basis of the quality of life but perhaps in reality on the basis of macro-economics.

Other Countries

The American state of Oregon allows assisted suicide in more restricted circumstances, but not euthanasia. In 1996

Australia's Northern Territory approved, but later revoked, a law allowing medically assisted suicide. In Britain there has been intense debate about legislating on the issue but no new laws have yet been passed. It would not surprise many if Right-to-Die advocates lobbied the European Parliament to implement the Dutch law on euthanasia and assisted suicide throughout the European Union. Although certain aspects of the law (in relation to minors and those suffering psychologically rather than physically) might be deemed contentious, it could be foisted on other nations as a fundamental human right.

Euthanasia opponents, which include many religious groups and organisations representing the disabled, question whether any system of safeguards, no matter how complex and well monitored, can really stop abuse, and maintain that the medical profession's first rule of "do no harm" is the best protection for the elderly and vulnerable from having their lives terminated for the convenience of others or on grounds of cost.

More palliative care, relieving pain at the end of life with drugs and other treatments, is a far better approach. Allowing some doctors to become killers will undermine confidence in the medical profession as a whole. And legalising euthanasia is also likely to make it more common and this is an appalling prospect.

People in favour of euthanasia contend that much euthanasia occurs under the guise of palliative care, when doctors give a terminally ill patient so much of a pain-killing drug that it shortens their life, a practice known euphemistically as "double effect". Many countries tolerate this, as long as the primary aim of the medication is to relieve pain, not end life. But advocates of legalised euthanasia maintain that turning a blind eye to such practices makes it much more difficult to regulate them, and to guard against abuse. They argue that it is better to admit this is going on and to have it regulated. It is certainly in the interest of society to find out exactly what is going on but that does not necessarily mean automatically accepting and legitimising existing practice. Clarity and guidelines are needed.

Dutch Lessons

Both sides have used evidence from the Dutch experience. About 3% of deaths are due to euthanasia. But this figure masks some disturbing trends. In 1995 an extensive survey of Dutch doctors found that about one-third of deaths by euthanasia, some 0.7% of all deaths, were deliberately brought about by doctors without the patient's request. The researchers accounted for this by explaining that such deaths occurred almost entirely because the patient had become what doctors call "incompetent" (permanently comatose) or because the patient suddenly deteriorated, to the point of being unable to say what he wanted. These figures may mask a more disturbing trend. By broadening the definition of those eligible for euthanasia, to include those chronically as well as terminally ill the Dutch have made the bullying of patients into agreeing to euthanasia more possible.

Prior to Legislation

Dutch doctors received a large number of requests for help in dying, 8,900 in 1990 and 9,700 in 1995. In 1990, about 1.7% of all deaths in the country were from active voluntary euthanasia; in 1995, the figure was 2.4%. Grey-area deaths—administering painkillers in large doses—stayed roughly the same, at about 19% of all deaths, and deaths arising from the decision to forgo treatment increased from around 18% to just over 20%. In most cases, the doctors estimated that life had been shortened by less than a week.

Dutch research reveals that pain was not a particularly significant factor in leading people to ask for death. In the Netherlands, only 5% of requests for assisted suicide or euthanasia come from those who describe themselves as being in unbearable pain. About 90% of people who opted for suicide were cancer patients between 55 and 75.

Euthanasia and assisted suicide are not easy to market in the USA. Voters have rejected euthanasia initiatives in Washington and California. Many were repulsed by the image of doctors giving their patients lethal injections. Learning from these defeats, Oregon limited it, successfully, to assisted suicide.

Although both assisted suicide and euthanasia have been presented as empowering patients by giving them control over their death, assisted suicide has been seen as protecting against potential medical abuse since the final act is in the patient's hands. But there is little protection in assisted suicide. People who are helpless or seriously ill are vulnerable to influence or coercion by physicians or relatives eager to be rid of a burden or to gain an inheritance. [150]

Supporters of assisted suicide and euthanasia tend to present a case history designed to show how necessary assisted suicide or euthanasia was in that particular instance. Such cases may rely either on nightmarish images of unnecessarily prolonged dying or on predictions of severe disability. Those who participate in the death (relatives,

---

[150] Yale Kamisar, "Physician-Assisted Suicide: The Last Bridge to Active Voluntary Euthanasia," *Examining Euthanasia*, ed. John Keown, Cambridge University Press; Yale Kamisar, "Are Laws against Assisted Suicide Unconstitutional?" Hastings Center Report 23, no. 3, 1993, pp. 33-41; Herbert Hendin, "Seduced by Death: Doctors, Patients and the Dutch Cure," *Issues in Law and Medicine* 10, no. 2, 1994, pp. 123-68; Carlos Gomez, *Regulating Death: Euthanasia and the Case of the Netherlands*, New York: Free Press, 1991.

euthanasia advocates and physicians) are celebrated as championing the dignity of the patient, who is usually presented as a heroic figure. Many people in the media seem keen to advance their atheistic agenda as campaigns for much-needed social reform.

When mainstream news channels advocate euthanasia and assisted suicide by invariably focusing on worse-case scenarios this contributes to the normalisation of these practices. The media has begun a battle for the minds and hearts of people on this matter and research, statistics and reasoned debate pales into insignificance in comparisons to such dramas. The power of such images is very persuasive.

Popping your Clogs

The current situation in the Netherlands is that patients who qualify for an induced death need not be terminally ill. There is no criminal stigma associated with euthanasia or assisted suicide. Previously if a doctor terminated a patient's life he/she was required to notify the local coroner and report the circumstances of the death to one of five regional review committees. The committee (comprised of at least one lawyer, a doctor and an ethicist) was then obliged to submit a report to the Public Prosecution Service for final review, even if the doctor followed all the established guidelines.

Currently the regional review committee is obligated to report a euthanasia or assisted suicide death to the Public Prosecution Service only if the committee thinks that the doctor did not comply with the criteria of due care. If the committee feels that the doctor acted appropriately, then the case is closed and no report to the Prosecution Service is required.[151] Doctors are not obligated to report patient killings until after the patient is dead.

Reporting noncompliance has been a major problem for the Dutch government in the past. A study, published in 1996, found that the majority of Dutch doctors (59%) did not report voluntary euthanasia and assisted-suicide deaths, and cases of involuntary euthanasia (without patients' knowledge or consent) are rarely if ever reported.[152]

Termination of life without consent is common. Data from the 1991 government-sponsored Remmelink Report clearly indicated that the majority of all euthanasia deaths in the Netherlands are involuntary.[153] 55% of Dutch doctors interviewed in 1995 indicated that "they had ended a patient's life without his or her explicit request" or "they had never done so but that they could conceive of a situation in which they would."[154]

Euthanasia for Minors

Generally, it has been the contention of the government and medical establishment that minors should also have the right to request euthanasia. Children with terminal illnesses, proponents argue, are often more mature than many adults, and they deserve the right to have their suffering ended.

---

[151] Ministry of Justice Press Release; CNN.com, 28 November, 2000.

[152] Van der Wal et al., "Evaluation of the Notification Procedure for Physician-Assisted Death in the Netherlands," *New England Journal of Medicine* (NEJM), 28 November, 1996, pp. 1706-1707.

[153] *Medical Decisions About the End of Life*, vol. 1, The Hague, 19 September, 1991, p. 72.

[154] Van der Maas et al., "Euthanasia, Physician-Assisted Suicide, and Other Medical Practices Involving the End of Life in the Netherlands, 1990-1995," *NEJM*, 28, November, 1996, p. 1701.

When the 2001 euthanasia law was originally proposed, it contained a provision allowing minors 12 and over to request and obtain an assisted death, even if their parents objected. Because of intense criticism both nationally and internationally, that provision was amended. The measure now stipulates that children age 12 - 15 can still be euthanized or assisted in suicide, but the consent of at least one parent or guardian is required. Minors 16 or 17 years-old can decide to have their lives ended without parental consent.

Advance Directives

The law sanctions advance directives authorising euthanasia and assisted suicide. It expressly validates written declarations—signed by patients long before the onset of incompetence—regarding their "termination of life" wishes. These declarations give doctors the right to decide whether patients' lives should be terminated if they become unable to make decisions for themselves.

Euthanasia breaches a taboo. People are rightly sensitive to the euthanasia mentality given Hitler's systematic extermination of children and adults considered physically or mentally disabled. Everyone has the right to die naturally. It is not a doctor's job to judge whose life is worth saving and whose is not.

When euthanasia and physician-assisted suicide was legalised in the Netherlands the Council of Europe expressed vehement opposition to the measure, stating that it violates Article 2 of the European Convention on Human Rights which mandates that no individual should be intentionally deprived of life unless that person has been convicted of a crime serious enough to impose the death penalty. Council spokesman Edeltraud Gatterer called on the Dutch Senate to defeat the bill when it came up for the final vote.

Follow the Leader

Following the introduction of the Dutch law in 2001 there were people in other countries such as the USA, Canada, Australia and England that wanted to see similar legislation introduced in their countries. They were playing a deadly game of "follow the leader". Immediately after the Dutch bill passed the Lower House, Australia's Philip Nitschke (founder of Exit International) told a New South Wales (NSW) parliamentary forum that voluntary euthanasia should be included in a NSW bill of rights.[155] In England, Voluntary Euthanasia Society head Malcolm Hurwitt told reporters that the Dutch vote "removes many of the arguments against euthanasia here."[156]

Dying to Kill

The Dutch Voluntary Euthanasia Society (DVES) actively promoted the passage of the euthanasia bill. While pleased overall by the measure's provisions, the DVES said it did not get everything it wanted, specifically the killing of people who are simply tired of living. DVES spokesperson Walburg de Jong said "We think that if you are old, you have no family near, and you are really suffering from life then it [euthanasia] should be possible" adding "We have to start this discussion, but we say, let's get this first part passed because it will also help a lot of people."[157]

A month before the Lower House debated the new euthanasia law a Dutch court ruled that Dr Philip Sutorius was medically justified when he helped 86-year-old Edward Brongersma commit suicide. As discussed earlier Brongersma

---

[155] *Sydney Morning Herald*, 29 November, 2000.
[156] *U.K. Yahoo News*, 28 November, 2000.
[157] *CNN.com*, 24 November, 2000.

was not physically ill or in pain. He had said that he was simply "tired of life" and his aging "hopeless existence." The Dutch government had claimed that the new euthanasia law would never allow doctors to kill patients like Brongersma. But the government's own prosecution sought only a token three-month suspended sentence for the doctor.[158]

As observed in a *Wall Street Journal* (Europe) editorial: "There is a slippery slope here. If we someday find ourselves as callous toward human life as were the ancient Romans, it may be remembered that it all began in the name of compassion with a people who tended toward the 'progressive' ideas, the Dutch."[159]

Maine Referendum

The ripples of the political debate in the Netherlands extended to the other side of the Atlantic pond. On 7 November, 2000, Maine voters in the USA joined ranks with those in Washington State, California, and Michigan by defeating a ballot measure that would have legalised assisted suicide. The measure, the Maine Death with Dignity Act (MDWDA), was placed on the ballot as Question 1: "Should a terminally ill adult who is of sound mind be allowed to ask for and receive a doctor's help to die?" The voters responded: 51% no, 49% yes, a close call.

The Oregon Experience

The MDWDA's defeat was essentially a rejection of Oregon's way of dealing with end-of-life difficulties—sanctioned killing.

---

[158] *British Medical Journal*, 11 November, 2000, p1174.
[159] Editorial, *Wall Street Journal* (Europe), 1 December, 2000.

But in spite of those legislative defeats, national right-to-die advocates targeted Maine as a state likely to advance their cause. Rita Marker, International Anti-Euthanasia Task Force (IAETF) executive director, explained, "The demographics of Maine are very much like those of Oregon. It's clear that the poor and minorities, for example, really oppose [assisted suicide]."[160]

It was clear from the start that the message was "Follow Oregon." The MDWDA was closely modelled after the Oregon law, which also bears the title "Death with Dignity Act." At various stages throughout the campaign, numerous Oregonians either endorsed the measure in writing or actually went to Maine to support the legalisation effort. Among those were Oregon's chief epidemiologist Dr Katrina Hedberg, co-author of Oregon's two annual assisted-suicide reports, both favouring the practice; Ann Jackson, executive director of the Oregon Hospice Association; Eli Stutsman, Oregon lawyer and long-time right-to-die activist; Barbara Coombs Lee, chief author of the Oregon law and executive director of the assisted-suicide advocacy group Compassion in Dying Federation; and Barbara Roberts, former governor of Oregon.

Kate Roberts, director of Mainers for Death with Dignity said, "We've looked to Oregon a lot in this campaign to talk to people about what's happened there."[161]

Opposition Coalition Formed

While the pro-assisted suicide camp was relying heavily on its collaboration with Oregon's key players to sell the MDWDA, an impressive, broad-based coalition was forming

---

[160] *Wall Street Journal*, 10 November, 2000.
[161] *Statesman Journal*, Salem: OR, 5 November, 2000.

in opposition to the measure. Groups representing various aspects of the medical profession, patients' rights, disability rights, ethical issues, and respect life concerns all banded together to form Maine Citizens Against the Dangers of Physician-Assisted Suicide.[162]

After their campaigns in Washington, California, and Michigan, assisted-suicide advocates blamed their losses on the fact that each time their opponents had more money with which to work. In Maine, that was not the case. In fact, data released the week before the election by the Maine Commission on Governmental Ethics and Election Practices showed that "Yes" campaign had raised a total of $1.6 million (the vast majority of which came from outside Maine), whereas the "No" campaign collected only about $957,474.[163]

Money was not the reason the MDWDA lost. According to Maine pollster Patrick Murphy (President of Strategic Marketing Services) the "No" campaign had, "superior advertising and hit home their message better than their opponents by creating doubts in people's minds."[164]

The "No" campaign ads were so effective that the "Yes" camp enlisted the aid of Oregon's John Kitzhaber, a former emergency room physician, to appear in a TV ad countering one of the "No" ads featuring Oregon physician Thomas

---

[162] Included among those groups were Maine Developmental Disabilities Council, Maine Medical Association, Maine Hospice Council, Maine Chapter of Not Dead Yet, Maine Hospital Association, Alpha-One, Maine Osteopathic Association, Maine Psychiatric Association, Maine Society of Anesthesiologists, Maine Medical Directors Association, Catholic Diocese of Portland, Organisation of Maine Nursing Executives, and the Maine Chapter of the American Cancer Society.

[163] *Bangor Daily News*, 8 November, 2000.
[164] *Sun-Journal*, Lewiston: ME, 14 November, 2000.

Reardon.[165] Reardon, immediate past president of the American Medical Association, stated in the ad that doctors in Oregon, "can prescribe 60 to 100 pills" to assist a suicide, that disturbing complications can cause family members to panic and call 911, and that lethal prescriptions can be sent in the mail—all assertions the coalition could back up with documentation. The ad concluded with Reardon saying, "And I don't want Maine to make the same mistake we made."[166] In the Kitzhaber ad, the governor declared that he wanted to "set the record straight" about the Oregon law. "Here's the truth," he said, "It's working well."[167]

Barbara Coombs Lee was also recruited to defend the Oregon law and to counter the Reardon ad. She told reporters that the ad contained false information, like the reference to the 60 to 100 pills in a lethal prescription. She said that Reardon was wrong because the barbiturates used to kill patients do not come in pill form but rather in capsules that can be opened to place the contents in liquid.[168]

Both Kitzhaber and Lee insisted that no assisted-suicide under the Oregon law had ever resulted in complications warranting a 911 call, despite the fact that just such a case was the subject of a 2-part article by columnist David Reinhard published in Oregon's largest newspaper, *The Oregonian*.[169]

Polls Tell the Story

The progressive decline in support for the MDWDA was a direct indication of just how effective the "No" campaign was in educating Maine voters about the dangers and abuses

---

[165] John Kitzhaber became Governor.
[166] Transcript, No on 1 Ad, "Same Mistake"
[167] *Register Guard*, 28 October, 2000.
[168] *Kennebec Journal*, 25 October, 2000.
[169] *Oregonian*, 23 March, 2000 and 26 March, 2000.

inherent in assisted-suicide practice. In August 2000, polls showed that 71% of Mainers supported the MDWDA.[170] By the end of September, support dropped to 67%.[171] In mid-October, support tumbled to only 54%, with a further decline by the end of October to 52%.[172] When voters actually cast their votes on November 7, support was down to 49%. Dr Laurel Coleman spokesperson for the "No" campaign said, "The more we tell the truth...the less people like the proposed law."[173] Rita Marker (IAETF) said, "The gut reaction is to like the idea of 'death with dignity'. But as people begin to take a closer look within the context of health care today—managed care, the need to save money, how cost-effectiveness will play a part—opinion starts to change."[174]

---

[170] *Portland Press Herald*, 24 August, 2000.
[171] *Bangor Daily News*, 27 September, 2000.
[172] *Press Herald*, 18 October, 2000 and 30 October, 2000.
[173] No on 1 Press Release, 24 October, 2000.
[174] *Wall Street Journal*, 10 November, 2000.

CHAPTER 9 Dutch Disease

The euthanasia agenda has not taken root in other places nearly as effectively as it has in the Netherlands.[175] There is much effort currently being exerted to protect broad-leaf trees in Britain against destruction from foreign insects, which are proving to be very dangerous pests. Some years ago many elm trees in Ireland, the UK and the USA were destroyed because of a disease known as "Dutch Elm Disease".[176] This was caused by fungus affecting elm trees and spread by the elm bark beetle. Although believed to be originally native to Asia, the disease was accidentally introduced into America and Europe, where it devastated native populations of elms, which had not had the opportunity to evolve resistance to the disease. There is imminent danger that the Dutch euthanasia and assisted suicide disease will spread to Britain and further afield if measures are not taken to protect the human species from its own perverse inclinations to introduce self-destructive codes of medical practice.

It is not certain if euthanasia and physician-assisted suicide will find acceptance in other European countries. The

---

[175] Though the assisted suicide issue has found fertile soil in other countries such as Belgium, Luxemburg, Switzerland and also in the United States in Oregon, Montana, Vermont and Washington and in Latin America in Colombia.

[176] The name "Dutch elm disease" refers to its identification in 1921 and later in the Netherlands by Dutch phytopathologists Bea Schwarz and Christine Buisman who both worked with Professor Johanna Westerdijk. The disease is not specific to the Dutch elm hybrid.

Dutch have legalised both prostitution, and the smoking of cannabis but neither of these have been legalised in Britain, the USA, or many other countries. Therefore, perhaps the feeling that the Dutch influence will be all-pervasive is unwarranted. Other factors may inhibit acceptance of euthanasia and physician-assisted suicide, such as, the historic religious culture of any given nation. Perhaps these things will find wider acceptance in societies that have a historically Protestant culture. Protestantism is more individualistic than Roman Catholicism, especially concerning social issues.

Australia[177]

In 2000 euthanasia activists in Australia announced plans to set up a secret laboratory to test the effectiveness of common weeds to kill patients. Leading that project was Dr Philip Nitschke, the doctor responsible for the deaths of four patients under the now defunct Northern Territory law which had legalised euthanasia. After that law was overturned by Australia's national parliament, Nitschke began holding how-to euthanasia clinics throughout the country.

Reportedly, Nitschke and his fellow activists have raised substantial funds from foreign sources. The underground laboratory enables patients to send in plant samples to be tested for lethal effects (such as Hemlock, the weed responsible for Socrates' death in 399 BC). Nitschke has pointed out, it is not illegal to grow hemlock, and it is a common weed all across Australia.

Nitschke also said that he did not believe people would use the lab to establish the best substances to use to murder someone or to commit suicide because of depression. He said

---

[177] The Australian situation, Dr Philip Nitschke and Exit International will be examined in more detail in the chapter entitled "Exit International".

that if a person wanted to murder someone, they wouldn't want to wait for the lab to suggest a "peaceful way" to do it.[178]

Indecent Haste

In February, 1999 in Perth, Australia, just two hours after cancer patient Freeda Hayes told her doctor and her brother and sister that she wanted to die, her wish was granted in the form of a fatal mixture of drugs. The trio was subsequently charged with murder. An autopsy confirmed that Hayes' death was not from natural causes and that one of the lethal drugs contained in her blood stream was a paralysing agent to prevent her breathing. Her doctor, Daryl Alan Stephens, was accused of actually giving her the lethal injection. "Whatever his motivation may have been" said Prosecutor David Dempster "there can only be one intention—the intention to kill." But, despite the facts of the case, Perth Magistrate Jeremy Packington dropped all the charges, saying the case was based on circumstantial evidence.[179]

Removing Food and Fluids is not a Violation of Human Rights Act

British High Court Judge Dame Elizabeth Butler-Sloss ruled (in 2000) that the right-to-life provision in Britain's Human Rights Act does not affect a doctor's right to withhold or withdraw tube feeding from patients thought to be in a permanent vegetative state (PVS).

---

[178] *South China Morning Post*, 24 October, 2000; *Herald Sun*, 23 October, 2000; *Courier Mail*, 28 September, 2000.

[179] *The Age*, 28 November, 2000 and *Sydney Morning Herald*, 30 November, 2000.

The Human Rights Act incorporates the provisions of the European Convention on Human Rights into British law. The cases before the British High Court purportedly involved two articles from the Act—Article 2, stating, "Everyone's right to life shall be protected by law," and Article 3, banning "inhuman and degrading treatment."

The cases in question involved two women referred to only by their initials. Mrs M, 49, reportedly had been in a PVS for three years as a result of an anaesthesia accident that occurred during surgery. Ms H, 36 and an epileptic, had been only "near-PVS" (she responded to external stimuli) since she went into cardiac arrest.

The families of both women wanted their feeding stopped. John Grace, the lawyer arguing for the withdrawal of tube feeding on behalf of the two hospital trusts caring for the women, described PVS in court as "a twilight zone of suspended animation where death commences whilst life continues - A living death."

Initially it was reported that the official solicitor representing the two women was expected to argue that withholding their tube feeding would violate their right to life. However, during the hearing, official solicitor Ben Emmerson agreed with the opposing lawyer, John Grace, that the existing nutrition and hydration guidelines established some years ago by the House of Lords—allowing the starvation and dehydration of Tony Bland, a young man brain-damaged during a soccer riot—were compatible with Article 2 of the Human Rights Act. Judge Butler-Sloss agreed and so ruled.[180]

---

[180] *British Medical Journal*, 14 October, 2000 and *London Times*, 2 October, 2000.

Zurich Allows Assisted Suicide in Homes for the Elderly

The city of Zurich in Switzerland sanctions assisted suicide for elderly people in residential/nursing homes. Until the directive was issued on 26 October, 2000, members representing pro-euthanasia organisations, such as Exit International, were not allowed to enter the homes. Suicide of any type was strictly prohibited on the premises. Now access is allowed at the elderly resident's request. Society has changed. People now place a high value on the right to self-determination. If such personal autonomy is enshrined as a supreme value then it becomes increasingly difficult to defend prohibitions that are understood as a human right. One fears that such suicide decisions are often the result of severe depression because of loneliness. It is not hard to imagine an elderly person, who knows that his son or daughter is struggling to pay £3,000 per month for nursing home care, would contemplate assisted suicide if the option is made available. It is not hard to imagine that some sons or daughters would nudge their parents in that direction.

Equality

Terminally-ill adults considering assisted suicide could be under social pressures and could be coerced into making that decision. To legalise assisted suicide implies that the lives of those disabled by terminal illness are undignified and of less value. Civilised society values equality and that means valuing disabled lives as much as others.

Deep-Continuous Sedation

The rate of deep-continuous sedation has also risen astronomically in the Netherlands. The 2001 euthanasia report indicates that about 5.6% of all deaths in the Netherlands were related to deep-continuous sedation. The 2005 euthanasia report indicates that about 8.2% of all deaths in the Netherlands were related to deep-continuous sedation.[181] The 2010 euthanasia report indicates that about 12.3% of all euthanasia deaths are related to deep-continuous sedation. The rate of deep-continuous sedation has more than doubled in the Netherlands since 2001 and has risen by 50% since 2005. There is a growing concern about the abuse of terminal sedation guidelines in the Netherlands.[182] How often are deaths by deep-continuous sedation actually euthanasia?[183] Combined with the growth in the use of terminal sedation for people who are not otherwise dying (slow euthanasia) and the number of unreported euthanasia deaths, one must conclude that there are abuses occurring in the Netherlands.

Termination Without Request or Consent

The guidelines for euthanasia have devalued patients and failed to protect the vulnerable. They have been violated so often that they might as well not exist at all. According to the guidelines when ending a life a physician must be convinced that the patient's request was voluntary, well-considered, and lasting. But many studies of Dutch euthanasia practice have shown that Dutch doctors routinely kill patients who have

---

[181] See the New England Journal of Medicine
http://www.nejm.org/doi/full/10.1056/NEJMsa071143#t=article

[182] Michael Cook, "Doubts emerge about Dutch guidelines for terminal sedation",
http://www.alexschadenberg.blogspot.ca/2012/07/doubts-emerge-about-dutch-guidelines.html

[183] Dr. Peter Saunders, "Dutch doctors turn to 'continuous deep sedation' to keep official euthanasia figures low", 11 July, 2012, http://www.alexschadenberg.blogspot.ca/2012/07/dutch-doctors-turn-to-continuous-deep.html

not asked to be poisoned. The favoured method of killing in the Netherlands is an overdose of barbiturates followed by a lethal dose of curare. In the Netherlands, this practice is known as "termination without request or consent" and is not even formally considered euthanasia in the statistics compiled by the government.

The evidence of decades demonstrates that such involuntary euthanasia is rampant. Indeed, in its 1997 ruling refusing to create a constitutional right to assisted suicide (Washington v. Glucksberg) the United States Supreme Court quoted a 1991 Dutch government study finding that in 1990 doctors committed "more than 1000 cases of euthanasia without an explicit request" and "an additional 4,941 cases where physicians administered lethal morphine overdoses without the patients' explicit consent." That means in 1990, nearly 6,000 of approximately 130,000 people who died in the Netherlands that year were involuntarily euthanized — approximately 4% of all Dutch deaths.

The law states that the physician must be convinced the patient is facing unremitting and unbearable suffering. Notice that this guideline does not require that the patient be dying or, for that matter, even be actually physiologically ill. Indeed, there have been several documented cases of euthanasia based on depression or suicidal ideation. For example, a Dutch documentary reported on the euthanasia of a young woman in remission from anorexia. Worried that her eating disorder would return, she asked her doctor to kill her. He did and the authorities refused to prosecute.

The most infamous case of this sort involved a physically healthy woman who had become obsessed about being buried between her two dead children. She bought a cemetery plot, had her children buried one on each side of her planned grave, and then asked a psychiatrist named

Boutdewijn Chabot to assist her suicide. He met with her four times over approximately five weeks and never attempted treatment. He then assisted her suicide. The Dutch Supreme Court refused to punish him, ruling that suffering is suffering and it does not matter whether it is physical or emotional, to justify euthanasia.

Another documented euthanasia that violated this and other guidelines was depicted in a Dutch documentary. Henk Dykma had asymptomatic HIV infection. Fearing future afflictions that might befall him, Henk asked his doctor to kill him. The film shows the doctor telling Henk that he might live for years at his current state of seemingly healthful living. When Henk still proclaims a desire to die, the doctor speaks with a colleague but never consults a psychiatrist or psychologist. He then helps kill Henk on 28 July, a date, we are told, which had symbolic importance for the patient.

This killing, like those of the anorexic young woman and the bereaved mother, was clearly not a matter of last resort, as the guidelines claim to require. Henk and his doctor did not explore all other options available to him before ending his life. Indeed, psychiatric treatment, which might have alleviated Henk's obvious anxiety about being HIV-positive, was never even discussed or attempted. Nor was Henk advised of the steps that could be taken to alleviate his suffering should he fall ill. The doctor did not even wait until Henk had actual symptoms of AIDS. There is a word for that level of care — abandonment — and it demonstrates the utter hollowness of the Dutch protective guidelines.

The guidelines stipulate that the physician must inform the patient about their situation and prospects. This guideline presumes that the physician(s) involved will have sufficient expertise to adequately inform the patient about their condition and options for treatment or palliation. The Dutch medical system is primarily made up of general practitioners, rather than specialists, who may not have the training, expertise, or desire to know the many treatment alternatives that may be available. Moreover, there are few hospices in the Netherlands, meaning that the many compassionate and dignified methods of alleviating suffering in the dying may never be discussed with patients who ask to be killed.

The Dutch guidelines stipulate that the physician must have reached the firm conclusion with the patient that there was no other reasonable alternative solution. The cases already described illustrate the ineffectiveness of this guideline. Another prime example of its uselessness is the killing by Dr Henk Prins of a three-day old infant born with Spina Bifida and limb anomalies. Euthanasia is not just a geriatric issue as it has entered Dutch paediatric wards too. A 1997 study in the British medical journal, *The Lancet*, revealed that about 8% of all infants who die in the Netherlands are killed by doctors. Spina Bifida is a condition in which there is an opening at the spine that may cause disability or death. Prins - a gynaecologist, not a paediatrician or expert in Spina Bifida - killed the child at the request of her parents, because, he later testified, the baby screamed in agony when touched. No wonder the baby was in pain! Prins never closed the wound in her back. In other words, the doctor killed his patient without first attempting proper medical treatment. Yet, rather than punishing Prins, the trial judge praised him for his "integrity and courage" wishing him well in any further legal proceedings he might face.

Dutch euthanasia is a human-rights disaster. Not only does the practice devalue the lives of the most defenceless people, but once killing became an acceptable answer to one problem, it soon became a solution to one hundred. Indeed, in their years of euthanasia practice, Dutch doctors have gone from killing terminally ill patients who ask for it, to chronically ill patients who ask for it, to disabled patients who ask for it, to depressed patients who ask for it, to babies who by definition cannot ask for it, to thousands of patients without request or consent. Now, the last remaining impediment to killing by doctors — its technically illegal status — has been dismantled and even teenagers beginning at the age of sixteen will be able to receive euthanasia without parental consent.

The theologian and philosopher, Richard John Neuhaus, was once asked, "Do you believe there is a euthanasia slippery slope?" His answer hit the mark, "Yes, like I believe that there is a Hudson River." We ignore the lessons of the Netherlands at our own peril.

CHAPTER 10 Ethical Definitions and Historical Debate

Consideration of the issues of euthanasia and assisted suicide from an ethical point of view must begin with clear definitions of the terms. So, even though we have been examining these issues in some detail it is necessary at this stage to clarify exactly what we mean by these terms.

Euthanasia means "good death".[184] Generally, it refers to the practice of intentionally ending a life in order to relieve pain and suffering. As such, it is a deliberate intervention undertaken with the express intention of ending a life, to relieve intractable suffering.[185] It is generally understood as termination of life by a doctor at the request of a patient.[186] As such, euthanasia is an active area of research in contemporary bioethics.[187]

Assisted suicide is when one or more individuals help another person commit suicide, i.e. directly, intentionally, and voluntarily cause his or her own death. "Assistance" may

---

[184] The word euthanasia comes from the Greek Εὐθανασία (εὖ, transliterated *eu* means 'good' and θάνατος transliterated *thanatos* means 'death').

[185] Harris, NM. (Oct 2001). "The euthanasia debate", *Journal of the Royal Army Medical Corps* 147 (3): pp. 367–70.

[186] Euthanasia is categorized in different ways, which include voluntary, non-voluntary and involuntary. These distinctions will be elucidated later.

[187] P. Borry, P. Schotsmans, K. Dierickx, "Empirical research in bioethical journals: A quantitative analysis", *Journal of Medical Ethics*, April 2006, 32 (4): pp. 240–245.

mean providing one with the means (drugs or equipment) to end one's own life, but may extend to other actions. It differs from euthanasia, which is when another person ends the life. When the person is seeking practical assistance and approval from medical professionals, it is commonly called physician-assisted suicide.

The current waves of global public debate have been on-going for decades, centring on legal, religious, and moral conceptions of suicide and a personal "right to death." The practice may be legal, illegal, or undecided, depending on the culture or jurisdiction.

Definition

Like other terms borrowed from history, "euthanasia" has had different meanings depending on usage. The first apparent use of the term "euthanasia" belongs to the historian Suetonius who described how the Emperor Augustus, "dying quickly and without suffering in the arms of his wife, Livia, experienced the 'euthanasia' he had wished for."[188] The word euthanasia was first used in a medical context by Francis Bacon in the seventeenth century, to refer to an easy, painless, happy death, during which it was a "physician's responsibility to alleviate the 'physical sufferings' of the body." Bacon referred to an "outward euthanasia"— the term "outward" he used to distinguish from a spiritual concept—the euthanasia "which regards the preparation of the soul."[189]

In current usage, one approach to defining euthanasia has been to mirror Suetonius, regarding it as the "painless

---

[188] Philippe Letellier, chapter: "History and definition of a Word", in *Euthanasia: Ethical and Human Aspects* by Council of Europe.
[189] Brian Vickers, *Francis Bacon: The Major Works*, Oxford World's Classics, Oxford University Press, USA, 2008, p. 630.

inducement of a quick death".[190] However, it is argued that this approach fails to properly define euthanasia, as it leaves open a number of possible actions which would meet the requirements of the definition, but would not be seen as euthanasia. In particular, these include situations where a person kills another, painlessly, but for no reason beyond that of personal gain; or accidental deaths which are quick and painless, but not intentional.[191]

Thus another approach is to incorporate the notion of suffering into the definition. The definition offered by the *Oxford English Dictionary* incorporates suffering as a necessary condition, with "the painless killing of a patient suffering from an incurable and painful disease or in an irreversible coma."[192] This approach can be seen as a part of other works, such as Marvin Khol and Paul Kurtz's "a mode or act of inducing or permitting death painlessly as a relief from suffering."[193] However, focusing on this approach to defining euthanasia may also lead to counter examples. Such definitions may encompass killing a person suffering from an incurable disease for personal gain (such as to claim an inheritance), and commentators such as Tom Beauchamp and

---

[190] Marvin Kohl, *The Morality of Killing*, New York: Humanities Press, 1974, p. 94. A similar definition is offered by Blackburn (1994) with "the action of causing the quick and painless death of a person, or not acting to prevent it when prevention was within the agent's powers".

[191] Tom L Beauchamp, Arnold I. Davidson, "The Definition of Euthanasia", *Journal of Medicine and Philosophy*, 1979, 4 (3): pp.294–312 and Heather Draper, "Euthanasia" in Ruth Chadwick, *Encyclopedia of Applied Ethics* second edition, Academic Press, 2011.

[192] *Oxford Dictionary*, Oxford University Press.

[193] Marvin Kohl; Paul Kurtz. "A Plea for Beneficient Euthanasia", in Marvin Kohl, *Beneficient Euthanasia*, Buffalo, New York: Prometheus Books, 1975, p. 94.

Arnold Davidson have argued that doing such would constitute "murder simpliciter" rather than euthanasia.[194]

The third element incorporated into many definitions is that of intentionality – the death must be intended, rather than being accidental, and the intent of the action must be a "merciful death".[195] Michael Wreen argued that: "the principal thing that distinguishes euthanasia from intentional killing simpliciter is the agent's motive: it must be a good motive insofar as the good of the person killed is concerned."[196] This is a view mirrored by Heather Draper, who also spoke about the importance of motive, arguing that: "the motive forms a crucial part of arguments for euthanasia, because it must be in the best interests of the person on the receiving end."[197] Definitions such as that offered by the House of Lords Select Committee on Medical Ethics take this path, where euthanasia is defined as, "a deliberate intervention undertaken with the express intention of ending a life, to relieve intractable suffering."[198] Beauchamp and Davidson also highlight Baruch Brody's, "an act of euthanasia is one in which one person...(A) kills another person (B) for the benefit of the second person, who actually does benefit from being killed."[199]

---

[194] Tom L. Beauchamp; Arnold I. Davidson, "The Definition of Euthanasia", *Journal of Medicine and Philosophy*, 1979, 4 (3): pp. 294–312.

[195] Ibid.

[196] Michael Wreen, "The Definition of Euthanasia", *Philosophy and Phenomenological Research*, 48 (4): 1988, pp. 637–653 [639].

[197] Heather Draper, "Euthanasia" in Ruth Chadwick, *Encyclopedia of Applied Ethics* second edition, Academic Press, 2011.

[198] N. M. Harris, "The Euthanasia Debate", *Journal of the Royal Army Medical Corps* 147 (3): October 2001, pp. 367–370.

[199] Baruch Brody, "Voluntary Euthanasia and the Law", in Marvin Kohl, *Beneficient Euthanasia*, Buffalo, New York: Prometheus Books, 1975, p. 94, quoted in Beauchamp & Davidson, 1979, p 295.

Draper argued that any definition of euthanasia must incorporate four elements: an agent and a subject; an intention; a causal proximity, such that the actions of the agent lead to the outcome; and an outcome. Based on this, she offered a definition incorporating those elements, stating that euthanasia "must be defined as death that results from the intention of one person to kill another person, using the most gentle and painless means possible, that is motivated solely by the best interests of the person who dies."[200] Prior to Draper, Beauchamp and Davidson had also offered a definition which includes these elements, although they offered a somewhat longer account and one that specifically discounts foetuses in order to distinguish between abortions and euthanasia:

> In summary, we have argued ... that the death of a human being, A, is an instance of euthanasia if and only if (1) A's death is intended by at least one other human being, B, where B is either the cause of death or a causally relevant feature of the event resulting in death (whether by action or by omission); (2) there is either sufficient current evidence for B to believe that A is acutely suffering or irreversibly comatose, or there is sufficient current evidence related to A's present condition such that one or more known causal laws supports B's belief that A will be in a condition of acute suffering or irreversible comatoseness; (3) (a) B's primary reason for intending A's death is cessation of A's (actual or predicted future) suffering or irreversible comatoseness, where B does not intend A's death for a different primary reason, though there may be

[200] Heather Draper, "Euthanasia" In Ruth Chadwick, *Encyclopedia of Applied Ethics*, Academic Press, 2011, p. 176.

other relevant reasons, and (b) there is sufficient current evidence for either A or B that causal means to A's death will not produce any more suffering than would be produced for A if B were not to intervene; (4) the causal means to the event of A's death are chosen by A or B to be as painless as possible, unless either A or B has an overriding reason for a more painful causal means, where the reason for choosing the latter causal means does not conflict with the evidence in 3b; (5) A is a nonfetal organism.[201]

Wreen, in part responding to Beauchamp and Davidson, offered a six-part definition:

Person A committed an act of euthanasia if and only if (1) A killed B or let her die; (2) A intended to kill B; (3) the intention specified in (2) was at least partial cause of the action specified in (1); (4) the causal journey from the intention specified in (2) to the action specified in (1) is more or less in accordance with A's plan of action; (5) A's killing of B is a voluntary action; (6) the motive for the action specified in (1), the motive standing behind the intention specified in (2), is the good of the person killed.[202]

Wreen also considered a seventh requirement: "(7) The good specified in (6) is, or at least includes, the avoidance of

[201] Tom L. Beauchamp, Arnold I. Davidson, "The Definition of Euthanasia", *Journal of Medicine and Philosophy* 4 (3): 1979, pp. 303-304.
[202] Michael Wreen, "The Definition of Euthanasia", *Philosophy and Phenomenological Research* 48 (4): 1988, pp. 637–640.

evil", although Wreen noted he was not convinced that the restriction was required.[203]

In discussing his definition, Wreen noted the difficulty of justifying euthanasia when faced with the notion of the subject's "right to life". In response, Wreen argued that euthanasia has to be voluntary, and that "involuntary euthanasia is, as such, a great wrong."[204] Other commentators incorporate consent more directly into their definitions. For example, in a discussion of euthanasia presented in 2003 by the European Association of Palliative Care (EAPC) Ethics Task Force, the authors offered: "Medicalized killing of a person without the person's consent, whether non-voluntary (where the person in unable to consent) or involuntary (against the person's will) is not euthanasia: it is murder. Hence, euthanasia can be voluntary only."[205]

Although the (EAPC) Ethics Task Force argued that both non-voluntary and involuntary euthanasia could not be included in the definition of euthanasia, there is discussion in the literature about excluding one but not the other.[206]

[203] Op. cit. pp. 637–653 [645].

[204] Ibid.

[205] Lars Johan Materstvedt; Clark, David; Ellershaw, John; Førde, Reidun; Boeck Gravgaard, Anne-Marie; Müller-Busch, Christof; Porta i Sales, Josep; Rapin, Charles-Henri (2003). "Euthanasia and physician-assisted suicide: a view from an EAPC Ethics Task Force". *Palliative Medicine* 17 (2): pp. 97–101.

[206] Ibid.

Classification of Euthanasia

Euthanasia may be classified according to whether a person gives informed consent into three types: voluntary, non-voluntary and involuntary.[207]

There is a debate within the medical and bioethics literature about whether or not the non-voluntary (and by extension, involuntary) killing of patients can be regarded as euthanasia, irrespective of intent or the patient's circumstances. In the definitions offered by Beauchamp and Davidson and, later, by Wreen, consent on the part of the patient was not considered to be one of their criteria, although it may have been required to justify euthanasia.[208] However, others see consent as essential.

Voluntary Euthanasia

Euthanasia conducted with the consent of the patient is termed voluntary euthanasia. When the patient brings about his or her own death with the assistance of a physician, the term "assisted suicide" is often used instead. Assisted suicide is legal in the Netherlands, Switzerland and the USA states of Oregon, Washington and Montana.

---

[207] R. W. Perrett. "Buddhism, euthanasia and the sanctity of life", *Journal of Medical Ethics* 22 (5): October 1996, pp. 309–313. See also Hugh LaFollette, *Ethics in Practice: An Anthology.* Oxford: Blackwell, 2002, pp. 25–26.
[208] Michael Wreen, "The Definition of Euthanasia", *Philosophy and Phenomenological Research* 48 (4): 1988, pp. 637–653. Tom L. Beauchamp; Arnold I. Davidson. "The Definition of Euthanasia", *Journal of Medicine and Philosophy* 4 (3): 1979, pp. 294–312.

Non-Voluntary Euthanasia

Euthanasia conducted where the consent of the patient is unavailable is termed non-voluntary euthanasia. Examples include child euthanasia, which is illegal worldwide but decriminalised under certain specific circumstances in the Netherlands under the Groningen Protocol.

Involuntary Euthanasia

Euthanasia conducted against the will of the patient is termed involuntary euthanasia.

Passive and Active Euthanasia

Voluntary, non-voluntary and involuntary euthanasia can all be further divided into passive or active variants.[209] Passive euthanasia entails the withholding of common treatments, such as antibiotics, necessary for the continuance of life. Active euthanasia entails the use of lethal substances or forces, such as administering a lethal injection, to kill and is the most controversial means.[210]

Doctrine of Double Effect

The doctrine of double effect; also known as the principle of double effect (often abbreviated as DDE or PDE), rule of double effect, double-effect reasoning; or simply double effect, is a set of ethical criteria which Christians, and

---

[209] J. Rachels, "Active and Passive Euthanasia", *New England Journal of Medicine* 292 (2), January 1975, pp. 78–80.

[210] I think the phrase "passive euthanasia" is inappropriate for treatments or withdrawal of treatments that result in death. To describe it as such minimises the vast moral difference between euthanasia and palliative care and makes it seem just a matter of semantics.

some others, use for evaluating the permissibility of acting when one's otherwise legitimate act (for example, relieving a terminally ill patient's pain) will also cause an effect one would normally be obliged to avoid (for example, the patient's death). Double-effect originates in Thomas Aquinas's treatment of homicidal self-defence, in his work *Summa Theologiae*.[211] This set of criteria states that an action having foreseen harmful effects is practically inseparable from the good effect and is justifiable if the nature of the act is itself good, or at least morally neutral; the agent intends the good effect and not the bad either as a means to the good or as an end itself; the good effect outweighs the bad effect in circumstances sufficiently grave to justify causing the bad effect and the agent exercises due diligence to minimise the harm.[212]

Intentional Harm Versus Side Effects

Although different writers state and employ double effect differently, they share the position that consequentially similar acts having different intentional structures make for ethically different acts. Therefore, for example, advocates of double effect typically consider the intentional terror bombing of non-combatants having as its goal victory in a legitimate war morally out of bounds, while holding as ethically in bounds an act of strategic bombing that similarly harms non-combatants with foresight but without intent as a side effect of destroying a legitimate military target. Because advocates of double effect propose that consequentially similar acts can be morally different, double effect is most often criticised by consequentialists who consider the

---

[211] *Summa Theologiae*, IIa-IIae Q. 64, art. 7.

[212] T. A. Cavanaugh, *Double-Effect Reasoning: Doing Good and Avoiding Evil*, Oxford: Clarendon Press, p. 36.

consequences of actions entirely determinative of the action's morality.

In their use of the distinction between intent and foresight without intent, advocates of double effect make three arguments. First, that intent differs from foresight, even in cases in which one foresees an effect as inevitable. Second, that one can apply the distinction to specific sets of cases found in military ethics (terror bombing/strategic bombing), medical ethics (craniotomy/hysterectomy), and social ethics (euthanasia). Third, that the distinction has moral relevance, importance, or significance.

The doctrine consists of four conditions that must be satisfied before an act is morally permissible. First the nature-of-the-act condition so the action must be either morally good or indifferent. Second, the means-end condition, so the bad effect must not be the means by which one achieves the good effect. Third, the right-intention condition whereby the intention must be the achieving of only the good effect, with the bad effect being only an unintended side effect. Fourth, the proportionality condition whereby the good effect must be at least equivalent in importance to the bad effect.

The second of these four conditions is an application of the more general principle that good ends do not justify evil means.[213]

Medicine

A vaccine manufacturer typically knows that while a vaccine will save many lives, a few people may get sick or die

---

[213] Mark Timmons, *Moral Theory: An Introduction*, Rowman & Littlefield 2003, p. 80. The apostle Paul asked the rhetorical question, "And why not do evil that good may come?" (Romans 3:8), which presupposes that such an approach is wrong.

from side effects of vaccination. The manufacture of a drug is in itself morally neutral. Lives are saved as a result of the vaccine, not as a result of the deaths due to side effects. The bad effect, the deaths due to side effects, does not further any goals of the manufacturer, and hence is not intended as a means to any end. Finally, the number of lives saved is much greater than the number lost, and so the proportionality condition is satisfied. This is more a case of side effects/benefit analysis than of a real principle application and is common in medicine.

The principle of double effect is frequently cited in cases of pregnancy and abortion. A doctor who believes abortion is always morally wrong may still remove the uterus or fallopian tubes of a pregnant woman, knowing the procedure will cause the death of the embryo or foetus, in cases in which the woman is certain to die without the procedure (examples cited include aggressive uterine cancer and ectopic pregnancy). In these cases, the intended effect is to save the woman's life, not to terminate the pregnancy, and the effect of not performing the procedure would result in the greater evil of the death of both the mother and the foetus.[214]

In cases of terminally ill patients who would hasten their deaths because of unbearable pain, or whose caregivers would do so for them (euthanasia, physician-assisted suicide, etc.), a principle of "double effect death" could be applied to justify the deliberate administration of a pain-killer in potentially unsafe doses — not in an attempt to end life, but with a conscious disregard of the possibility. The USA Supreme Court has voiced support for this principle in its

---

[214] Alison McIntyre, "Doctrine of Double Effect", In Edward N. Zalta, *Stanford Encyclopedia of Philosophy*, 2006 edition.

deliberations over the constitutionality of physician-assisted suicide.[215]

War

The principle appears useful in war situations. In a war, it may be morally acceptable to bomb the enemy headquarters to end the war quickly, even if civilians on the streets around the headquarters might die as, in such a case, the bad effect of civilian deaths is not disproportionate to the good effect of ending the war quickly, and the deaths of the civilians is a side effect and not intended by the bombers, either as ends or as means.

On the other hand, to bomb an enemy orphanage in order to terrorise the enemy into surrender would be unacceptable, because the deaths of the orphans would be intended, in this case, as a means to ending the war early, contrary to the second condition.

Criticisms

Consequentialists, in particular, reject the notion that two acts can differ in their moral permissibility, if both have exactly the same consequences, or expected consequences. John Stuart Mill, a nineteenth-century advocate of the utilitarian version of consequentialism, argues that it is a mistake to confuse the standards for right action with a consideration of our motives to perform a right action:

---

[215] Vacco v. Quill and Washington v. Glucksberg, both in 1997. See: Kathryn E. Tucker, "Legal Advocacy to Improved Care and Expand Options at the End of Life," in *Physician-Assisted Dying: The Case for Palliative Care & Patient Choice*, edited by T.E. Quill and M.P. Battin (Johns Hopkins University Press, 2004). The Court made it clear that a "medical death" hastened by palliative measures was permissible.

He who saves a fellow creature from drowning does what is morally right, whether his motive be duty, or the hope of being paid for his trouble; he who betrays the friend that trusts him, is guilty of a crime, even if his object be to serve another friend to whom he is under greater obligations.[216]

According to Mill, scrutiny of motives or intentions will show that almost all good behaviour proceeds from questionable intentions.[217] Therefore, Mill argues that moral analysis should ignore matters of intention, and so one should reject the doctrine of double effect, which appeals to a distinction between intended and unintended consequences.

History

According to the historian N. D. A. Kemp, the origin of the contemporary debate on euthanasia started in 1870.[218] Nevertheless, euthanasia was debated and practiced long before that date in Ancient Greece and Rome where it was supported by Socrates, Plato and Seneca. Although Hippocrates appears to have spoken against the practice, writing (as previously noted), "I will not prescribe a deadly drug to please someone, nor give advice that may cause his death."[219]

---

[216] John Stuart Mill, *Utilitarianism*, London: Parker, Son and Bourn, 1863, p. 26.

[217] Ibid.

[218] Nick Kemp. *Merciful Release*, Manchester University Press, 2002.

[219] Noting there is some debate in the literature about whether or not this was intended to encompass euthanasia see: Kyriaki Mystakidou; Efi Parpa; Eleni Tsilika; Emanuela Katsouda; Lambros Vlahos; "The Evolution of Euthanasia and Its Perceptions in Greek Culture and Civilization", *Perspectives in Biology and Medicine* 48 (1), 2005, pp. 97–

Euthanasia was strongly opposed in the Judeo-Christian tradition. Thomas Aquinas argued that the practice of euthanasia contradicted the natural human instinct for survival.[220] This view was also held by Francois Ranchin (1565–1641), a French physician and professor of medicine, and Michael Boudewijns (1601–1681), a physician and teacher.[221] Nevertheless, there were voices arguing for euthanasia, such as John Donne in 1624.[222] In 1678, the publication of Caspar Questel's *De Pulvinari Morientibus Non Subtrahend, (On The Pillow Of Which The Dying Should Not Be Deprived)*, initiated debate on the topic. Questel described various customs which were employed at the time to hasten the death of the dying, (including the sudden removal of a pillow, which was believed to accelerate death), and argued against their use, as doing so was "against the laws of God and Nature."[223] This view was shared by many who followed, including Philipp Jakob Spener, Veit Riedlin and

---

98. Michael Stolberg "Active Euthanasia in Pre-Modern Society, 1500–1800: Learned Debates and Popular Practices". *Social History of Medicine* 20 (2), 2007, pp. 206–207. Benjamin Gesundheit: Avraham Steinberg; Shimon Glick; Reuven Or; Alan Jotkovitz "Euthanasia: An Overview and the Jewish Perspective", *Cancer Investigation* 24 (6), 2006.

[220] Michael Manning, "Historical Timeline – Euthanasia." Euthanasia – ProCon.org. Web.
http://euthanasia.procon.org/view.resource.php?resourceID=000130

[221] Michael Manning, "Historical Timeline – Euthanasia." Euthanasia – ProCon.org. Web.
http://euthanasia.procon.org/view.resource.php?resourceID=000130
. Gesundheit, Benjamin; Steinberg, Avraham; Glick, Shimon; Or, Reuven; Jotkovitz, Alan "Euthanasia: An Overview and the Jewish Perspective". Cancer Investigation 24(6), 2006, p. 623.

[222] Marya Mannes, "Euthanasia vs. the Right to Life". *Baylor Law Review* 27, 1975, p. 69.

[223] Michael Stolberg, "Active Euthanasia in Pre-Modern Society, 1500–1800: Learned Debates and Popular Practices", *Social History of Medicine* 20 (2), 2007, pp. 209–211.

Johann Georg Krünitz.[224] In spite of opposition, euthanasia continued to be practiced. It involved techniques such as bleeding, suffocation and removing people from their beds to be placed on the cold ground.[225]

Some have suggested that suicide and euthanasia were more acceptable under Protestantism and during the Age of Enlightenment.[226] Thomas More wrote of euthanasia in *Utopia*, although it is not clear if More was intending to endorse the practice.[227] Other cultures have taken different approaches: for example, in Japan, suicide has not traditionally been viewed as a sin, and accordingly the perceptions of euthanasia are different from those in other parts of the world.[228]

Beginnings of the Contemporary Euthanasia Debate

In the mid-1800s, the use of morphine to treat "the pains of death" emerged, with John Warren recommending its use in 1848. A similar use of chloroform was revealed by Joseph Bullar in 1866. However, in neither case was it recommended that the use should be to hasten death. In 1870 Samuel Williams, a schoolteacher initiated the contemporary euthanasia debate through a speech given at the Birmingham

---

[224] Op. cit. p. 211.

[225] Op. cit. pp. 211–214.

[226] Benjamin Gesundheit; Avraham Steinberg; Shimon Glick; Reuven Or; Alan Jotkovitz, "Euthanasia: An Overview and the Jewish Perspective", *Cancer Investigation* 24(6), 2006, p. 623.

[227] Michael Stolberg, "Active Euthanasia in Pre-Modern Society, 1500–1800: Learned Debates and Popular Practices", *Social History of Medicine* 20 (2), 2007, p. 208–209.

[228] Izumi Otani, "Good Manner of Dying" as a Normative Concept: "Autocide", "Granny Dumping" and Discussions on Euthanasia/Death with Dignity in Japan", *International Journal of Japanese Society* 19 (1), October, 2010, pp. 49–63.

Speculative Club in England, which was subsequently published in a one-off publication entitled *Essays of the Birmingham Speculative Club*, the collected works of a number of members of an amateur philosophical society.[229] Williams' proposal was to use chloroform to deliberately hasten the death of terminally ill patients:

> That in all cases of hopeless and painful illness, it should be the recognised duty of the medical attendant, whenever so desired by the patient, to administer chloroform or such other anaesthetic as may by-and-bye supersede chloroform – so as to destroy consciousness at once, and put the sufferer to a quick and painless death; all needful precautions being adopted to prevent any possible abuse of such duty; and means being taken to establish, beyond the possibility of doubt or question, that the remedy was applied at the express wish of the patient.[230]

The essay was favourably reviewed in *The Saturday Review*, and an editorial speaking against the essay appeared in *The Spectator*.[231] From there it proved to be influential, and other writers came out in support of such views: Lionel Tollemache wrote in favour of euthanasia, as did Annie Besant, the essayist and reformer who later became involved with the National Secular Society, considering it a duty to society to "die voluntarily and painlessly" when one reaches the point of becoming a "burden".[232] *Popular Science* also analysed the issue in May 1873, assessing both sides of the

---

[229] Ezekiel Emanuel, "The history of euthanasia debates in the United States and Britain", *Annals of Internal Medicine* 121 (10), 1994, p. 794.

[230] Ibid.

[231] Nick Kemp, *Merciful Release*, Manchester University Press, 2002.

[232] Ian Dowbiggin, *A Concise History of Euthanasia: Life, Death, God, and Medicine*, Rowman & Littlefield, 2007, pp. 51, 62–64.

argument.[233] Nevertheless, Kemp notes that at the time, medical doctors did not participate in the discussion; it was "essentially a philosophical enterprise... tied inextricably to a number of objections to the Christian doctrine of the sanctity of human life."[234]

Early Euthanasia Movement in the United States

The rise of the euthanasia movement in the United States coincided with the so-called Gilded Age. This was a time of social and technological change that encompassed an "individualistic conservatism that praised laissez-faire economics, scientific method, and rationalism". It was a time of industrialisation and conflict between corporations and labour unions.[235] It was also a time that saw the development of the modern hospital system, seen as a factor in the emergence of the euthanasia debate.[236]

Robert Ingersoll argued for euthanasia, stating in 1894 that where someone is suffering from a terminal illness, such as terminal cancer, they should have a right to end their pain through suicide. Felix Adler offered a similar approach, although, unlike Ingersoll, Adler did not reject religion, instead arguing from an ethical framework. In 1891, Adler argued that those suffering from overwhelming pain should have the right to commit suicide, and, furthermore, that it

---

[233] *Popular Science Monthly*, Vol.3, May 1873, pp. 90-96
http://books.google.ie/books?id=-B8DAAAAMBAJ&lpg=PA90&pg=PA90&redir_esc=y#v=onepage&q&f=false

[234] Nick Kemp, *Merciful Release*, Manchester University Press, 2002.

[235] Ezekiel Emanuel, "The history of euthanasia debates in the United States and Britain", *Annals of Internal Medicine* 121 (10), 1994, p. 794.

[236] Demetra Pappas, "Recent historical perspectives regarding medical euthanasia and physician assisted suicide", *British Medical Bulletin* 52 (2), 1996, pp. 386–387.

should be permissible for a doctor to assist – thus making Adler the first prominent American to argue for physician-assisted suicide in cases where people were suffering from chronic illness.[237] Both Ingersoll and Adler argued for voluntary euthanasia of adults suffering from terminal ailments.[238] However, Dowbiggin argues that by breaking down prior moral objections to euthanasia and suicide, Ingersoll and Adler made it possible for others to stretch the definition of euthanasia.[239]

America also saw the first attempt to legalise euthanasia, when Henry Hunt introduced legislation into the General Assembly of Ohio in 1906.[240] Hunt did so at the behest of Anna Hall, a wealthy heiress who was a major figure in the euthanasia movement during the early twentieth century in the United States. Hall had watched her mother die after an extended battle with liver cancer, and had dedicated herself to ensuring that others would not have to endure the same suffering. Towards this end, she engaged in an extensive letter writing campaign, recruited Lurana Sheldon and Maud Ballington Booth, and organised a debate on euthanasia at the annual meeting of the American Humane Association in 1905 – described by Jacob Appel as the first significant public debate on the topic in the twentieth century.[241] Hunt's bill called for the administration of an anaesthetic to bring about a patient's death, so long as the person is of lawful age and sound mind, and was suffering from a fatal injury, an

---

[237] Ian Dowbiggin, A Merciful End: The Euthanasia Movement in Modern America, Oxford University Press. 2003, pp. 10–13.

[238] Ibid.

[239] Ian Dowbiggin, A Merciful End, 2003, p. 13.

[240] Jacob Appel, "A Duty to Kill? A Duty to Die? Rethinking the Euthanasia Controversy of 1906", Bulletin of the History of Medicine 78 (3), 2004, p. 614.

[241] Op. cit. pp. 614–616.

irrecoverable illness or great physical pain. It also required that a physician hear the case, required informed consent in front of three witnesses, and then required the attendance of three physicians who had to agree that the patient's recovery was impossible. A motion to reject the bill outright was voted down, but the bill itself failed to pass, 79 to 23.[242]

Along with the Ohio euthanasia proposal, 1906 also witnessed the creation of a second bill. Assemblyman Ross Gregory introduced a proposal to permit euthanasia to the Iowa legislature. However, the Iowa legislation was far broader in scope than that offered in Ohio. It allowed for the death of any person of at least ten years of age who suffered from an ailment that would prove fatal and cause extreme pain, should they be of sound mind and express a desire to artificially hasten their death. In addition, it allowed for infants to be euthanized if they were sufficiently deformed and permitted guardians to request euthanasia on behalf of their wards. The proposed legislation also imposed penalties on physicians who refused to perform euthanasia when requested - a six–twelve month prison term and a fine of between $200 and $1000. Unsurprisingly, the proposal proved to be controversial.[243] It engendered considerable debate but failed to pass, having been withdrawn from consideration after being passed to the Committee on Public Health.[244] After 1906 the euthanasia debate reduced in intensity, resurfacing periodically but not returning to the

---

[242] Ezekiel Emanuel, "The history of euthanasia debates in the United States and Britain", *Annals of Internal Medicine* 121 (10), 1994, 796. Jacob Appel "A Duty to Kill? A Duty to Die? Rethinking the Euthanasia Controversy of 1906", *Bulletin of the History of Medicine* 78 (3), 2004, pp. 618-619.

[243] Jacob Appel, "A Duty to Kill? A Duty to Die? Rethinking the Euthanasia Controversy of 1906", *Bulletin of the History of Medicine* 78 (3), 2004, pp. 619-621.

[244] Op. cit. p. 623.

same level of debate until the 1930s in the United Kingdom.[245]

1930s in Britain

The Voluntary Euthanasia Legalisation Society was founded in 1935 by Charles Killick Millard (now called Dignity in Dying), a movement that campaigned for the legalisation of euthanasia in Great Britain.

In January 1936, King George V was given a fatal dose of morphine and cocaine in order to hasten his death. At the time he was suffering from cardio-respiratory failure, and the decision to end his life was made by his physician, Lord Dawson.[246] Although this remained a secret for over fifty years, the death of George V coincided with proposed legislation in the House of Lords to legalise euthanasia. The legislation came through the British Volunteer Euthanasia Legalisation Society.[247]

Euthanasia opponent Ian Dowbiggin argues that the early membership of the Euthanasia Society of America (ESA) reflected how many perceived euthanasia at the time, often seeing it as a eugenics matter rather than an issue concerning individual rights.[248] Dowbiggin argues that not every eugenist joined the ESA "solely for eugenic reasons" but he postulates that there were clear ideological connections between the eugenics and euthanasia movements.[249]

---

[245] Ezekiel Emanuel, "The history of euthanasia debates in the United States and Britain", *Annals of Internal Medicine* 121 (10), 1994, p. 796.
[246] J. H. R. Ramsay, "A king, a doctor, and a convenient death", *British Medical Journal* 308, May 2011, p. 1445.
[247] Edward Gurney, "Is There a Right to Die – A Study of the Law of Euthanasia", *Cumberland-Samford Law Review* 3, 1972, p. 237.
[248] Ian Dowbiggin, *A Merciful End*, OUP, 2003, pp. 10–13.
[249] Ibid.

Nazi Euthanasia Programme (Action T4)

Nazi doctors did more than conduct bizarre experiments on concentration-camp inmates; they supervised the entire process of medical mass murder, from selecting those who were to be exterminated to disposing of corpses. Robert Jay Lifton has written about the Nazi doctors and shows that this medically supervised killing was done in the name of "healing" as part of a racist programme to cleanse the Aryan body politic.[250] After the German eugenics campaign of the 1920s for forced sterilisation of the "unfit" it was but one step to euthanasia which in the Nazi context meant systematic murder of Jews. Building on interviews with former Nazi physicians and their prisoners, Lifton presents a disturbing portrait of careerists who killed to overcome feelings of powerlessness. He includes a chapter on Josef Mengele and one on Eduard Wirths, the "kind", "decent" doctor (as some inmates described him) who set up the Auschwitz death machinery.

Lifton analyses the terrible, seemingly contradictory phenomenon of doctors becoming agents of mass murder. He paints a picture of the Nazi transmutation of values that allowed medical killing to be seen as a therapeutic healing of the body politic. Based on arresting historical scholarship and personal interviews with Nazi and prisoner doctors, he traces the inexorable logic leading from early Nazi sterilisation and euthanasia of its own citizens to mass extermination of European Jews and other "racial undesirables." Ultimately Lifton's book asks how doctors rationalised being "killer-healers." He provides a multifaceted evaluation of genocide,

---

[250] Robert Jay Lifton, *Medical Killing and the Psychology of Genocide: The Nazi Doctors* (Basic Books 1986) - 2000-Da Capo Press edition (1988).

of the seductive power of Nazi ideology, and of the psychological processes involved.

The killing of a severely disabled infant in Nazi Germany on the 24 July, 1939 was described in a BBC "Genocide under the Nazis" *Timeline* as the first "state-sponsored euthanasia".[251] Parties that consented to the killing included Hitler's office, the parents and the Reich Committee for the Scientific Registration of Serious and Congenitally Based Illnesses.[252] *The Telegraph* noted that the killing of the disabled infant—whose name was Gerhard Kretschmar, born blind, with missing limbs, subject to convulsions, and reportedly "an idiot"— provided "the rationale for a secret Nazi decree that led to 'mercy killings' of almost 300,000 mentally and physically handicapped people".[253] While Kretchmar's killing received parental consent, most of the 5,000 to 8,000 children killed afterwards were forcibly taken from their parents.[254]

The euthanasia campaign of mass murder gathered momentum on 14 January, 1940 when the "handicapped" were killed with gas vans and killing centres, eventually

---

[251] *Genocide Under the Nazis Timeline*: 24 July 1939 BBC. Quotation: "The first state-sanctioned euthanasia is carried out, after Hitler receives a petition from a child's parents, asking for the life of their severely disabled infant to be ended. This happens after the case has been considered by Hitler's office and by the Reich Committee for the Scientific Registration of Serious and Congenitally Based Illnesses, whose 'experts' have laid down the basis for the removal of disabled children to special 'paediatric clinics'. Here they can be either starved to death or given lethal injections. At least 5,200 infants will eventually be killed through this programme".

[252] *Genocide Under the Nazis Timeline*: 24 July 1939 BBC.

[253] Irene Zoech (in Berlin) "Named: the baby boy who was Nazis' first euthanasia victim", *Telegraph*, 12 October, 2003.

[254] *Genocide Under the Nazis Timeline*: 24 July 1939 BBC.

leading to the deaths of 70,000 adult Germans.[255] Lifton contrasts this programme with what he considers to be a genuine euthanasia. He explains that the Nazi version of euthanasia was based on the work of Adolf Jost, who published *The Right to Death* (*Das Recht auf den Tod*) in 1895. Lifton writes:

> Jost argued that control over the death of the individual must ultimately belong to the social organism, the state. This concept is in direct opposition to the Anglo-American concept of euthanasia, which emphasizes the individual's 'right to die' or 'right to death' or 'right to his or her own death,' as the ultimate human claim. In contrast, Jost was pointing to the state's right to kill...Ultimately the argument was biological: 'The rights to death [are] the key to the fitness of life.' The state must own death—must kill—in order to keep the social organism alive and healthy.[256]

In modern terms, the use of "euthanasia" in the context of Action T4 is seen to be a euphemism to disguise a programme of genocide, in which people were killed on the grounds of "disabilities, religious beliefs, and discordant individual values."[257]

---

[255] Genocide Under the Nazis Timeline: 14 January 1940 BBC. Quotation: "The 'euthanasia campaign' gathers momentum in Germany, as six special killing centres and gas vans, under an organisation code-named T4, are used in the murder of 'handicapped' adults. Over 70,000 Germans will be killed in this act of mass murder – it is the first time poison gas will be used for such a purpose".

[256] Robert Jay Lifton, *The Nazi Doctors*, Basic Books 1986, p. 46.

[257] A. Michalsen; K. Reinhart ""Euthanasia": A confusing term, abused under the Nazi regime and misused in present end-of-life debate", *Intensive Care Medicine* 32 (9), September 2006, pp. 1304–1310.

Compared to the discussions of euthanasia that emerged post-war, the Nazi programme may have been worded in terms that appear similar to the modern use of "euthanasia" but there was no "mercy" and the patients were not necessarily terminally ill.[258] But Ian Dowbiggin writes that "the origins of Nazi euthanasia, like those of the American euthanasia movement, predate the Third Reich and were intertwined with the history of eugenics and Social Darwinism, and with efforts to discredit traditional morality and ethics."[259]

Euthanasia Debate

Historically, the euthanasia debate has tended to focus on a number of key concerns. According to euthanasia opponent Ezekiel Emanuel, proponents of euthanasia have presented four main arguments. First, that people have a right to self-determination, and thus should be allowed to choose their own fate. Second, assisting a subject to die might be a better choice than requiring that they continue to suffer. Third, the distinction between passive euthanasia (which is often permitted and active euthanasia, which is not) is not substantive or that the underlying principle (the doctrine of double effect) is unreasonable and unsound. Fourth, permitting euthanasia will not necessarily lead to unacceptable consequences.

Similarly, Emanuel argues that there are four major arguments presented by opponents of euthanasia. First, not all deaths are painful. Second, alternatives, such as cessation of active treatment, combined with the use of effective pain relief, are available. Third, the distinction between active and passive euthanasia is morally significant. Fourth, legalising

---

[258] Ibid.
[259] Ian Dowbiggin, *A Merciful End*, OUP, 2003, p. 65.

euthanasia will place society on a slippery slope, which will lead to unacceptable consequences.[260]

Elisabeth Kübler-Ross, an eminent Swiss-American psychiatrist encouraged the hospice care movement, believing that euthanasia prevents people from completing their "unfinished business".[261]

Theological and Philosophical Support for Euthanasia

Catholicism has an official position of unqualified opposition to any form of euthanasia. According to its catechism, "Intentional euthanasia, whatever its form or motives, is murder. It is gravely contrary to the dignity of the human person and the respect due to the living God, his Creator." However, there are Catholic voices expressing disagreement with that position.

The Australian philosopher, Max Charlesworth, is one. He takes a position, which has been characteristic of Christian supporters of voluntary euthanasia, affirming that God has created human beings to make their own decisions and to accept responsibility for themselves and their neighbours. He says:

> It's not 'playing God' to seek freely to control the direction of my life and it's not 'playing God' to seek freely to control the mode of my dying. For a Christian, God is not honoured by a person (made in

---

[260] Wesley J. Smith. *Forced Exit*, New York: Times Books, 1997. Ezekiel Emanuel "The history of euthanasia debates in the United States and Britain", *Annals of Internal Medicine* 121 (10), 1994, pp. 797-8.

[261] A pioneer in near-death studies and the author of the groundbreaking book *On Death and Dying* (1969) where she first discussed her theory of the five stages of grief.

the 'image' of God) abdicating her autonomy and freedom of will and passively submitting to 'fate.'[262]

Hans Küng, a well-known Catholic theologian, has taken a similar position. In his view:

> God, who has given men and women freedom and responsibility for their lives, has also left to dying people the responsibility for making a conscientious decision about the manner and time of their deaths. This is a responsibility which neither the state, nor the church, neither a theologian, nor a doctor can take away.[263]

For Küng, "...precisely because I am convinced that death is not the end of everything, I am not so concerned about an endless prolongation of my life—certainly not under conditions that are no longer compatible with human dignity."[264]

Similar views have been expressed by Protestant Christians. Kenneth Ralph, a Uniting Church Minister, has argued that, "self-determination is central to what it means to be a human being or a person" and resists the arbitrary removal of the responsibility of self-determination in the manner of one's death. For such people the interests of the individual have priority over any social, political, or religious project to which he or she might be conscripted. They argue that there is no religious value in requiring extreme and hopeless suffering of individuals against their will, subsuming their good to the good of society or the common good. They

---

[262] Rev. Dr. Andrew Dutney Monash, *Bioethics Review* Vol. 16 No. 2 (April 1997). Cited on the Website *Christians Supporting Choice for Voluntary Euthanasia* http://www.christiansforve.org.au/BibleFacts.html
[263] Ibid.
[264] Ibid.

would contend that such use of persons defaces the image of God in them and is to that extent irreligious.

Bible-believing Christians who uphold the sanctity of human life and the sovereignty of God in the creation, continuation and cessation of life would agree that one should be allowed to die with dignity. That might mean refusing treatment, asking not to be resuscitated and receiving pain-relief medication and palliative care. However, that is not the same thing as euthanasia or physician-assisted suicide. In fact, the theology of those who support euthanasia and physician assisted suicide is what might be called "cat theology." A dog looks at his owner and thinks, "He feeds me and takes care of me – he must be God" whereas a cat looks at his owner and thinks, "He feeds me and takes care of me - I must be God". The theology that upholds a view that euthanasia and physician-assisted suicide is man-centred whereas the theology, which views these things as morally wrong, is God-centred. When human will is elevated above the will of God, it leads to subjectivism and arbitrariness in morality. The Word of God ought to be the absolute authority in all matters of faith and practice. It ought to guide and govern those who profess to be "Christian".

CHAPTER 11 Dignitas

D ignitas is a group that claims it "helps" those with terminal illness and severe physical and mental illnesses to die assisted by qualified doctors and nurses. Additionally, they say they provide assisted suicide for people provided that they are of sound judgement and submit to an in-depth medical report prepared by a psychiatrist that establishes the patient's condition, as required by Swiss courts.[265]

History and Operation

Dignitas was founded in 1998 by Ludwig A. Minelli, a Swiss lawyer. Swiss laws provide that assistance to suicide is only illegal if it is motivated by self-interest. As a result, Dignitas claims to ensure that it acts as a neutral party by proving that, aside from non-recurring fees, they have nothing to gain from the deaths of its members.

The person who wishes to die meets several Dignitas personnel, in addition to an independent doctor, for a private consultation. The independent doctor assesses the evidence provided by the patient and is met on two separate occasions, with a time gap between each of the consultations.[266] Legally admissible proof that the person wishes to die is also created, i.e. a signed affidavit,

---

[265] USA - "A suicide right for the mentally ill? A Swiss case opens a new debate". Ncbi.nlm.nih.gov., 18 March, 2011, Retrieved 12 July, 2011.

[266] "Paralysed player killed himself", BBC News, 10 December, 2008, Retrieved 1 October, 2013.

countersigned by independent witnesses. In cases where a person is physically unable to sign a document, a short video film of the person is made in which they are asked to confirm their identity, that they wish to die, and that their decision is made of their own free will, without any form of coercion. This evidence of informed consent remains private and is preserved only for use in any possible legal dispute.

Finally, a few minutes before the lethal overdose is provided, the person is once again reminded that taking the overdose will surely kill them. Additionally, they are asked several times whether they want to proceed, or take some time to consider the matter further. This gives the person the opportunity to stop the process. However, if at this point the person states that they are determined to proceed, a lethal overdose is provided and ingested.[267]

Suicide Method

In general, Dignitas uses the following protocol to assist suicides: an oral dose of an antiemetic drug, followed approximately one hour later by a lethal overdose of powdered pentobarbital dissolved in a glass of water or fruit juice. If necessary, the drugs can be ingested via a drinking straw. The pentobarbital overdose depresses the central nervous system, causing the person to become drowsy and fall asleep within five minutes of drinking it and anaesthesia progresses to coma as the person's breathing becomes shallower. Death is caused by respiratory arrest, which occurs within thirty minutes of ingesting the pentobarbital.

In a few cases in 2008, Dignitas used helium gas as a suicide method instead of a pentobarbital overdose. This

---

[267] "If you drink this, you will die': Father reveals what paralysed rugby son was told before he took poison in Swiss suicide", *Daily Mail*, 11, December 2008.

avoids the need for medical supervision and prescription controlled drugs, and is therefore cheaper.[268]

Statistics

Ludwig Minelli said in an interview in March 2008 that Dignitas had assisted 840 people to die, 60% of them Germans.[269] By 2010, that number had exceeded a thousand assisted suicides.[270] 21% of people receiving assisted dying in Dignitas do not have a terminal or progressive illness, but rather "weariness of life".[271]

Costs and Finances

According to Ludwig Minelli, Dignitas charges its patients €4,000 (£3,182/$5,263.16) for preparation and suicide assistance, or €7,000 (£5,568/$9,210.53) in case of taking over family duties, including funerals, medical costs and official fees.[272] Despite being a non-profit organisation, Dignitas has repeatedly refused to open its finances to public scrutiny.[273]

---

[268] "Euthanasia group Dignitas films gas and plastic bag deaths", *Daily Mail*, 19 March, 2008.

[269] Wenn Sie das trinken, gibt es kein Zurück *Tagesspiegel de*. Retrieved 1 October, 2013.

[270] Bruce Falconer, "Death Becomes Him", *The Atlantic*, 1 March 2010.

[271] S. Fischer; C. A. Huber; L. Imhof; Imhof, R. Mahrer; M. Furter, SJ. Ziegler; G. Bosshard, "Suicide assisted by two Swiss right-to-die organisations", *Journal of Medical Ethics* 34 (11), November, 2008, pp. 810–814.

[272] Wenn Sie das trinken, gibt es kein Zurück *Tagesspiegel de*. These figures are based on 2008 costs and exchange rates.

[273] Craig Whitlock, "Branching out to serve a growing but dying market", *Washington Post*, 1 November, 2005

Suicide Tourism

Although the assisted suicide market is largely German, as of March 2012, approximately 180 British citizens had travelled to Switzerland from the UK to die at one of Dignitas' rented apartments in Zurich.

In July 2009, British conductor Sir Edward Downes and his wife Joan died together at a suicide clinic outside Zürich "under circumstances of their own choosing." Sir Edward was not terminally ill, but his wife was diagnosed with rapidly developing cancer.[274] In March 2010, British "comics" artist John Hicklenton ended his life at the Dignitas clinic following a ten-year battle with multiple sclerosis.[275]

Allegations by Dignitas Ex-Employee

Soraya Wernli (a nurse employed by Dignitas for two-and-a-half years, until March 2005), accused the organisation of being a "production line of death concerned only with profits".[276] Wernli claimed many wealthy and vulnerable people bequeathed "vast sums" to Minelli in addition to standard fees and some were not terminally ill.[277] She also complained some patients died in pain and she resigned after an alleged incident in which a new type of machine left a client suffering for seventy hours.[278] Dignitas denied all allegations and pointed out that Wernli left Dignitas several

---

[274] Leigh Lundin, "YOUthanasia". Criminal Brief, August 2, 2009, Retrieved August 27, 2009.

[275] "Judge Dredd artist dies at centre", BBC News. 26 March, 2010. Retrieved 1 October, 2013.

[276] Allan Hall "Cashing in on despair? Suicide clinic Dignitas is a profit obsessed killing machine, claims ex-worker", Daily Mail, 25 January, 2009.

[277] Op. cit.

[278] Op. cit.

years ago.[279] Minelli said that "If the state prosecutors feel I'm making myself rich they should start legal proceedings."[280]

Reaction of Local Swiss People and Organisations

Director Ludwig Minelli has described the difficulties that Dignitas has faced over the years. In Sept 2007, it was evicted, blocked or locked out of three apartments, and so Minelli offered assisted dying to two German men in a car. In October, 2007 Dignitas was prevented from working in a private house by the local council and refused rooms on an industrial site. In December, 2007 an interim judgement prevented Dignitas from working in a building next to a busy brothel.

Patient Selection

Although Dignitas (and Exit International) provide little or no data into their activities, it is known that 21% of people receiving assistance by Dignitas do not have a terminal or progressive illness.[281]

Cremation Urns in Lake Zurich

In April 2010, police divers found a group of over sixty cremation urns in Lake Zurich. Each of the urns bore the logo of the Nordheim crematorium used by Dignitas. Soraya Wernli (the former employee mentioned above) had told

---

[279] Op. cit.

[280] Patrick Sawer (in Zurich), "Dignitas founder accused of profiting from assisted suicides", *The Telegraph*, 10 January, 2009.

[281] S. Fischer; C. A. Huber; L. Imhof; Imhof, R. Mahrer; M. Furter, SJ. Ziegler; G. Bosshard, "Suicide assisted by two Swiss right-to-die organisations", *Journal of Medical Ethics* 34 (11), November, 2008, pp. 810–814. It is also stated here that and 65% of women attending Exit International do not have a terminal or progressive illness.

The Times newspaper eighteen months previously that Dignitas had dumped at least three-hundred urns in the lake. She claimed that Minelli dumped them there himself, but later asked his daughter and another member of staff to do it. In 2008 two members of Dignitas were caught trying to pour the ashes of twenty dead people into the lake.[282]

Dignitas in the Media

In 2008, the documentary film "Right to Die?" was broadcast on Sky *Real Lives* (rebroadcast on PBS Frontline in March 2010 as *The Suicide Tourist*). Directed by Oscar-winning Canadian John Zaritsky, it depicts the assisted suicide of several people who have gone to Switzerland to end their lives. It includes the story of Craig Ewert, a 59-year-old retired university professor who suffered from a motor neuron disease. Ewert travelled to Switzerland where he was assisted by Dignitas. The documentary shows him passing away with Mary, his wife of 37 years, at his side. It was shown on the Swiss television network SF1 and is available as a web movie on the Dignitas website.

The BBC produced a film entitled, *A Short Stay in Switzerland* telling the story of Dr Anne Turner, who made the journey to the Dignitas assisted suicide clinic. On 24 January 2006, the day before her 67th birthday, she ended her life. The film was shown on BBC1 on 25 January 2009.[283]

As already mentioned British maestro Sir Edward Downes, who conducted the BBC Philharmonic and the Royal Opera orchestras, struggled in his later years (but was

---

[282] Roger Boyes, "Ashes dumped in Lake Zurich put Dignitas back in the spotlight", *The Times* (London), 28 April, 2010.

[283] Andrea Thompson, "Anne, if you drink this you will die': Why we stood by and allowed our mother to commit suicide", *Daily Mail*, 18 January, 2009.

not terminally ill) as his hearing and sight failed, died with his wife, who had terminal cancer, at an assisted suicide clinic in Switzerland in July 2009. He was 85 and she was 74.[284] French lesbian theorist and translator, Michele Causse chose to die on her birthday (30 July 2010) in association with Dignitas.[285]

On 13 June 2011, BBC 2 aired a documentary called "Terry Pratchett: Choosing to Die", featuring author and Alzheimer's disease sufferer Terry Pratchett guiding viewers through an assisted suicide that took place at Dignitas facilities in Switzerland. Peter Smedley, a British hotelier and millionaire, and his wife Christine allowed Pratchett to film Smedley's deliberate consumption of prepared barbiturate in order to kill himself as Christine comforted Smedley in his demise. The documentary received a highly polarised reaction in the United Kingdom, with some praise for the programme as "brave", "sensitive" and "important" whilst it also gathered accusations of "pro-death" bias from anti-euthanasia groups and of encouraging the view that disability was a good reason for killing, from disability groups.[286]

The corporation acknowledged that it had received 1,060 complaints. This is a significant number to have registered their disapproval of the documentary. It received only 82 "appreciations" of the programme.

This documentary elicited many comments which re-ignited the debate on Britain's assisted suicide laws. Alistair

---

[284] Leigh Lundin, (August 2, 2009). "YOUthanasia" Criminal Brief (Retrieved August 20, 2013) http://criminalbrief.com/?p=7887

[285] "France Soir", http://michele-causse.com/MicheleCausse

[286] Catherine Gee, "Terry Pratchett: Choosing to Die, BBC Two, review", The Telegraph, 13 June, 2011. Ceri Radford, "Terry Pratchett: Choosing to Die is important TV, not a tasteless polemic", The Telegraph, 13 June, 2011. "BBC flooded with complaints over Choosing to Die documentary", The Telegraph, 14 June, 2011.

Thompson, a spokesman for the Care Not Killing Alliance said "This is pro-assisted suicide propaganda loosely dressed up as a documentary. The evidence is that the more you portray this, the more suicides you will have." The Rt. Rev. Michael Nazir-Ali, the former Bishop of Rochester said:

> I think an opportunity has been bypassed of having a balanced programme – the thousands of people who use the hospice movement and who have a good and peaceful death, there was very little about them. This was really propaganda on one side. Life is a gift and it has infinite value and we are not competent to take it, we do not have the right to take it, except perhaps in the most extreme circumstances of protecting the weak.[287]

Dr Peter Saunders, campaign director for the Care Not Killing Alliance said:

> We felt the programme was very unbalanced and one-sided and did not put the counter-arguments. Our biggest concern was that it really breached just about all the international and national guidelines on portrayal of suicide by the media. We are very worried about the danger of copycat suicide or suicide contagion. We have written to the Secretary of State for Health and the Secretary of State for Culture to ask them to carry out an urgent investigation into the way that assisted suicide has

---

[287] "BBC flooded with complaints over Choosing to Die documentary", *The Telegraph*, 14 June, 2011.
http://www.telegraph.co.uk/culture/tvandradio/bbc/8574762/BBC-flooded-with-complaints-over-Choosing-to-Die-documentary.html

been covered by the BBC and its link to English suicide rates.[288]

Liz Carr, a disability campaigner said, "I, and many other disabled older and terminally ill people, are quite fearful of what legalising assisted suicide would do and mean and those arguments aren't being debated, teased out, the safeguards aren't being looked at. Until we have a programme that does that, then I won't be happy to move onto this wider debate."[289]

Emma Swain, the BBC's Head of Knowledge Commissioning said, "The film does show some other perspectives but it is not critical that every film we make is completely impartial and balanced."[290] A clear admission that it was not impartial and balanced! Nola Leach, chief executive of CARE said "I rather thought that we had moved on from the days when people gathered in crowds to watch other people die. That the BBC should facilitate this is deeply disturbing. One wonders whether the BBC has any interest in treating this subject impartially."[291]

Damian Thompson, Editor of *Telegraph Blogs* added a note of levity to his complaint "As for the BBC, I wonder what the moral status is of exploiting a writer with a degenerative brain disease to nudge us towards a creepy change in the law – at our expense, of course. I would

---

[288] "BBC flooded with complaints over Choosing to Die documentary", *The Telegraph*, 14 June, 2011.
http://www.telegraph.co.uk/culture/tvandradio/bbc/8574762/BBC-flooded-with-complaints-over-Choosing-to-Die-documentary.html

[289] "BBC flooded with complaints over Choosing to Die documentary", *The Telegraph*, June 14, 2011.
http://www.telegraph.co.uk/culture/tvandradio/bbc/8574762/BBC-flooded-with-complaints-over-Choosing-to-Die-documentary.html

[290] Ibid.

[291] Ibid.

threaten to withhold my licence fee in protest, but the Beeb [i.e. the BBC] is utterly relentless in tracking down evaders and the last thing I want is to wake up in a Swiss clinic with a syringe staring me in the face.[292]

---

[292] Ibid.

CHAPTER 12 Dignity in Dying

Dignity in Dying is a United Kingdom nationwide campaigning organisation. It is funded by voluntary contributions from members of the public, and it claims to have in excess of 25,000 actively subscribing supporters. The organisation declares it is independent of any political, religious or other affiliations, and has the stated primary aim of campaigning for individuals to have greater choice and more control over end-of-life decisions, so as to alleviate any suffering they may be undergoing as they near the end of their life.

Dignity in Dying campaigns for greater choice, control and access to a full range of medical and palliative services at the end-of-life. This includes providing terminally ill adults with the option of a painless, assisted death, within legal safeguards. It declares that its campaign looks to bring about a generally more compassionate approach to the end-of-life.

Dignity in Dying points out that in the 2010 British Social Attitudes survey 82% of the general public believed that a doctor should probably or definitely be allowed to end the life of a patient with a painful incurable disease at the patient's request.[293] This was further analysed to show 71% of religious people and 92% of non-religious people supported this statement.

---

[293] British Social Attitudes Survey, 2009-2010.

Origins

In 1931 Dr Charles Killick Millard, the Medical Officer of Health for Leicester (from 1901 to 1935) gave the Presidential address at the Annual General Meeting of the Society of Medical Officers of Health. In the address, he advocated the "Legalisation of Voluntary Euthanasia" which prompted considerable debate in Britain involving doctors, clerics and the wider public. Millard's proposal was that in the case of terminal illnesses the law should be changed "to substitute for the slow and painful death a quick and painless one."[294]

The organisation was set up in December 1935 under the name Voluntary Euthanasia Legalisation Society (VELS).[295] The initial meeting that set the society up was held at the headquarters of the British Medical Association free of charge, despite the BMA not supporting the aims of the society. During the debate, forty members of a Catholic youth association disrupted the meeting.[296]

The foundation of the society followed an offer of £10,000 (a considerable amount at the time) from Mr O. W. Greene, a terminally-ill man in London. The initial offer was retracted and no posthumous endowment was left to the Society after Greene learned that the prospective Society would only be supporting legalisation of euthanasia for those with incurable conditions.[297]

The first chairman was C. J. Bond, a consulting surgeon at the Leicester Royal Infirmary. Millard was made the first

---

[294] Nick Kemp, *Merciful Release*, Manchester University Press, 2002.

[295] William Stewart, *An A-Z of Counselling Theory and Practice*, Nelson Thornes, 2005, p. 158.

[296] "Doctors Urge Mercy Death Be Legalised", *Rochester Journal*, Associated Press. 11 December 1935, p.65.

[297] Nick Kemp, *Merciful Release*, Manchester University Press, 2002.

Honorary Secretary.[298] Other members of the Executive Committee were drawn from Bond and Millard's social milieu in Leicester, including Astley V. Clarke from the Leicester Royal Infirmary; Rev. Dr R. F. Rattray, a Unitarian minister and principal of University College, Leicester; Canon F. R. C. Payne of Leicester Cathedral; Rev. A. S. Hurn; Frederick Attenborough, also a former principal of University College, Leicester; and H. T. Cooper, the honorary solicitor of the Committee.[299]

The society did not attempt to build a popular movement at first but attempted to build, according to Kemp, "a network of distinguished sympathisers able to influence policy at high levels."[300] The society had a Consultative Medical Council and a Literary Group and was endorsed by a variety of authors, "progressive" reformers, feminists and supporters of the Fabian Society.[301] Early supporters included Henry Havelock Ellis, Vera Brittain, Cicely Hamilton, Laurence Housman, H. G. Wells, Harold Laski, George Bernard Shaw, Eleanor Rathbone MP, G. M.

---

[298] Leicester Literary & Philosophical Society, Presidents Gallery: Charles Killick Millard MD DSc (1870 - 1952)
http://www.le.ac.uk/litandphil/presidents/1917.html
[299] Nick Kemp, Merciful Release, Manchester University Press, 2002.
[300] Ibid.
[301] The Fabian Society is a British socialist organisation whose purpose is to advance the principles of socialism via gradualist and reformist, rather than revolutionary, means. It is best known for its initial ground-breaking work beginning late in the 19th century and continuing up to World War I. The society laid many of the foundations of the Labour Party and subsequently affected the policies of states emerging from the decolonisation of the British Empire, especially India. Today, the society functions primarily as a think tank and is one of 15 socialist societies affiliated with the Labour Party. Similar societies exist in Australia (the Australian Fabian Society), Canada (the Douglas-Coldwell Foundation and the now disbanded League for Social Reconstruction) and in New Zealand.

Trevelyan, W. Arbuthnot Lane, and a variety of peers including Lord Woolton of Liverpool (Conservative) and Lord Moynihan who had been the President of the Royal College of Surgeons.

Incidentally, the Fabian Society is still active in the UK. Eighty-year-old retired medical doctor Michael Irwin set up a suicide support group in April 2013 called "Die-alogue" which shares advice on euthanasia. The idea for the group came from the Brighton and Hove Fabian Society, where he has given talks. This is Britain's first suicide support group. Irwin, who lives in Surrey, launched this support group in in Hove, East Sussex. The group plans to help each other travel abroad to commit suicide if necessary. Irwin and his group is now providing financial, moral and emotional support to people travelling abroad to the Dignitas clinic in Switzerland. Around 180 Britons are thought to have died at Dignitas, which exploits liberal Swiss laws. Irwin has also been in contact with an 83-year-old dementia sufferer who plans to die at Dignitas.[302] The British man would be the first to end his life at the Swiss clinic purely because of dementia.

In 2011 Dr Irwin revealed how a 91-year-old from Eastbourne had contacted him about Dignitas. He did not take her to Switzerland but police officers interviewed him, making no arrest. Dr Irwin has been investigated in the past over assisted suicide – an offence carrying a 14-year jail sentence – but has never been arrested. The Suicide Act 1961 states that: "a person who aids, abets, counsels or procures the suicide of another, or an attempt by another to commit suicide, shall be liable to prosecution." The police have an obligation to investigate such matters and people engaged in such activity should be prosecuted.

---

[302] Anthony Bond and Mark Duell, *Daily Mail*, 19 March, 2013.

The first attempt to pass legislation to make euthanasia legal in Britain was the Voluntary Euthanasia (Legalisation) Bill 1936 introduced to the House of Lords by Arthur Ponsonby.[303] The debate was not split along party political grounds and the government considered it "outside the proper range of government intervention and to be one which should be left to the conscience of the individual members of the House". The Hunterian Society held a debate on 16 November, 1936 to discuss whether "the practice of voluntary euthanasia would be unjustifiable" and the Bill was opposed by the British Medical Association.[304]

1950s to 1980s

On 28 November 1950, the next attempt was made by Lord Chorley of Kendal, a Vice-President of the society, who brought a pro-voluntary euthanasia motion before the House of Lords. The motion was so widely condemned it was withdrawn without a division. According to N. D. A. Kemp, the attempt was an "ignominious failure", as were similar attempts to produce more liberal legislation generally on abortion, homosexuality and divorce.[305]

Following the death of the Killick Millard (Honorary Secretary) and the resignation of Lord Denman (President of the Society) and the deaths of two prominent supporters of the society, E.W. Barnes and Dr N.I. Spriggs, a new Honorary Secretary was found in R. S. W. Pollard who moved the society from Leicester to be based in London. The society also changed tactics: moving away from courting the medical and

---

[303] The Earl of Listowel, "Foreword" to A. B. Downing, Barbara Smoker (eds.), *Voluntary Euthanasia: Experts Debate the Right to Die*, Owen, 1986, pp. 5–7.
[304] Nick Kemp, *Merciful Release*, Manchester University Press, 2002.
[305] Ibid.

legal elites to trying to build up a mass movement to exert "grass-roots pressure" and efforts were made to bring up the topic in civic society groups like Rotary Clubs, local newspaper editorials etc.[306]

From 1955 onwards "Legalisation" was dropped from the name along with "Voluntary" to make it the Euthanasia Society (although some sources place it at 1960).[307] The Euthanasia Society placed adverts in the London Underground and on mainline railway services in the south of England with the wording, "The Euthanasia Society believes that incurable sufferers should have the right to choose a Merciful Death". In 1960, the chairman, C. K. MacDonald died and was replaced by Leonard Colebrook. Maurice Millard replaced him temporarily. In 1962, he was replaced by the Unitarian minister Rev. A. B. Downing, and in 1964, C. R. Sweetingham was made secretary.[308]

Prominent people who supported the society during the 1960s included the legal academic and president of the Law Reform Association, Glanville Williams. Williams gave a paper entitled "Voluntary euthanasia: the next step" at the Annual General Meeting of the society in 1955. Williams' ethical justification of euthanasia argued against the principle of double effect and for a utilitarian approach to the questions in medical ethics including both voluntary euthanasia and abortion. His proposal would have allowed a physician to put as a defence to a homicide, assault or bodily

---

[306] Ibid.

[307] A. B. Downing, Barbara Smoker (eds.), *Voluntary Euthanasia: Experts Debate the Right to Die*, Peter Owen Publishers; 2nd (revised) edition, 1986, pp. 255–259.

[308] Nick Kemp, *Merciful Release*, Manchester University Press, 2002.

harm charge that the person was incurably and fatally ill if the doctor was acting in good faith.[309]

According to Kemp, the public association of euthanasia with eugenics and Nazi atrocities marred attempts in the 1950s to promote voluntary euthanasia, but such setbacks were short-lived.[310] The next legislative attempt was started in 1967 with a bill drafted by Mary Rose Barrington, a member of the executive committee of the Euthanasia Society and barrister. Attempts were made to find an MP willing to introduce it to the Commons but eventually Lord Raglan, a member of the National Secular Society, introduced it to the Lords in 1969.[311]

The word "Voluntary" was reinstated to the name in 1969 to become the Voluntary Euthanasia Society.[312] It was also known as Exit (not to be confused with Exit International) from 1979 but this was reverted in 1982.[313] During the period it was known as "Exit", the secretary of the society, Nicholas Reed, was convicted of conspiracy to variously aid and abet or counsel a number of suicides. He was jailed for two and a half years, although this was reduced to 18 months on appeal. Reed had supported Mark Lyons, a seventy-year old man who provided pills and alcohol to several sick people. Lyons was given a two-year suspended sentence.[314] The society had voted in 1979 to publish a

---

[309] These proposals mirror those of James Rachels discussed below.

[310] Nick Kemp, *Merciful Release*, Manchester University Press, 2002.

[311] Ibid.

[312] A. B. Downing, Barbara Smoker (eds.), *Voluntary Euthanasia: Experts Debate the Right to Die*, Peter Owen Publishers; 2nd revised edition, 1986, p. 255–259.

[313] A. B. Downing, Barbara Smoker (eds.), *Voluntary Euthanasia: Experts Debate the Right to Die*, Peter Owen Publishers; 2nd revised edition, 1986, p. 255–259.

[314] Alison Benjamin, "Exit strategy", *The Guardian*, 25 January 2006.

"Guide to Self-Deliverance", a booklet which described suicide methods. This was challenged by the Attorney General in 1982 under s2 of the Suicide Act 1961, and after a brief attempt to fight back against this the distribution of the booklet was suspended in 1983.[315]

After the name was changed back following the conviction of Reed and Lyons, Lord Jenkins of Putney introduced an amendment to the Suicide Act to introduce a defence for those who acted "on behalf of the person who committed suicide and in so acting behaved reasonably and with compassion and in good faith" but this was defeated 48 votes to 15.[316]

In 1988, the Voluntary Euthanasia Society, as it was then, attempted to place a full-page newspaper advertisement in the *Evening Standard* showing twenty-four young men with advanced emphysema with the words "A day in the life of an emphysema sufferer" and accompanied by "We believe that he should have the right to choose a peaceful and dignified death." The British Medical Association contacted the Advertising Standards Authority to block publication of the ad, and a representative of the British Lung Foundation condemned the advert, saying, "fears of patients with lung disease should not be exploited in this way."[317]

1990s

In 1990, the group campaigned for the early release of Anthony Cocker, who was convicted of murder after killing his wife Esther after she begged him to end her suffering from

---

[315] Nick Kemp, *Merciful Release*, Manchester University Press, 2002.
[316] Ibid.
[317] Charles Oulton, "Anger at euthanasia advert", *Sunday Times*, 31 July 1988.

multiple sclerosis.[318] In 1992, the society supported Dr Nigel Cox, who was prosecuted and convicted for murder for shortening the life of a patient at the Royal Hampshire County Hospital.[319]

2000 to Present [320]

Dignity in Dying was the new name endorsed by members at the annual general meeting in 2005. The name change was made to "get away from the suggestion that you can only achieve dignity in dying with euthanasia."[321]

Dignity in Dying has a range of patrons, including people who have been associated with high-profile cases connected with Dignity in Dying's campaigns, such as Lesley Close (sister of John Close), Brian Pretty (husband of Diane Pretty) and Heather Pratten. Other patrons include prominent individuals from the worlds of business, politics, the arts and religion, such as Terry Pratchett, Jonathan Miller, Patricia Hewitt, Zoë Wanamaker, Simon Weston, Anthony Grayling and Matthew Wright.

Lord Joffe who joined the society in the 1970s has made recent legislative attempts.[322] The first bill was introduced in the 2003 session and the Bill has been reintroduced

---

[318] Angela Johnson, "'Right to die' campaign finds growing support: Angela Johnson examines the debate about legalising voluntary euthanasia, an issue which arouses strong passions", *The Guardian*, 25 August 1990.

[319] John Furbisher, "Euthanasia supporters say it is time to change the law", *Sunday Times*, 20 September 1992.

[320] Time of writing, October, 2013.

[321] Angela Johnson, "'Right to die' campaign finds growing support: Angela Johnson examines the debate about legalising voluntary euthanasia, an issue which arouses strong passions", *The Guardian*, 25 August 1990.

[322] Hélène Mulholland, "A matter of life and death", *The Guardian*, 24 October 2005.

repeatedly since.[323] The Joffe Bill led to the formation of the anti-euthanasia group Care Not Killing.[324]

Diane Pretty

Diane Pretty (1958-2002) was a British woman from Luton who became notable after being the focus of a debate about the laws of euthanasia in the United Kingdom during the early part of the twenty-first century. She had attempted to change British law so she could end her own life because of the pains and problems that she endured because of the terminal illness motor neurone disease. She stated "I want to have a quick death without suffering, at home surrounded by my family."[325]

Pretty had been diagnosed with motor neurone disease several years before. Over time, the disease worsened and made it impossible for her to move or communicate easily even though her mental faculties remained normal. The illness resulted in her having to be looked after round the clock by her husband and nurses, meaning that she could not commit suicide, which she had said she would do if she was able to.[326] She stated a wish that her husband should be able to assist her in ending her life, but this is classed as assisted suicide, which is illegal in the United Kingdom.

Pretty took her case to court using the Human Rights Act to argue that the Director of Public Prosecutions should make

---

[323] "Bid to legalise assisted suicide", BBC News, 20 February, 2003. "Assisted Dying for the Terminally Ill Bill [HL]", Public Bills before Parliament, United Kingdom Parliament, 8 January, 2004.

[324] "Anti-euthanasia alliance launched", BBC News, 31 January 2006.

[325] Husband pays tribute to Diane Pretty, BBC, 13 May, 2002. Panorama: *Please Help Me Die* was screened on BBC One on the evening of the day she died.

[326] Clare Dyer (legal correspondent), "Diane Pretty makes final 'death with dignity' plea" *The Guardian*, 20 March 2002.

a commitment not to prosecute anybody involved in helping her to die. British courts did not accept Pretty's arguments, with the House of Lords, eventually turning her case down.[327] The European Court of Human Rights refused to acknowledge that the European Convention on Human Rights provided a right to die, and her appeal to that court also failed.[328]

Diane Pretty died aged forty-three on 11 May 2002, as her health had deteriorated over the last several months of her life due to a series of lung and chest problems.[329]

Partnership

Dignity in Dying has a non-campaigning partner charity, Compassion in Dying, which carries out research to do with end-of-life matters, provides the general public with access to advance decisions and also works to provide information about a person's rights at the end-of-life. They are also associated with Healthcare Professionals for Assisted Dying, a group formed by Dignity in Dying supporter and general practitioner Ann McPherson.[330]

In May 2011, Dignity in Dying noted the result of a referendum in Zurich, Switzerland, which showed overwhelming support for assisted dying and voted to reject the restriction of assisted dying services in Zurich to the

---

[327] The Queen on the Application of Mrs Diane Pretty (Appellant) v. Director of Public Prosecutions (Respondent) and Secretary of State for the Home Department (Interested Party) www.parliament.uk

[328] ECHR, Pretty v. the United Kingdom, application no. 2346/02

[329] Diane Pretty dies, BBC, 12 May, 2002.

[330] "Assisted suicide campaigner Ann McPherson dies" (Obituary), The Guardian, 30 May 2011.

residents of the city. The organisation called the result a "brave decision" on the part of the Swiss people.[331]

Activities

Dignity in Dying campaigns for patient choice at the end-of-life and supports palliative care, increased funding and the provision of hospice care. It also campaigns for new legislation to permit assisted dying within strict safeguards, and promotes the concept and use of advance decisions in England and Wales. The group has repeatedly published opinion polls showing considerable public support for a change to the law on assisted dying as well as showing support from doctors and disabled people.[332]

Dignity in Dying's stated view is that everyone has the right to a dignified death. They interpret this to mean that everybody should be able to choose where they die, who else would be present at that time and the treatment options they would welcome or not. A person should have access to information on their end-of-life options from qualified experts and their caregivers, family and friends should also be able to access high quality care and support. Ultimately an individual should have the right to plan for and then take personal control over their own death, including the medication and pain relief they wish to receive or not.

---

[331] "BBC News, 15 May, 2011". Bbc.co.uk.

[332] Chris Mihill, "'No surprise' as poll shows 79pc back legalisation of euthanasia", *The Guardian*, 26 April 1993. "Briton dies after landmark euthanasia ruling", ABC News Online. 4 December 2004. Thomson Prentice, "More GPs would 'support euthanasia for Aids victims'", *The Times*, 27 April 1987. H. Trowell, *The Unfinished Debate on Euthanasia*, SCM Press Ltd, Appendix B: "Doctors and Euthanasia", 1973, p. 167. This is a response to a BMA document, and it cites the National Opinion Polls which say 35.8% of GPs said "they would be prepared to administer euthanasia if legally permissible".

Dignity in Dying also outlines how it goes about campaigning. They encourage their supporters to campaign for a change to the current laws so that a terminally ill, mentally competent adult who feels their suffering has become unbearable can opt for an assisted death, subject to strict rules and safeguards. They lobby politicians and other decision-makers, and seek to educate legal and healthcare professionals and the public in general to support this drive towards obtaining a comprehensive national end-of-life strategy and working procedures. They would generally attempt to "empower" terminally ill people (and their families and friends) so that they can obtain a better experience as their end-of-life approaches, including access to information on current rights and such plans as Advance Decisions.

Arguments and Opposition

One of Dignity in Dying's main arguments is that their proposals for a comprehensive strategy around the issue of assisted dying would provide safeguards and protection for an individual from, for example, the coercive pressures to die that some people believe can be exerted by families of the frail or relatively disadvantaged on occasions. Dignity in Dying argue that at the moment not only can unscrupulous people do this in a relatively unchecked way, but that the legal authorities can generally carry out investigations only after a person's death, whereas under their plans there would be safeguards and checks upfront to ensure a person was fully informed and counselled as to their rights and options and additionally protected from possible malign influences.

Dignity in Dying also state that their proposals would alleviate a great deal of the stress and worry that approaching death can bring to a person, particularly one suffering significant pain from a terminal illness. The use of Advanced Decisions can help significantly but they also believe that if a right to an Assisted Death is available then the very knowledge of this fact can alleviate many of the worries an individual might have. Dignity in Dying supporters argue that the recent trends towards the use of the Dignitas clinic in Switzerland and press stories regarding botched suicides and do-it-yourself advice would be stopped because individuals would know that when and if they wished to finally request an assisted death in the UK, it would be available. They contend that studies from parts of the world that have legalised assisted suicide report that many plans put in place for an early death are not taken up as people end up dying naturally, with the peace of mind brought about by knowing that an assisted death was available if pain and suffering had got too much.

For example, in the US state of Oregon in 2007, it was reported that of the 30,000 deaths in the state that year, 10,000 people considered an assisted death, around 1,000 spoke to their doctor about it, 85 actually got a prescription and just 49 went on to have an assisted death.[333]

Dignity in Dying is often opposed by some religious believers and groups such as Care Not Killing. Many people of a religious persuasion rightly take the view that all life is sacred and that only natural processes (and God) should determine a person's death. Dignity in Dying argue (rather simplistically) that if a person does not wish to take advantage of a change in the law which would allow for an assisted death then that is down to personal choice. However, it strongly opposes opponents who would try to deny an individual the right to a personal choice in the

---

[333] Ann Jackson presentation October 2009 to a symposium on end-of-life practices in Washington State.

matter by blocking enabling legislation. In reality, a change in the law in the UK would be a seismic movement that would have serious repercussions for everybody.

The introduction of the sort of legislation supported by Dignity in Dying would be a "slippery slope" towards more liberal and permissive laws. Additionally, some disability rights campaigners are concerned that an assisted dying law would lead to extra pressure on some disabled persons to seek a premature death, as they might consider their lives to be devalued. The 2007 British Social Attitudes survey interestingly reported that 75% of people with a disability believed that a person with a terminal and painful illness from which they were certain to die should be allowed an assisted death.[334] But it depends on how such questions are framed. Phrases like "dignity in dying", "mercy-killing", "compassion in death" and others are hijacked by pro-euthanasia pressure groups and those who oppose these practices appear to oppose the concept of a dignified, painless and peaceful death. But this is not so. Everybody wants a dignified, painless and peaceful death and palliative care offers this.

Dignity in Dying point to other parts of the world that have some form of assisted dying or similar legislation, which they say is generally popular and supported by the majority, such as the Netherlands. Dignity in Dying supports the legislation of assisted death, whereby a doctor prescribes a life-ending dose of medication to a mentally competent, terminally ill adult at the patient's request, and which the patient administers. But the reality in the Netherlands is that one does not have to be terminally ill to avail of this service. Another argument used by Dignity in Dying regarding the use of the Dignitas organisation in Switzerland is that the

---

[334] British Social Attitudes survey: 2007.

availability of assisted dying in Switzerland is simply "outsourcing" the problem.[335]

Practicalities

James Rachels in *The End of Life: Euthanasia and Morality* supports voluntary euthanasia but argues that proposals put forward by Dignity in Dying and by other voluntary euthanasia supporters are often impractical. Rachels describes the proposal of the Euthanasia Society (as it then was) as requiring the person be over twenty-one, "suffering from a disease involving severe pain and of an incurable and fatal character", submitting an application with two medical signatories to a third-party "Euthanasia Referee" who would interview the patient. If that person were satisfied, the patient would have to wait seven days and the euthanasia procedure would have to be done "in the presence of an official witness". Rachels argues that this procedure, along with a more complex one then proposed by the Euthanasia Society of America, were "unworkably cumbersome" and "so elaborate, and take so much time, that they are hardly conducive to the 'quick and easy' death that is the whole point of euthanasia...by the time he could go through it all, he might already be dead."[336]

Rachels instead proposes that a better route to implementing legal euthanasia would be to provide a defence to homicide offences of "mercy" killing:

> ...what would happen in court under this proposal is very much like what often happens now. Many juries are already functioning as though mercy-

---

[335] Martin Beckford, "14% rise in British members of Dignitas", *Daily Telegraph*, 23 January 2012.

[336] James Rachels, *The End of Life: Euthanasia and Morality*, Oxford University Press, 1986, pp. 183–187.

killing were an acceptable defence: when faced with genuine mercy-killers, they refuse to convict. The main consequence of my proposal would be to sanction officially what these juries already do.[337]

Advance Decisions

Advance decisions have been allowed in Britain since the passing of the Mental Capacity Act 2005. Essentially, they allow an individual to write down their wish to refuse life-sustaining treatment, so that if they are no longer able to communicate they can be assured that doctors and other medical staff know what their wishes are and that they are legally binding. Additionally, a person can also state in their advance decision what life-sustaining treatment they do wish, although doctors do not ultimately have to respect that request.

---

[337] Op. cit.

CHAPTER 13 Exit International

Exit International is an international non-profit organisation advocating legalisation of euthanasia and assisted suicide. It was previously known as the Voluntary Euthanasia Research Foundation (VERF). Exit International was founded in Australia by Dr Philip Nitschke in 1997 after the over-turning of the world's first Voluntary Euthanasia law—the Rights of the Terminally Ill (ROTI) Act. During the time the ROTI Act was in force Dr Nitschke became the first physician in the world to administer a legal, lethal, voluntary injection.[338] The organisation had 3,500-members in 2011.[339] Their average age is 75.[340]

Activities

In 2010, Exit International unveiled the first pro-euthanasia billboard in Australia on the Hume Highway near Sydney. The billboard wording was:

> "**85%** of Australians support
>
> ## Voluntary Euthanasia
>
> Our government doesn't!
>
> **Make them listen**

---

[338] "Exit International", www.exitinternational.net
[339] Dominic Kennedy, "Suicide expert Philip Nitschke launches UK tour" - *Times Online*, (London: News Intl.).
[340] Barbie Dutter, "Pensioners defy death drug laws", *The Daily Telegraph*, 21 April 2011.

The plan had previously met with opposition when the Australian Advertising Standards Bureau wrote to Exit International, informing them that the advertisement may be illegal as it would contravene state laws on aiding or abetting suicide.[341] Exit International successfully countered by arguing that the language used on the billboard did not argue for euthanasia, but instead referred only to public support for the act.[342]

In September 2010, Billboards Australia blocked Nitschke's billboard advertising campaign.[343] Billboards Australia cited a section of the NSW Crimes Act that outlaws the aiding or abetting of suicide or attempted suicide. Nitschke was told to provide legal advice outlining how his billboard did not break this law, a request Nitschke described as "ludicrous", pointing out that the billboards urge "political change and in no way could be considered to be in breach of the crimes act."[344] Nitschke said he had sought a legal opinion from prominent human rights lawyer Greg Barns.[345] The lawyer was able to convince Billboards Australia to rescind its ruling, in part.[346]

Prior to the billboard, Exit International had developed a pro-voluntary euthanasia television advertisement that was

---

[341] Danny Rose, "Another blow for euthanasia campaign", *Shepparton News*, August 2011.
[342] "Euthanasia billboard approved", *The Sydney Morning Herald*, 4 October 2010.
[343] Danny Rose, "Another blow for euthanasia campaign", *Shepparton News*, August 2011.
[344] Danny Rose, "Another blow for euthanasia campaign", *Shepparton News*, August 2011.
[345] Danny Rose, "Another blow for euthanasia campaign", *Shepparton News*, August 2011.
[346] "Euthanasia billboard approved". smh.com.au. 4 October 2010.

due to screen in 2010. "The Gruen Transfer" prompted the advertisement.[347] Two advertising agencies had been requested to create a pro-euthanasia advertisement to "market the unmarketable." Although the winning entry was not able to be used by Exit International, they employed the successful advertising agency. The resulting advertisement was to screen on 12 September, but was unable to be shown after approval for the advertisement was withdrawn two days prior to screening, legal concerns in regard to the promotion of euthanasia and suicide being cited as the cause.[348]

Philip Nitschke

Philip Nitschke is an Australian medical doctor, humanist, author and founder and director of the pro-euthanasia group Exit International. He campaigned successfully to have a legal euthanasia law passed in Australia's Northern Territory and assisted four people in ending their lives before the law was overturned by the Federal government. Nitschke says he was the first doctor in the world to administer a legal, voluntary, lethal injection.[349] Nitschke has complained that he and his group are regularly subject to harassment by authorities and

---

[347] The Gruen Transfer was an Australian television programme focusing on advertising, which debuted on ABC1 on 28 May 2008 and ran for four seasons. The programme was hosted by Will Anderson with a panel of advertising industry experts. The title refers to the Gruen transfer, the response to designed disorientation cues in retail environments. The show's debut episode drew an audience of nearly 1.3 million, the highest debut for an entertainment programme in the ABC's history at that time.

[348] Paula Kruger, "Pro-euthanasia TV ad banned", *Australian Broadcasting Corporation*, 10 September 2010.

[349] "Dr. Death says Britain ignoring end-of-life needs", Reuters. 7 May 2009.

has written on his personal mixed feelings on assisted suicide and the influence of religion on opposition to it.[350]

Career

Born in 1947 in rural South Australia, Nitschke studied physics at the University of Adelaide, gaining a Ph.D. from Flinders University in laser physics in 1972. Rejecting a career in the sciences, he instead travelled to the Northern Territory to take up work with the Aboriginal land rights activist, Vincent Lingiari and the Gurindji at Wave Hill.

After the return of land by then Prime Minister Gough Whitlam, Nitschke became a Northern Territory Parks and Wildlife ranger. However, a serious accident to his foot saw him return to university, graduating from Sydney University Medical School in 1988.

Since assisting four people in ending their lives, Nitschke has provided advice to others who have ended their lives, most notably Nancy Crick, aged 69. On 22 May 2002, Crick, in the presence of over 20 friends and family (but not Nitschke), took a lethal dose of barbiturates, went quickly to sleep, and died within twenty minutes. Nitschke had encouraged Nancy Crick to enter palliative care, which she did for a number of days before returning home again. She had undergone multiple surgeries to treat bowel cancer, and was left with multiple, dense, inoperable bowel adhesions that left her in constant pain and diarrhoea and tied to the toilet, but she was not terminally ill at the time of her

---

[350] "Euthanasia group raided over suicide", *The Australian*, 12 November 2009. "Euthanasia group quizzed over death", *The Canberra Times*. "The World Today – Exit members threatened by raids: Nitschke" 13 November, 2009. "Atheism and Euthanasia", in Warren Bonett (Editor), *The Australian Book of Atheism*. Melbourne, Victoria: Scribe, 2010, pp. 193–200.

death.[351] Nitschke said the scar tissue from previous cancer surgery had caused her suffering. "She didn't actually want to die when she had cancer. She wanted to die after she had cancer treatment," he said.[352]

A 2004 documentary film, *Mademoiselle and the Doctor* focused on the quest of a retired Perth professor, Lisette Nigot, a healthy 79-year-old, to seek a successful method of voluntary euthanasia.[353] She sought advice from Nitschke. Nigot took an overdose of medication that she had bought in the United States and died, just before her 80th birthday.[354] In a note to Nitschke, thanking him for his support, she described him as a crusader working for a worthwhile humane cause. "After 80 years of a good life, I have enough of it" she wrote, adding, "I want to stop it before it gets bad."

Nitschke made headlines in New Zealand when he announced plans to accompany eight New Zealanders to Mexico where the drug Nembutal, capable of producing a fatal overdose, can be purchased legally.[355] He also made headlines, even angering some fellow right-to-die advocates, when he presented his plan to launch a "death ship" that would have allowed him to circumvent local laws by

---

[351] "Radio National Breakfast – 27 May 2002 – Nancy Crick's Cancer". www.abc.net.au. "Spotlight shifted onto Crick doctor" www.smh.com.au. 30 May 2002. Dale Paget, "Crick had no cancer: report", 8 June 2004, www.theage.com.au

[352] Dale Paget, "Crick had no cancer: report – National – www.theage.com.au", 8 June 2004, Melbourne: theage.com.au

[353] "Mademoiselle and the Doctor", Australian Screen, 2004.

[354] "Healthy woman thanks Dr. Nitschke, then kills herself", www.smh.com.au

[355] "NZ offered Mexican Suicide Drug Trip", *The Age* (Melbourne), 6 February 2007.

euthanizing people from around the world in international waters.[356]

In the 2007 Australian federal election, Nitschke ran against the Australian politician Kevin Andrews in the Victoria seat of Menzies but was unsuccessful.[357] On 2 May 2009, British Immigration officials at Heathrow Airport detained Nitschke for nine hours after arriving for a visit to the UK to lecture on voluntary euthanasia and end-of-life choices. Nitschke said it was a matter of free speech and that his detention said something about changes to British society, which were "quite troubling."[358] Nitschke was told that he and his wife were detained because the workshops may contravene British law.[359] However, although assisting someone to commit suicide in the UK is illegal, the law does not apply to a person lecturing on the concept of euthanasia, and Nitschke was allowed to enter. Dame Joan Bakewell, the British Government's "Voice of Older People" said the current British law on assisted suicide was "a mess" and that Nitschke should have been made more welcome in the UK.[360]

In 2009, Nitschke helped to promote Dignified Departure, a 13-hour, pay-television programme on doctor-assisted suicide in Hong Kong and mainland China. The

---

[356] "InternationalTaskForce.org – Update – 2000, Number 2". www.internationaltaskforce.org

[357] "Election results for the seat of Menzies (Australian Electoral Commission)". 26 November 2007.

[358] "BBC NEWS – Euthanasia doctor held at airport", news.bbc.co.uk., 2 May 2009.

[359] Ibid.

[360] "Welcome Dr. Death, says 'spokesman' for elderly", *The Christian Institute*, http://www.christian.org.uk/news/welcome-dr-death-says-spokesman-for-elderly/

programme aired in October that year in China on the Family Health channel, run by the official China National Radio.[361]

Dying with Dignity

On 29 April 2009 Nitschke said "It seems we demand humans to live with indignity, pain and anguish whereas we are kinder to our pets when their suffering becomes too much. It simply is not logical or mature. Trouble is we have had too many centuries of religious claptrap."[362] He works mainly with older people from whom he gains inspiration, saying, "You get quite inspired and uplifted by the elderly folk who see this as quite a practical approach."[363]

In July 2009, Nitschke said he no longer believed voluntary euthanasia should only be available to the terminally ill, but that elderly people afraid of getting old and incapacitated should also have a choice.[364]

Palliative Care

Palliative care specialists claim that many requests for euthanasia arise from fear of physical or psychological distress in the patient's last days, and that widespread and equitable availability of specialist palliative care services will reduce requests for euthanasia. Nitschke is dismissive of this argument: "We have too many people who have the best

---

[361] "'Dr. Death' Nitschke Sells Euthanasia to China Before TV Show - Bloomberg.com". www.bloomberg.com

[362] Saffron Howden, "His choice to live or die", *Lismore Northern Star*, 2 July 2009.

[363] Ibid.

[364] "Give all elderly the right to die – Nitschke", News Corp. 8 July 2009.

palliative care in the world and they still want to know that they can put an end to things."[365]

Younger People and Suicide

Australian statistics published in *The Age* revealed that people in their twenties, thirties and forties have died from overdosing on Nembutal, the drug that Nitschke recommends for dying by suicide.[366] Nitschke responded that his organisation has made every attempt to filter who they provide information to but he accepts that despite the disclaimer on the *Peaceful Pill* website, anyone, including depressed teenagers, could access the information. He said this is the risk Exit International has taken to help vast numbers of elderly and seriously ill people.[367] Nitschke argues, "There will be some casualties when you put this information out there, and these are casualties which are tragic...but this has to be balanced with the growing pool of older people who feel immense wellbeing from having access to this information."[368] Nitschke believes that people's right to control death is as fundamental as their right to control life.[369]

Books

Killing Me Softly: Voluntary Euthanasia and the Road to the Peaceful Pill, was published in 2005. This book explains the philosophy behind Nitschke's work at Exit International.

---

[365] Greg Baxter, "Does the freedom to die enhance lives?" *Irish Medical Times*, 28 March, 2010.

[366] Melissa Jenkins, "Young Aussies 'told of euthanasia pill'", Melbourne: theage.com.au, 15 February 2010.

[367] Julia Medew, (15 February 2010) "The Death Trap", Melbourne: theage.com.au.

[368] Ibid.

[369] Greg Baxter. "Does the freedom to die enhance lives?" *Irish Medical Times*, 28 March, 2010.

Part biography, part political call-to-arms, *Killing Me Softly* documents the events around the world's first right-to-die law and provides analysis of the medico-legal model behind the voluntary euthanasia debate. It also discusses how a "peaceful pill" would revolutionise voluntary euthanasia in the same way the contraceptive pill transformed birth control.

In January 2007, he published the controversial book *The Peaceful Pill Handbook* which was prohibited by Australian federal censorship regulator, the Office of Film and Literature Classification at the end of February 2007.[370] The New Zealand Office of Film and Literature Classification banned the book in New Zealand on 8 June 2007, not because it advocates euthanasia, but because it gives instructions on drug manufacture and other acts deemed criminal. In May 2008, it was allowed for sale in New Zealand if sealed and an indication of the censorship classification was displayed.[371]

The Peaceful Pill Handbook is a book giving instructions on how to perform suicide. It was originally published in the U.S. in 2007 and was written by the Australian doctors Philip Nitschke and Fiona Stewart. It describes legal and moral aspects of suicide and euthanasia (from an amoral position) and provides how-to instructions for several suicide methods. The primary focus of the book is on peaceful (non-violent and painless) suicide methods that can be used by seriously ill and elderly people. To distinguish between suitable and non-suitable methods Dr Nitschke introduces the Reliability-Peacefulness (RP) rating. One of the recommended suicide methods involves drinking pentobarbital, a drug available at

---

[370] "The Peaceful Pill Handbook Refused Classification Upon Review" (pdf), Classification Review Board, 24 February 2007.
[371] Office of Film & Literature Classification decision.

Mexican veterinary pharmacies that is only supposed to be sold "to licensed veterinarians who present a prescription."[372]

The book was initially banned in New Zealand since it was deemed to be objectionable. The ban in New Zealand was lifted in 2008.[373] The book is banned in Australia, in both printed and (according to Wiki-Leaks) online versions.[374] At the same time, the book was freely sold in other countries, in particular by Amazon.com in the USA. Since May 2008 it has been allowed for sale in New Zealand if sealed and, as already mentioned, an indication of the censorship classification is displayed. To circumvent the continuing import ban in Australia, an online for-pay e-book edition was launched in October 2008. The more expensive online edition includes videos and other material, not available with the printed book. The Australian government included the handbook website in its internet-filtering plan in 2009.[375]

Nitschke was involved in an argument in the press with the family of a woman suffering from post-natal depression who read the book and took the advice offered about travelling to Mexico. Her drawn-out death caused her family to attack the accuracy of the book's advice.[376] Nitschke responded by saying that there was no way of knowing, which drugs the woman, actually took and whether the drugs were still potent.

---

[372] Marc Lacey, "In Tijuana, a Market for Death in a Bottle", *The New York Times*, 21 July, 2008.

[373] "Ban on euthanasia book lifted in NZ", *Sydney Morning Herald*, 11 May, 2011.

[374] Michael Duffy, "Web filtering pulls plug on euthanasia debate", *Sydney Morning Herald*, 22May, 2009.

[375] Asher Moses, "Conroy urged to 'end net censorship farce", *Sydney Morning Herald*, 2 September, 2009.

[376] "Doctor caught in Mexican stand-off", *The Australian*. 19 December, 2008.

Because there are problems with the "Mexican option" (high cost of travel, high crime rate in Mexico, unreliability of drug availability, counterfeit or expired Nembutal) Nitschke announced in December 2008 that he now supported the use of a do-it-yourself euthanasia device that relied only on easily available items.[377] Later in 2009 he announced the availability of a testing kit to help people determine if the Nembutal they had bought was still potent.

Final Exit: The Practicalities of Self-Deliverance and Assisted Suicide for the Dying is a controversial 1991 self-help book by Derek Humphry, founder of the Hemlock Society in California and past president of the World Federation of Right to Die Societies.[378] A newspaper journalist and author who helped his wife, Jean, end her life with an intentional overdose of medication after a long and painful decline from terminal cancer. Humphry wrote the book as a how-to guide for terminally ill people who wish to end their lives. The controversy arose not only from the intense debate over whether one should have a right to end one's own life, and whether anyone, especially medical professionals, can ethically assist self-chosen euthanasia, but also because the information in the book can be used by anyone, not just the terminally ill.

The book covers many aspects of planning and carrying out "self-deliverance", from the decision of whether and when one is ready to die, to the careful protection of anyone assisting one's preparations, to the legal and financial preparations for those one leaves behind. But the bulk of the work consists of the advantages and disadvantages and the processes for a variety of suicide methods.

---

[377] Kim Wheatley, "New death device to be launched in Adelaide", *Adelaide Now*, 16 December, 2008.
[378] Published by Dell, 1992.

In 2000, a Supplement to *Final Exit* was published with a new chapter on a method using helium gas as an alternative not requiring controlled prescription drugs. In 2001, marking the book's 10th anniversary, this information was included in the revised third edition of the book. In 2005, an electronic addendum to the third edition was released, offering refinements to the helium bag technique. The addendum was updated May 2009.

Success of the Book

In 1991, the first edition was the number one bestselling nonfiction book in America for eighteen weeks and has sold over a million copies. An updated edition was published in 2011 by Dell, New York. *Final Exit* has been translated into twelve languages and is banned by law only in France. It remains in print in English, Spanish, Italian and other languages.

In April 2007, the editors and book critics of the American national newspaper *USA Today* selected *Final Exit* as one of the twenty-five most memorable books of the last quarter century. Humphry subsequently put the information in this book onto a VHS video (2000) and a DVD (2006), both available through ERGO.

The ethicist Peter Singer included it on a list of his top ten books (he lists it tenth) in *The Guardian*.[379]

References in Pop Culture

Industrial metal band *Fear Factory* uses quotes from Humphry's video in the last track, "Final Exit", of their seventh studio album, *Mechanize*. In a Christmas episode of *Mystery Science Theater 3000* Dr Forrester gives TV's Frank a

---

[379] Peter Singer, "Peter Singer's top 10 books", *The Guardian*, 6 April 2001.

copy of the book as a gift after he reveals that he stole Frank's blood to pay for it. In episode eleven of the sixth season of *Married with Children*, Al Bundy can be seen reading this book while in bed. The legendary comedian Bill Hicks incorporates this book in several of his bootleg shows as a build-up to one of his controversial sketches on how euthanasia can make movies more interesting and believable, quoting a phrase, "Put 'em in the movies..."

Australian Censorship

On 22 May 2009 it was disclosed in the press (citing wikileaks.org) that the Australian Government had added the online *Peaceful Pill Handbook* (hosted at www.yudu.com to the blacklist maintained by the Australian Communications and Media Authority used to filter internet access to citizens of Australia.[380] Australian Communications Minister Stephen Conroy planned to introduce legislation just before the 2010 election to make internet service providers block a blacklist of "refused classification" websites. The blacklist includes Exit's websites and other similar sites. Nitschke at the time said the proposals were the "final nail in the coffin for euthanasia advocacy" in Australia, where people are banned from discussing end-of-life issues over the phone, buying books about it or importing printed material on it. "The one avenue we had open to us was the internet, and now it looks like it will be part of Conroy's grand plan to provide a so-called clean feed to Australia. It's outrageous."[381]

In April 2010, Nitschke began holding a series of "Hacking Master-classes" to teach people how to circumvent

---

[380] Michael Duffy, "Web filtering pulls plug on euthanasia debate", smh.com.au, 22 May 2009.
[381] Asher Moses, "Big Brother laws to be brought in for web", *The Age* (Melbourne) 16 December 2009.

the Australian internet filter.[382] Access to Nitschke's online *Peaceful Pill Handbook* was blocked during trials of the government's filter. A government spokeswoman said euthanasia would not be targeted by the proposed filter, but confirmed that, "The website for accessing an electronic version of the *Peaceful Pill Handbook* was classified as 'refused classification' because it provided detailed instruction in crimes relating to the possession, manufacture and importation of barbiturates."[383] Nitschke said Exit International would investigate if it could set up its own proxy server or virtual private network (VPN) tunnel, so its members had a safe way of accessing its information.[384]

Television

On 10 September 2010, Nitschke complained that the Commercials Advice self-regulator of advertising content on Australian commercial television had prevented the television screening of a paid advertisement from Exit International in which an actor depicted a dying man who requested the option of voluntary euthanasia. Commercials Advice reportedly cited Section 2.17.5 of the Commercial Television Code of Practice: Suicide. Not surprisingly the advertisement was felt to condone the practice of suicide. Nitschke responded that the acts of Commercials Advice constitute

---

[382] Cortlan Bennett, "Euthanasia workshops 'to fight filter'", smh.com.au, 4 April 2010.

[383] Ibid.

[384] Geesche Jacobsen, "Elderly learn to beat euthanasia firewall", smh.com.au, 6 April 2010.

Note: VPN extends a private network across a public network, such as the internet. It enables a computer to send and receive data across shared or public networks as if it were directly connected to the private network, while benefitting from the functionality, security and management policies of the private network. This is done by establishing a virtual point-to-point connection through the use of dedicated connections, encryption, or a combination of the two.

interference with the right to free speech. But there have to be limits to free-speech. One cannot be allowed to shout the word "fire" repeatedly in a cinema if there is no fire. To do so would constitute reckless endangerment. Free speech should not be used to promote hatred or incitement to violence because these things are detrimental to society and what Exit International is advocating is also detrimental to society.

Similar TV commercials, planned for use during Nitschke's Canadian lecture tour of 2010, were likewise banned by the Television Bureau of Canada, after lobbying by anti-euthanasia groups.[385]

Euthanasia Techniques

Nitschke created devices to aid people who want euthanasia, including a product called the "exit bag" (a large plastic bag with a drawstring allowing it to be secured around the neck) and the "Co-Gen" (or "Co-Genie") device. The Co-Gen device generates the deadly gas carbon monoxide, which is inhaled with a facemask.[386]

In December 2008, Nitschke released details of a euthanasia machine to the media. He called it "flawless" and "undetectable", saying the new process uses ordinary household products including a barbecue gas bottle — available from hardware stores — filled with nitrogen.[387] Nitschke developed a process in which patients lose consciousness immediately and die a few minutes later. He

---

[385] Les Perreaux, "Ad campaign for assisted suicide banned from Canadian airwaves", *The Globe and Mail*, Toronto, 27 September 2010.
[386] "Nitschke launches suicide machine – smh.com.au", www.smh.com.au, 3 December 2002
[387] Kim Wheatley, "Adelaide Now: Dr Philip Nitschke launches 'flawless' euthanasia device", www.news.com.au, 17 December 2008.

said: "So it's extremely quick and there are no drugs. Importantly this doesn't fail – it's reliable, peaceful, available and with the additional benefit of un-detectability."[388]

Barbiturate Testing Kit

In 2009 Nitschke made a barbiturate testing kit available, initially launched in the UK, then Australia.[389] He said Exit International made the kit available in response to growing demand for something to test the Nembutal obtained from Mexico, often delivered in the post without labels. "They want to be sure they have the right concentration," Nitschke said. The kits have chemicals that change colour when mixed with Nembutal. He was detained for an hour for questioning on arrival at Auckland Airport in New Zealand on a trip to hold public meetings and launch the kit.[390]

Pentobarbital Long-Storage Pill

In October 2009, Nitschke announced his intention to inform people at his workshops where to obtain a long-storage form of sodium pentobarbital (Nembutal) that manufacturers say could be stored for up to fifty years without degrading.[391] Liquid forms of pentobarbital degrade within a few years, while the solid form (a white, crystalline powder) does not. Nitschke intends to advise people on how to reconstitute the pill into liquid form for ingestion if and when it ever becomes appropriate. He said that he sees it as a

---

[388] Kim Wheatley, "Doctor Philip Nitschke to launch 'undetectable' death machine", The Australian, 18 December 2008.

[389] Jamie Doward, "'Dr. Death' sells euthanasia kits in UK for £35", The Guardian, 29 March 2009.

[390] "Nitschke held over drug kits in NZ", ABC News, Australian Broadcasting Corporation, July 2009.

[391] "Nitschke to promote illegal pill – ABC News (Australian Broadcasting Corporation)", www.abc.net.au.

way of keeping people accurately informed and allowing them to make viable choices. The provision of this information would be consistent with good medical care, in his view.[392]

Nitrogen Canisters

In 2012, Nitschke started a beer-brewing company (Max Dog Brewing) for the purpose of importing nitrogen canisters. Nitschke stated that the gas cylinders can be used for both brewing and, if required, to end life at a later stage in a "peaceful, reliable and totally legal" manner.[393] Nitschke said nitrogen "was undetectable even by autopsy, which was important to some people."[394] An Australian anti-euthanasia campaigner complained to the Australian Health Practitioner Regulation Agency (AHPRA) about the canisters.[395]

Following a 2013 workshop showcasing Nitschke's nitrogen gas product, the AMA's WA branch president and general practitioner, Richard Choong, said that he was strongly opposed to it, regardless of its technical legality, since "any machine that can help you kill yourself can be abused, misused and maliciously used."[396] Nitschke responded that without such information most elderly people who want

---

[392] Ibid.

[393] Mike Sexton, "Euthanasia campaigner under scrutiny", *ABC*, 18 December 2012.

[394] Aleisha Orr, "Euthanasia group to show West Aussies how to die 'well'". *WA Today*, 3 May 2013.

[395] Dennis Shanahan, "Euthanasia expert Philip Nitschke accused of gas import scam", *The Australian*, 31 August 2012. AHPRA undertook to investigate. As of 3 May, 2013 the investigation is not complete. See: "'Dr. Death' to fight nitrogen complaint", *Nine MSN*, 3 May 2013.

[396] Courtney Trenwith, "'Horrendous, hidden' waiting list new priority for AMA WA", *Fairfax*, "AMA outraged over euthanasia device", *ABC*. 5 May 2013.

to end their lives hang themselves, which is "an embarrassment and shame."[397] But surely the real embarrassment and shame is that such people, often lonely and depressed are not helped to find hope and companionship and to die with courage and dignity. All Nitschke really does is make the tragedy of suicide more efficient.

Awards and Recognition

In 1996, Nitschke received the Rainier Foundation Humanitarian Award. Once upon a time in a saner world it was people like Mother Theresa who won such awards. In 1998, Nitschke was recognised as the Australian Humanist of the Year by the Council of Australian Humanist Societies. How odd that one who helps to bring the tragedy of suicide into families and communities should be honoured in such a way. He has twice been a finalist for Australian of the Year (2005 and 2006). His nomination sullies and devalues the award and makes Australia look weird.

It is upsetting that a series of public meetings by Exit International have been held in recent years to encourage people, especially the elderly to learn about their "right" to die. Exit International meetings are held in two parts. First, there is a public meeting. These free and open meetings discuss the legislative history and current political status of assisted suicide and voluntary euthanasia around the world. Second, there are Exit workshops. These practical information sessions are based on The Peaceful Pill eHandbook, include question and answer sessions. Topics include Barbiturates: online/offline sources, testing, administration issues and warnings. Prescription/non-

---

[397] Emily Moulton, "Outrage over euthanasia advocate Philip Nitschke and killing machine", The Sunday Times, 5 May, 2013.

prescription drugs: combinations and legal issues. Gases and poisons, risks, safety (ironically), legal issues, suicide notes, death certificates, autopsies, need-to-know rights, obligations, and "insights". Dr Philip Nitschke presents all Exit International meetings and Workshops. Attendance at Exit Workshops is reserved for those over 50 years and people who are seriously ill. Notice that attendance is not restricted to the terminally ill. Exit International workshops are held regularly in most cities of the western world.

Sadly, society is losing its sense of community. The Christian church has a significant role to play in not only upholding the sanctity of life and moral values but also in creating transformed and transforming communities where people belong and understand their preciousness in the eyes of God. It is well known that the elderly are susceptible to depression. Why? Loneliness and feelings of worthlessness weigh heavily upon them. How terribly sad that having contributed so much to society and sacrificed so much for their children that they should end their days in such a way.

Recently a TV programme called "How not to Grow Old" was aired. It seems the natural ageing process must be countered at all cost. This has long been the poisoned idea of the cosmetics industry but now it is becoming more pervasive and insidious.

CHAPTER 14 Doctor Death

Jack Kevorkian (1928–2011), commonly known as "Dr Death", was an American pathologist and euthanasia activist.[398] He is best known for publicly championing a terminal patient's right to die by physician-assisted suicide. He claimed to have assisted at least 130 patients to that end and famously said "dying is not a crime."[399] However, killing is! In 1999, Kevorkian was arrested and tried for his direct role in a case of voluntary euthanasia. He was convicted of second-degree murder and served eight years of a 10- 25-year prison sentence. He was released on parole on 1 June 2007 on condition he would not offer suicide advice to any other person.[400]

Kevorkian was sentenced for the death of Thomas Youk, which Kevorkian videotaped. This was later aired on CBS's 60 Minutes. Australian euthanasia activist Dr Philip Nitschke and two other supporters wrote a letter to then President Bill Clinton asking him to pardon Jack Kevorkian. Here is an excerpt from a transcript of the letter, "We are writing to you, a leader of a democracy, to ask that you, as president, demand that Dr Kevorkian be given a pardon and released from prison. We...beg you to exercise your authority and have Dr Kevorkian restored to his rightful place in society—as a leader and a hero of reform." What a distorted

---

[398] Keith Schneider, "Dr. Jack Kevorkian Dies at 83; A Doctor Who Helped End Lives", *The New York Times*, 3 June, 2011.
[399] Samuel Wells and Ben Quash, *Introducing Christian Ethics*, John Wiley and Sons, 2010, p. 329.
[400] Monica Davey, "Kevorkian Speaks After His Release From Prison", *The New York Times*, 4 June, 2007.

understanding of leadership and heroism. People like Martin Luther King, Mohandas (Mahatma) Gandhi and William Wilberforce were leaders and champions of noble causes. Kevorkian hardly deserves to be defined as a "hero".

Most of Kevorkian's "patients" had no Terminal Illness

A study of 69 of Jack Kevorkian's assisted-suicide deaths from 1990 to 1998 revealed that only 25% involved people with a terminal condition, meaning they had less than six months to live. Of the 69 people whose lives Kevorkian claimed, five were found to have no "anatomical disease" whatsoever upon autopsy.

These findings, which were published as a letter in the *New England Journal of Medicine*, were the result of a two-year clinical analysis, conducted by psychologists from the University of South Florida, of data from the Oakland County, Michigan, medical examiner's office. Since autopsy procedures can vary among counties, Kevorkian-related deaths outside of Oakland County were excluded from the study. As noted, Kevorkian had claimed to have participated in about 130 deaths.

Researchers found that in 72% of the cases the individual had experienced a recent decline in health, a factor which could have precipitated their desire to die. 71% were women' and most of the 69 were either divorced, widowed, or had never married. 35% were experiencing pain, and 13% exhibited symptoms of depression. "Altogether," researchers concluded, "our findings underscore the vulnerability of women and groups of men (i.e., those not married and those coping with serious illness) to physician-assisted suicide and euthanasia" Dr Donna Cohen, co-author of the analysis said:

Kevorkian attracted a group of people who were desperate and depressed and didn't have the support systems to deal with their suffering...The issue isn't about the right for someone to die. It's the issue of the standards of practice that create safeguards for individuals who aren't getting proper care, support and counselling. We can do better as a society than to just kill people.

Oakland County's chief medical examiner and co-author Dr L.J. Dragovic said "This is a catastrophe. Five of those individuals just died in vain because they were led to believe that it was the only solution for their problems."

Diane Coleman, president and founder of the disability rights group Not Dead Yet said that Kevorkian has "been touted as a hero by so many, yet he did this. He robbed many disabled women and others of their lives by responding to their despair in a way society would never respond if they were not disabled women."

Early life

Kevorkian was born in Pontiac, Michigan. His parents were Armenian immigrants.[401] His real name was Jacob but he became known as "Jack".[402] In 1952, he graduated from the University of Michigan Medical School in the city of Ann Arbor.[403] He completed residency training in anatomical and

---

[401] Jack Kevorkian, *Glimmer IQs* (Paperback), World Audience, Inc., 2009.

[402] Neal Nicol and Harry Wylie, *Between the Dead and the Dying*, London: Satin Publications, 2006, pp. 32–33.

[403] Steven M Chermak and Frankie Y. Bailey, *Crimes and Trials of the Century*, Greenwood Publishing Group, 2007, pp. 101–102. See also: Edmond Y; Azadian Agop J.; Franchuk Hacikyan and S. Edward "History on the Move: Views, Interviews and Essays on Armenian Issues, "An

clinical pathology and briefly conducted research on blood transfusion. Unable to function effectively as a hospital pathologist, Kevorkian left the active practice of medicine and, for a time, was even homeless.[404] Kevorkian never married.[405]

Career

Over a period of decades, Kevorkian developed several controversial ideas related to death. In a 1959 journal article, he wrote:

> I propose that a prisoner condemned to death by due process of law be allowed to submit, by his own free choice, to medical experimentation under complete anaesthesia (at the time appointed for administering the penalty) as a form of execution in lieu of conventional methods prescribed by law.[406]

Senior doctors at the University of Michigan, Kevorkian's employer, opposed his proposal and Kevorkian chose to leave the University rather than stop advocating his ideas. Ultimately, he gained little support for his plan. He returned to the idea of using death row inmates for medical purposes after the Supreme Court's 1976 decision in Gregg v. Georgia re-instituted the death penalty. He advocated harvesting the organs from inmates after the death penalty was carried out

---

Interview with Dr. Jack Kevorkian" (Detroit: Wayne State University Press, 1999, p. 233.
[404] Biography, December 15, 2010.
http://thekevorkianpapers.com/about/biography
[405] "Jack Kevorkian", (Obituary) *The Daily Telegraph*, June 3, 2011.
[406] Jack Kevorkian, "Capital Punishment or Capital Gain", *The Journal of Criminal Law, Criminology, and Police Science* 50 (1), May - June 1959, pp. 50–51.

for transplant into sick patients, but failed to gain the cooperation of prison officials.[407]

As a pathologist at Pontiac General Hospital, Kevorkian experimented with transfusing blood from the recently deceased into live patients. He drew blood from corpses recently brought into the hospital and transferred it successfully into the bodies of hospital staff members. Kevorkian thought that the US military might be interested in using this technique to help wounded soldiers during battle, but the Pentagon was not interested.[408]

In the 1980s, Kevorkian wrote a series of articles for the German journal *Medicine and Law* that laid out his thinking on the ethics of euthanasia.[409]

In 1987, Kevorkian started advertising in Detroit newspapers as a physician consultant for "death counselling." Therefore, it is not as if he had many or even some patients who were seeking help on end of life issues and he felt compelled out of compassion to help. Rather he solicited the vulnerable by trawling a sea of despair.

His first public assisted suicide, of Janet Adkins, a 54-year-old woman diagnosed in 1989 with Alzheimer's disease, took place in 1990. Charges of murder were dropped on 13 December 1990, as there were, at that time, no laws in Michigan regarding assisted suicide.[410]

---

[407] Michael Betzold, "1993: Excerpt from 'Appointment with Doctor Death'", *Detroit Free Press*, 19 September 1993.

[408] Ibid.

[409] "The Kevorian Verdict: A Chronology", *Frontline*, May 1996. PBS. See also Jack Lessenberry, "Death becomes him", PBS.org. Vanity Fair, July 1994.

[410] "People v. Kevorkian; Hobbins v. Attorney General", *Ascension Health*, 1994.

The reason there are no laws in many places about assisted suicide is not that there is no opinion about it. Rather, one suspects that the very notion is so bizarre that right-thinking people would not have thought there was any need for such a law. However, the amoral vortex of contemporary culture is a force that has the power to pull society into the hitherto unimaginable.

In 1991, however, the State of Michigan revoked Kevorkian's medical license and made it clear that given his actions, he was no longer permitted to practice medicine or to work with patients.[411] According to his lawyer Geoffrey Fieger, Kevorkian assisted in the deaths of 130 terminally ill people between 1990 and 1998. But, as already shown, many of the people were not actually terminally ill. In each of these cases, the individuals themselves allegedly took the final action which resulted in their own deaths. Kevorkian allegedly assisted only by attaching the individual to a euthanasia device that he had devised and constructed. The individual then pushed a button, which released the drugs, or chemicals that would end his or her own life. Two deaths were assisted by means of a device which delivered the euthanizing drugs intravenously. Kevorkian called the device a "Thanatron" ("Death machine", from the Greek *thanatos* meaning "death").[412] Other people were assisted by a device which employed a gas mask fed by a canister of carbon monoxide, which Kevorkian called the "Mercitron" ("Mercy machine").[413]

---

[411] "Kevorkian medical license revoked", *Lodi News-Sentinel* (Michigan), Associated Press, 21 November, 1991. p. 8.
[412] "The Kevorkian Verdict: The Thanatron", *Frontline*, May 1996.
[413] Nicholas Jackson, "Jack Kevorkian's Death Van and the Tech of Assisted Suicide", *The Atlantic Monthly*, June 3, 2011.

Criticism and Kevorkian's Response

According to a report by the *Detroit Free Press*, 60% of the patients who committed suicide with Kevorkian's help were not terminally ill, and at least thirteen had not complained of pain. The report further asserted that Kevorkian's counselling was too brief (with at least 19 patients dying less than 24 hours after first meeting Kevorkian) and lacked a psychiatric exam in at least 19 cases, 5 of which involved people with histories of depression, though Kevorkian was sometimes alerted that the patient was unhappy for reasons other than their medical condition. In 1992, Kevorkian himself wrote that it is always necessary to consult a psychiatrist when performing assisted suicides because a person's "mental state is...of paramount importance."[414] Clearly, this was nothing more than a public relations statement designed to make him seem careful, considerate and compassionate.

The report also stated that Kevorkian failed to refer at least 17 patients to a pain specialist after they complained of chronic pain, and sometimes failed to obtain a complete medical record for his patients, with at least 3 autopsies of suicides Kevorkian had assisted with showing the person who committed suicide to have no physical sign of disease. Rebecca Badger, a patient of Kevorkian's and a mentally troubled drug abuser, had been mistakenly diagnosed with multiple sclerosis. The report also stated that Janet Adkins, Kevorkian's first patient, had been chosen without Kevorkian ever speaking to her, only with her husband, and that when Kevorkian first met Adkins two days before her assisted suicide he "made no real effort to discover whether Mrs Adkins wished to end her life", as the Michigan Court of

---

[414] Kirk Cheyfitz, "Suicide Machine, Part 1: Kevorkian rushes to fulfill his clients' desire to die", *Detroit Free Press*, 3 March, 1997.

Appeals put it in a 1995 ruling upholding an order against Kevorkian's activity.[415] According to *The Economist*:

Studies of those who sought out Dr Kevorkian, however, suggest that though many had a worsening illness...it was not usually terminal. Autopsies showed five people had no disease at all...Little over a third were in pain. Some presumably suffered from no more than hypochondria or depression."[416]

In fact (as mentioned earlier) they did not seek out Kevorkian rather it was he who sought them out. In response, Kevorkian's attorney Geoffrey Fieger published an essay in which he stated:

I've never met any doctor who lived by such exacting guidelines as Kevorkian...he published them in an article for the American Journal of Forensic Psychiatry in 1992. Last year he got a committee of doctors, the Physicians of Mercy, to lay down new guidelines, which he scrupulously follows.[417]

However, Fieger stated that Kevorkian found it difficult to follow his "exacting guidelines" due to "persecution and prosecution."[418] The facts discovered in subsequent investigation indicate that if Kevorkian had any guidelines they were far from "exacting". In a 2010 interview with Sanjay Gupta, Kevorkian stated an objection to the status of assisted suicide in Oregon, Washington, and Montana. Only in those three states is assisted suicide legal in the United States, and then only for terminally ill patients. To Gupta,

---

[415] Ibid.

[416] "Jack Kevorkian, champion of voluntary euthanasia, died on June 3rd, aged 83", *The Economist*, 9 June, 2011.

[417] Kirk Cheyfitz, "Suicide Machine, Part 1: Kevorkian rushes to fulfill his clients' desire to die", Detroit Free Press, 3 March, 1997.

[418] Ibid.

Kevorkian stated, "What difference does it make if someone is terminal? We are all terminal."[419] In his view, a patient did not have to be terminally ill to be assisted in committing suicide, but did need to be suffering. However, he also said in that same interview that he declined 4 out of every 5 assisted suicide requests, on the grounds that the patient needed more treatment or medical records had to be checked.[420] The facts suggest otherwise.

Art Career

Kevorkian was a jazz musician and composer. *The Kevorkian Suite: A Very Still Life* was a 1997 limited release CD of 5,000 copies from the "Lucid Subjazz" label. It features Kevorkian on the flute and organ playing his own works with "The Morpheus Quintet." It was reviewed in *Entertainment Weekly* online as "weird" but "good natured."[421] Kevorkian wrote all the songs but one. Perhaps they reflected something of his personality.

He was also an oil painter. His work tended toward the grotesque and macabre. Again, reflecting something of his personality, perhaps? He sometimes painted with his own blood, and had created pictures such as, "Of a child eating the flesh off a decomposing corpse."[422] Although hailed as a hero by many it seems he was unbalanced and disturbed. Of his known works, six were made available in the 1990s for print release. The Ariana Gallery in Royal Oak, Michigan is

---

[419] Dr. Sanjay Gupta,"Kevorian: "I have no regrets"", *CNN*, 14 June, 2010.

[420] "'Dr. Death's' view on life", *CNN*. 14 June, 2010.

[421] Andrew Essex, "Death Mettle", *Entertainment Weekly*, December 26, 1997. As of 1997, 1,400 units had been sold. The album was reviewed in jazzreview.com.

[422] "People v. Kevorkian; Hobbins v. Attorney General", *Ascension Health*, 1994.

the exclusive distributor of Kevorkian's artwork. The original oil prints are not for release.[423] Sludge metal band Acid Bath used his painting "For He is Raised" as the cover for their 1996 album *Paegan Terrorism Tactics*.[424] In 2011, his paintings became the centre of a legal entanglement between his sole heir and a Massachusetts museum.[425]

Trials

Kevorkian was tried four times for assisting suicides between May 1994 and June 1997. With the assistance of Fieger, Kevorkian was acquitted three times. The fourth trial ended in a mistrial.[426] The trials helped Kevorkian gain public support for his cause. After Oakland County prosecutor Richard Thompson lost a primary election to a Republican challenger, Thompson attributed the loss in part to the declining public support for the prosecution of Kevorkian and its associated legal expenses.[427]

Conviction and Imprisonment

On the 22 November 1998 broadcast of CBS News' *60 Minutes*, Kevorkian allowed the airing of a videotape he

---

[423] "The Kevorkian Verdict: The Ariana Gallery" (Press release), *Frontline*, May 1996.

[424] "Acid Bath – Paegan Terrorism Tactics Remastered, Reissued", Brave Words, 10 August, 2010.

[425] "Kevorkian Estate to Auction Disputed Paintings", *WDIV-TV*, ClickonDetroit.com, 2 November, 2011.

[426] Keith Schneider, "Dr. Jack Kevorkian Dies at 83; A Doctor Who Helped End Lives", *The New York Times*, June 3, 2011.

[427] "Prosecutor has last shot at Dr. Death", *Sun Journal* (Lewiston Maine), 1 November, 1996. p. 3A. Also: Robert Davis "Assisted Suicide", *USA Today*, 8 August 8, 1996, p. 3A. Thompson, the first Oakland County prosecutor in 24 years to lose an election, agreed that the controversy clearly was an issue in his defeat.

made on 17 September 1998, which depicted the voluntary euthanasia of Thomas Youk, aged fifty-two, who was in the final stages of Amyotrophic lateral sclerosis.[428] After Youk provided his consent (on 17 September, 1998) Kevorkian himself administered a lethal injection to Thomas Youk. This was highly significant, as all of his earlier clients had reportedly completed the process themselves. During the videotape, Kevorkian dared the authorities to try to convict him or stop him from carrying out "mercy killings". In doing so he displayed an arrogance that was his Achilles heel. Youk's family described the lethal injection as humane, not murder.

On 26 March 1999, Kevorkian was charged with second-degree murder and the delivery of a controlled substance by administering the lethal injection to Thomas Youk.[429] Because Kevorkian's license to practice medicine had been revoked eight years previously, he was not legally allowed to possess the controlled substance. Kevorkian discharged his attorneys and proceeded through the trial representing himself, a decision he later regretted.[430] This was another indication of his arrogance. The judge ordered a criminal defence attorney to remain available at trial as standby counsel for information and advice. Inexperienced in law but persisting in his efforts to represent himself, Kevorkian encountered great difficulty in

---

[428] Amyotrophic Lateral Sclerosis (ALS) – also referred to as Motor Neurone Disease (MND) in most Commonwealth countries, and as Lou Gehrig's disease in the United States– is a debilitating disease with varied etiology characterised by rapidly progressive weakness, muscle atrophy and fasciculations, muscle spasticity, difficulty speaking (dysarthria), difficulty swallowing (dysphagia), and difficulty breathing (dyspnea). ALS is the most common of the five motor neuron diseases.

[429] "The Kevorian Verdict: A Chronology", *Frontline*, May 1996. PBS.

[430] Keith Schneider, "Dr. Jack Kevorkian Dies at 83; A Doctor Who Helped End Lives", *New York Times*, 3 June, 2011.

presenting his evidence and arguments. He was not able to call any witnesses to the stand as the judge did not deem the testimony of any of his witnesses relevant.[431] After a two day trial, the Michigan jury found Kevorkian guilty of second-degree homicide.[432] Judge Jessica Cooper sentenced Kevorkian to serve 10–25 years in prison.

Statement from judge to Kevorkian

The statement from the judge to Kevorkian is worth citing here:

> This is a court of law and you said you invited yourself here to take a final stand. But this trial was not an opportunity for a referendum. The law prohibiting euthanasia was specifically reviewed and clarified by the Michigan Supreme Court several years ago in a decision involving your very own cases, sir. So the charge here should come as no surprise to you. You invited yourself to the wrong forum. Well, we are a nation of laws, and we are a nation that tolerates differences of opinion because we have a civilized and a nonviolent way of resolving our conflicts that weighs the law and adheres to the law. We have the means and the methods to protest the laws with which we disagree. You can criticize the law, you can write or lecture about the law, you can speak to the media or petition the voters. But you must always stay within the limits provided by the law. You may not break the law. You may not take the law into your own hands.

---

[431] Marie Higgins Williams, Pro Se Criminal Defendant, Standby Counsel, and the Judge: A Proposal for Better-Defined Roles, The. 71 U. Colo. L. Rev., 2000, p. 789.

[432] Keith Schneider, "Dr. Jack Kevorkian Dies at 83; A Doctor Who Helped End Lives", New York Times, 3 June, 2011.

In point of fact, the issue of assisted suicide was addressed in this state by referendum just last November. And while the proponents of that were out campaigning, you were with Thomas Youk. And the voters of the State of Michigan said "no." And they said no two-and-a-half to one.

But we are not talking about assisted suicide here. When you purposely inject another human being with what you know to be a lethal dosage of poison, that, sir, is murder. And the jury so found.

Now, you've vilified the jury and the justice system in this case. But every member of that jury had compassion and empathy for Thomas Youk. They had a higher duty that went beyond personal sympathy and emotion. They took an oath to follow the law, not to nullify it.

And I am bound by a very similar oath, sir.

No one is unmindful of the controversy and emotion that exists over end-of-life issues and pain control. And I assume that the debate will continue in a calm and reasoned forum long after this trial and your activities have faded from public memory.

But this trial is not about that controversy. The trial was about you, sir. It was about you and the legal system. And you have ignored and challenged the Legislature and the Supreme Court. And moreover, you've defied your own profession, the medical profession.

You stood before this jury and you spoke of your duty as a physician. You repeatedly speak of treating patients to relieve their pain and suffering. You don't have a license to practice medicine. The state of

Michigan told you eight years ago you may not practice medicine. You may not treat patients. You may not possess -- let alone inject -- drugs into another human being...

There are several valid considerations in sentencing. One of them is rehabilitation. But based upon the fact that you publicly and repeatedly announced your intentions to disregard the laws of this state, I question whether you will ever cease and desist...

Now, another consideration and perhaps even a stronger factor in sentencing is deterrence. This trial was not about the political or moral correctness of euthanasia. It was all about you, sir. It was about lawlessness. It was about disrespect for a society that exists and flourishes because of the strength of the legal system.

No one, sir, is above the law - no one. So let's talk just a little bit more about you specifically. You were on bond to another judge when you committed this offense, you were not licensed to practice medicine when you committed this offense and you hadn't been licensed for eight years. And you had the audacity to go on national television, show the world what you did and dare the legal system to stop you. Well, sir, consider yourself stopped. [433]

Kevorkian was sent to a prison in Coldwater, Michigan to serve his sentence.[434] After his conviction (and subsequent

---

[433] Jessica Cooper, "Statement from Judge to Kevorkian". *New York Times*, 14 April, 1999.

[434] Jessica Cooper, "Statement from Judge to Kevorkian", *New York Times*, 14 April, 1999.

losses on appeal), Kevorkian was denied parole repeatedly until 2007.[435]

In an MSNBC interview aired on 29 September 2005 Kevorkian said that if he were granted parole, he would not resume directly helping people die and would restrict himself to campaigning to have the law changed. On 22 December 2005 Kevorkian was denied parole by a board on the count of 7–2 recommending that parole not be granted.[436]

Reportedly terminally ill with Hepatitis C, which he contracted while doing research on blood transfusions, Kevorkian was expected to die within a year in May 2006.[437] After applying for a pardon, parole, or commutation by the parole board and Governor Jennifer Granholm, he was paroled for good behaviour on 1 June 2007. He had spent eight years and two and a half months in prison.[438]

Kevorkian was on parole for two years, under the conditions that he would not help anyone else die, or provide care for anyone older than sixty-two or disabled.[439]

---

[435] Paul Egan, "After 8 years, Kevorkian to go free", *The Detroit News*, 14 December, 2006.

[436] Rita Cosby, "'Dr. Death' speaks out from jail", MSNBC, 29 September 29, 2005.

[437] Steven Ettelt, "Jack Kevorkian Attorney Says His Health is in Serious Jeopardy". Lifenews.com, 6 December, 2005.

[438] "Jack Kevorkian Plans Run For Congress", CBS News (cbsnews.com). AP. 12 March, 2008. Lara Setrakian "Dying 'Dr. Death' Has Second Thoughts About Assisting Suicides", ABC News. USA: ABC, 1 June, 2007.

[439] "Kevorkian released from prison after 8 years". MSNBC (MSNBC), 1 June, 2007.

He was also forbidden by the rules of his parole from commenting about assisted suicide.[440]

Activities after His Release from Prison

Kevorkian gave a number of lectures upon his release. He lectured at universities such as the University of Florida, Nova Southeastern University, and the University of California, Los Angeles.[441] His lectures were not limited to the topic of euthanasia. He also discussed such topics as tyranny, the criminal justice system, politics, the Ninth Amendment to the United States Constitution and Armenian culture.[442] He appeared on Fox News Channel's *Your World* with Neil Cavuto on 2 September 2009 to discuss health care reform.

On 15 and 16 April 2010, Kevorkian appeared on CNN's Anderson Cooper 360°.[443] Anderson asked, "You are saying doctors play God all the time?" Kevorkian said, "Of course. Anytime you interfere with a natural process, you are playing God."[444] Director Barry Levinson and actors Susan Sarandon and John Goodman, who appeared in *You Don't Know Jack*, a film based on Kevorkian's life, were interviewed alongside

---

[440] "Kevorkian criticizes attack on right-to-die group", mlive.com (Michigan Live), AP, 27 February, 2009. "Four arrested in 2 states in assisted-suicide probe", CNN (CNN), 26 February, 2009.

[441] Jack Stripling, "Kevorkian pushes for euthanasia", *Gainesville Sun*, 16 January, 2008. Andrew Ba Tran, "Jack Kevorkian unveils U.S. flag altered with swastika", *Sun-Sentinel*, 5 February 5, 2009. Suzy Strutner, "Right-to-die activist Dr Jack Kevorkian will share his ideology of death and story of life during Royce Hall lecture", *Daily Bruin*, 11 January, 2011.

[442] The Ninth Amendment (Amendment IX) to the United States Constitution, which is part of the Bill of Rights, addresses rights of the people that are not specifically enumerated in the Constitution.

[443] "Video: Mr Kevorkian on physician-assisted suicide", Anderson Cooper 360 (CNN), 15 April, 2010.

[444] Anderson Cooper, "Mr. Kevorkian Responds to Question about Playing God", 360 (CNN), 16 April, 2010.

Kevorkian. Kevorkian was again interviewed by Cavuto on *Your World* on 19 April 2010 about the film and Kevorkian's worldview. You *Don't Know Jack* premiered on 24 April, 2010 on HBO.[445] The film premiered on 14 April at the Ziegfeld Theater in New York City. Kevorkian walked the red carpet alongside Al Pacino, who portrayed him in the film.[446] Pacino received Emmy and Golden Globe awards for his portrayal, and personally thanked Kevorkian, who was in the audience, upon receiving both of these awards. Kevorkian stated that both the film and Pacino's performance "brings tears to my eyes – and I lived through it."[447]

2008 Congressional Race

On 12 March 2008, Kevorkian announced plans to run for United States Congress to represent Michigan's 9th congressional district against eight-term congressman Joe Knollenberg, Central Michigan University Professor Gary Peters, Adam Goodman and Douglas Campbell. Kevorkian ran as an independent and received 8,987 votes (2.6% of the vote).[448]

---

[445] *You Don't Know Jack*, HBO. 2010. Home Box Office (HBO) is an American premium cable and satellite television network that is owned by Home Box Office Inc., an operating subsidiary of Time Warner. HBO's programming consists primarily of theatrically released motion pictures and original television series, along with made-for-cable movies and documentaries, boxing matches and occasional stand-up comedy and concert specials.

[446] "Premiere of You Don't Know Jack at Ziegfeld Theatre" (Image gallery), Day Life.com (Getty Images), 14 April, 2010.

[447] Tara Krieger, "A New Life for Dr. Death", New York Law School, Legal As She Is Spoke, 2 November, 2010.
http://www.lasisblog.com/tag/jack-kevorkian/

[448] 2008 "Official Michigan General Candidate Listing", Michigan Department of State, 25 November, 2008.

Death

Kevorkian had struggled with kidney problems for years.[449] He was diagnosed with liver cancer, which "may have been caused by hepatitis C" according to his long-time friend Neal Nicol.[450] Kevorkian was hospitalised on 18 May, 2011, with kidney problems and pneumonia.[451] His condition grew rapidly worse and he died from a thrombosis on 3 June 2011, eight days after his 83rd birthday, at William Beaumont Hospital in Royal Oak, Michigan.[452] According to his attorney, Mayer Morganroth, there were no artificial attempts to keep him alive and his death was painless.[453] Kevorkian was buried in White Chapel Memorial Park Cemetery in Troy, Michigan.[454]

Legacy

Judge Thomas Jackson, who presided over Kevorkian's first murder trial in 1994, commented that he wanted to express sorrow at Kevorkian's death and that the 1994 case was brought under "a badly written law" aimed at Kevorkian, but he attempted to give him "the best trial possible." Maria Silveira, a professor of internal medicine, said she became involved with palliative care partly because of the attention Kevorkian brought to the complex issue of unintended suffering, adding that he had a tremendous

---

[449] "Dr. Jack Kevorkian dead at 83", CNN, 3 June, 2011.

[450] Joe Swickard and Pat Anstett, "Assisted suicide advocate Jack Kevorkian dies", *Detroit Free Press*, 3 June, 2011.

[451] Keith Schneider, "Dr. Jack Kevorkian Dies at 83; A Doctor Who Helped End Lives", *New York Times*, 3 June, 2011.

[452] Ibid.

[453] Joe Swickard and Pat Anstett, "Assisted suicide advocate Jack Kevorkian dies", *Detroit Free Press*, 3 June, 2011.

[454] "Politicians, officials and residents remember Kevorkian", *Detroit Free Press*, 3 June, 2011.

impact and fuelled the public awareness of unintended suffering and the need to address it. Geoffrey Fieger, Kevorkian's lawyer during the 1990s, gave a speech at a press conference in which he stated, "Dr Jack Kevorkian didn't seek out history, but he made history."[455] Many people have made history but that does not necessarily mean they made a positive contribution to history. Fieger said that Kevorkian revolutionised the concept of suicide by working to help people end their own suffering, because he believed physicians are responsible for alleviating the suffering of patients, even if that meant allowing patients to die.[456]

John Finn, medical director of palliative care at the Catholic St. John's Hospital, said Kevorkian's methods were unorthodox and inappropriate.[457] He added that many of Kevorkian's patients were isolated, lonely and potentially depressed and therefore in no state to mindfully choose whether to live or die.[458] The Catholic Church in Detroit said Kevorkian left behind a "deadly legacy" that denied scores of people their right to humane deaths.[459]

Derek Humphry, author of the suicide handbook, *Final Exit*, said Kevorkian was "too obsessed, too fanatical, in his interest in death and suicide to offer direction for the nation."[460] Howard Markel, a medical historian at the University of Michigan, said Kevorkian "was a major

---

[455] Brienne Prusak, "'U' Medical School alum Dr Kevorkian dies at 83", *The Michigan Daily*, June 2011.

[456] Ibid.

[457] "Mission and Values, St. John Health, as a Catholic health ministry", stjohnprovidence.org, 2011.

[458] Brienne Prusak, "'U' Medical School alum Dr Kevorkian dies at 83". *The Michigan Daily*, June 2011.

[459] Niraj Warikoo, "Archdiocese of Detroit: Kevorkian leaves 'deadly legacy'", *Detroit Free Press*, 3 June, 2011.

[460] Joe Swickard, Patricia Anstett and L.L. Brasier, "Jack Kevorkian sparked a debate on death", *Detroit Free Press*, 4 June, 2011.

historical figure in modern medicine."[461] Philip Nitschke, founder and director of *Exit International*, said that Kevorkian "...moved the debate forward in ways the rest of us can only imagine. He started at a time when it was hardly talked about and got people thinking about the issue. He paid one hell of a price, and that is one of the hallmarks of true heroism."[462]

The epitaph on Kevorkian's tombstone reads, "He sacrificed himself for everyone's rights."[463]

Heroism

This raises serious questions about the concept of heroism. What is heroic conduct? It has often been said that "beauty is in the eye of the beholder" and that seems to be true when it comes to understanding heroism. Traditionally heroism has been understood in terms of fulfilling a high purpose or attaining a noble end.

Illustration

On 2 January 2007, approximately seventy-five people waiting at a busy subway station in New York watched as a young man suffered a seizure and then fell from the platform onto the subway tracks. Onlookers watched in horror yet did nothing, but a man named Wesley Autry took action. He leapt down onto the tracks hoping to have time to drag the man out of the way of an oncoming train. When Autry realised that there was no time to move the other man, he instead held him down between the tracks as a train passed

---

[461] Brienne Prusak, "'U' Medical School alum Dr. Kevorkian dies at 83", *The Michigan Daily*, June 2011.

[462] Susan Donaldson James, "Jack Kevorkian, Godfather of Right-to Die-Movement, Dies Leaving Controversial Legacy – ABC News, 23 June, 2011.

[463] "Jack Kevorkian", *Find A Grave*, 4 December, 2011.

over the top of them. "I don't feel like I did something spectacular; I just saw someone who needed help. I did what I felt was right" he told *The New York Times* after the incident. That is heroic.

What makes certain people take heroic actions in the face of great danger? When one thinks about heroism, several recent examples might spring to mind. After the tragic theatre shooting in Aurora, Colorado during the summer of 2012, three women who survived the shooting revealed that their boyfriends had saved them. The three men had shielded their girlfriends with their own bodies and died as a result.

Heroism is something that is deeply valued across cultures, but how exactly do we define a hero? What is it that inspires some people to take heroic action?

Heroism involves behaviour or action on behalf of another person or for a moral cause. Four key elements of heroism may be identified. First, it is voluntary. Second, it is done in the service of people or communities in need. Third, it involves some type of risk, either physical, social, or in terms of quality of life. Fourth, it is done without the need for recompense or material gain.

Society rightly tends to think of heroes as exceptional people who achieve something great or advance a noble cause. The film industry portrays them as young, fit, intelligent, strong, resilient, selfless, caring, charismatic, reliable, and inspiring individuals. Such characters are involved in grand acts, which endanger their lives in order to save another person. However, this kind of portrayal overlooks the smaller, everyday acts performed to help another human being in need. Ordinary, everyday heroism is about helping others, doing good deeds and showing kindness where serious harm or major consequences are not usually a result.

It is possible that Kevorkian and others like him were well-motivated. His work involved significant risk to his career and liberty and people who do such things must be risk-takers who also possess a great deal of empathy. Kevorkian was probably a compassionate man who firmly believed he was an agent of mercy. However, he was no Florence Nightingale. What is generally perceived as his altruistic endeavours may have had a more self-serving purpose as a means to ensure recognition, significance and status. His engagement in "self-sacrificing" behaviour ultimately led to long-term rewards, especially fame and "heroic" status. Perhaps this was the driving force behind his career.

Contemporary Crisis

A crisis has arisen in society concerning euthanasia and assisted suicide. Most people will fall into a trap of inaction by assuming that someone else will offer assistance, a phenomenon known as the "bystander effect". Because personal responsibility is diffused by the presence of others, we believe that someone else will take on the role of the hero. Albert Einstein said "The world is a dangerous place, not because of those who do bad things, but because of those who look on and do nothing."

If asked to list their heroes many people today would likely include pop culture figures from the music industry, professional athletes and actors. But a generation ago such a list would have included heroes from history such as Abraham Lincoln, Winston Churchill, Christopher Columbus, Neil Armstrong and so on. Contemporary culture has replaced heroes with celebrities. Society worships (pop-idols) people who haven't actually achieved anything significant. It is time to get back to focusing on what matters, because we need real heroes more than ever.

Many people engage in lifelong heroism such as professional nurses who regularly comfort the sick and dying. Such people are often inspired by a strong moral code and see their work as a vocation. Many heroes of history have had a strong moral compass. They lived by their Christian values and they were willing to endure personal risk to protect those values.

Persistence is a quality commonly shared by heroes. They are more likely to put a positive spin on negative events. When faced with a potentially life-threatening illness, people with heroic tendencies might focus on the good that might come from the situation such as a renewed appreciation for life or an increased closeness with loved ones.

Kevorkian's misguided mercy short-circuited all of the human potential to endure and transcend and to come to terms with the natural process of death with its profound spiritual implications. He killed people who needed to be helped to live. I don't wish to belittle Al Pacino's immense contribution to the arts, which I genuinely appreciate, but all that is now known about Kevorkian was in the public domain at the time the film was made and Pacino was either unaware of it or unconcerned about it. The former is negligent the latter is reckless. Commentary from an actor on such a serious ethical issue should be understood for what it probably was, an ill-considered personal opinion. It is merely the of view one celebrity endorsing a very dubious "hero". Kevorkian may have been motivated by a misguided sense of mercy but he was a deranged, deceitful, delusional and dangerous individual who brought the noble medical profession into disrepute.

CHAPTER 15 Palliative Care or Slippery Slope

Palliative care (from Latin *palliare*, to cloak) is an area of healthcare that focuses on relieving and preventing the suffering of patients. Unlike hospice care, palliative medicine is appropriate for patients in all disease stages, including those undergoing treatment for curable illnesses and those living with chronic diseases, as well as patients who are nearing the end of life. Palliative medicine utilises a multidisciplinary approach to patient care, relying on input from physicians, pharmacists, nurses, chaplains, social workers, psychologists, and other allied health professionals in formulating a plan of care to relieve suffering in all areas of a patient's life. This multidisciplinary approach allows the palliative care team to address physical, emotional, spiritual, and social concerns that arise with advanced illness.

Medications and treatments are said to have a palliative effect if they relieve symptoms without having a curative effect on the underlying disease or cause. This can include treating nausea related to chemotherapy or something as simple as morphine to treat the pain of a broken leg or ibuprofen to treat aching related to an influenza infection.

Although the concept of palliative care is not new, most physicians have traditionally concentrated on trying to cure patients. Treatments for the alleviation of symptoms were viewed as hazardous and seen as inviting addiction and other unwanted side effects.[464] Some doctors viewed morphine or other strong opiates as potentially hazardous because of the risk of addiction and because of potentially serious side effects if the dose is not carefully adjusted.

The focus on a patient's quality of life has increased greatly during the past twenty years. In the United States today, 55% of hospitals with more than 100 beds offer a palliative-care programme, and nearly one-fifth of community hospitals have palliative-care programmes.[465] A relatively recent development is the palliative-care team, a dedicated health care team that is entirely geared toward palliative treatment.

Scope of the Term

Palliative care is specialised medical care for people with serious illnesses. It is focused on providing patients with relief from the symptoms, pain, and the stress of a serious illness — whatever the prognosis. The goal is to improve quality of life for both the patient and the family as they are the central system for care.

A team of doctors, nurses, and other specialists who work together with a patient's other doctors to provide an extra layer of support provides palliative care. It is appropriate at any age and at any stage in a serious illness and can be provided along with curative treatment.

---

[464] J. E. D. Seymour and M. Winslow Clark, "Morphine use in cancer pain: from 'last resort' to 'gold standard', Poster presentation at the Third research Forum of the European Association of Palliative Care", *Palliative Medicine* 18 (4), 2004, p. 378.

[465] Joanne Lynn, *Sick To Death And Not going To Take It Anymore!: Reforming Health Care for the Last Years of Life"*, Berkeley: University of California Press, 2004, p. 72.

A World Health Organisation statement describes palliative care as:

...an approach that improves the quality of life of patients and their families facing the problems associated with life-threatening illness, through the prevention and relief of suffering by means of early identification and impeccable assessment and treatment of pain and other problems, physical, psychosocial and spiritual.[466]

More generally, however, the term "palliative care" may refer to any care that alleviates symptoms, whether or not there is hope of a cure by other means. Thus, palliative treatments may be used to alleviate the side effects of curative treatments, such as (as mentioned above) relieving the nausea associated with chemotherapy.

The term "palliative care" is increasingly used with regard to diseases other than cancer such as chronic, progressive pulmonary disorders, renal disease, chronic heart failure, HIV/AIDS, and progressive neurological conditions. In addition, the rapidly growing field of paediatric palliative care has clearly shown the need for services geared specifically for children with serious illness.

Palliative care provides relief from distressing symptoms, affirms life, and regards dying as a normal process. It intends neither to hasten nor to postpone death. It integrates the psychological and spiritual aspects of patient care, with chaplains playing a role. It offers a support system to help patients live as actively as possible and to help the family cope. It uses a team approach to address the needs of patients and their families. It will enhance quality of life. It is applicable early in the course of illness, in conjunction with

---

[466] "WHO Definition of Palliative Care", World Health Organisation.

other therapies that are intended to prolong life, such as chemotherapy or radiation therapy.

The goals of palliative treatment are concrete. It offers a support system to help the individual live as actively as possible and to sustain the individual's family.[467]

Comparison with Hospice Care

A distinction may be made between palliative care and hospice care. Hospice services and palliative care programmes share similar goals of providing symptom relief and pain management.[468] Palliative care services can be offered to any patient without restriction to disease or prognosis, and can be appropriate for anyone with a serious, complex illness, whether they are expected to recover fully, to live with chronic illness for an extended time, or to experience disease progression. In the USA hospice care under the Medicare Hospice Benefit, however, requires that two physicians certify that a patient has less than six months to live if the disease follows its usual course. This does not necessarily mean that if a patient is still living after six months in hospice he or she will be discharged from the service.

The philosophy and multi-disciplinary team approach are similar with hospice and palliative care. The biggest difference between hospice and palliative care is the patient: where they are in their illness especially related to prognosis and their goals/wishes regarding curative treatment.

---

[467] D. Walsh, W, Gombeski, P. Goldstein, D. Hayes, M. Armour, "Managing a palliative oncology program: the role of a business plan", Journal of Pain and Symptom Management 9 (2), February, 1994, pp. 109–18.
[468] R. R. Hill, "Clinical pharmacy services in a home-based palliative care program", American Journal of Health-System Pharmacy 64 (8), 15 April, 2007, pp. 806, 808, 810.

Outside the United States there is generally no such division of terminology or funding, and all such care with a primarily palliative focus, whether or not for patients with terminal illness, is usually referred to as palliative care.

Outside the United States the term hospice usually refers to a building or institution which specialises in palliative care, rather than to a particular stage of care progression. Such institutions may predominantly specialise in providing care in an end-of-life setting; but they may also be available for patients with other specific palliative care needs.

History

Palliative care began in the hospice movement and is now widely used outside of traditional hospice care. Hospices were originally places of rest for travellers in the fourth-century. In the nineteenth-century, a religious order established hospices for the dying in Ireland and England (London). The modern hospice is a relatively recent concept that originated and gained momentum in the United Kingdom after the founding of St. Christopher's Hospice in 1967. Dame Cicely Saunders, widely regarded as the founder of the modern hospice movement, founded it.

The hospice movement has grown dramatically in recent years. In the UK in 2005 there were just under 1700 hospice services consisting of 220 inpatient units for adults with 3156 beds, 33 inpatient units for children with 255 beds, 358 home care services, 104 hospice at home services, 263 day-care services, and 293 hospital teams. These services together helped over 250,000 patients in 2003 and 2004. Funding varies from 100% funding by the National Health Service to almost 100% funding by charities, but the service is always free to patients.

Hospice in the United States has grown from a volunteer-led movement to improve care for people dying alone, isolated, or in hospitals, to a significant part of the health care system. In 2005, more than 1.2 million individuals and their families received hospice care. Hospice is the only Medicare benefit that includes pharmaceuticals, medical equipment, twenty-four hour/seven day a week access to care and support for loved ones following a death. Most hospice care is delivered at home. Hospice care is also available to people in home-like hospice residences, nursing homes, assisted living facilities, veterans' facilities, hospitals, and prisons.

The first United States hospital-based palliative care programmes began in the late 1980s at a handful of institutions such as the Cleveland Clinic and Medical College of Wisconsin. Since then there has been a dramatic increase in hospital-based palliative care programmes, now numbering more than 1400. 80% of US hospitals with more than 300 beds have a programme.[469]

A 2009 study regarding the availability of palliative care in 120 USA cancer centre hospitals reported the following: Only 23% of the centres had beds that were dedicated to palliative care; 37% offered inpatient hospice; 75% have a median time of referral to palliative care to the time of death of 30 to 120 days.[470]

The results of a 2010 study in *The New England Journal of Medicine* showed that lung cancer patients receiving early palliative care experienced less depression, increased quality

---

[469] Center to Advance Palliative Care, www.capc.org.

[470] D. Hui, A. Elsayem, M. De la Cruz, et al., "Availability and integration of palliative care at US cancer centers". *The Journal of the American Medical Association* 303 (11), March 2010, pp. 1054–1061.

of life and survived 2.7 months longer than those receiving standard oncologic care.[471]

The first pan-European centre devoted to improving patient palliative care and end-of-life care was established in Trondheim, Norway in 2009. The centre is based at NTNU's Faculty of Medicine and at St. Olavs Hospital/Trondheim University Hospital and coordinates efforts between groups and individual researchers across Europe, specifically Scotland, England, Italy, Denmark, Germany and Switzerland, along with the USA, Canada and Australia.

Indications

Patients at all stages of treatment need some kind of palliative care to comfort them. In some cases, medical specialty professional organisations recommend that patients and physicians respond to an illness only with palliative care and not with a therapy directed at the disease. The following items are indications named by the American Society of Clinical Oncology as characteristics of a patient who should receive palliative care but not any cancer-directed therapy.[472]

The patient has low performance status, corresponding with limited ability to care for oneself. The patient received no benefit from prior evidence-based treatments. The patient is ineligible to participate in any appropriate clinical trial. The physician sees no strong evidence that treatment would be effective. These characteristics may be generally applicable to other disease conditions besides cancer.

---

[471] J.S Temel et al., "Early Palliative Care for Patients with Metastatic Non–Small-Cell Lung Cancer," *New England Journal of Medicine* 2010; 363:733-742, 19 August, 2010.

[472] The American Society of Clinical Oncology made this recommendation based on various cancers. "Five Things Physicians and Patients Should Question", Choosing Wisely: an initiative of the ABIM Foundation.

Assessment of Symptoms

A method for the assessment of symptoms in patients admitted to palliative care is the Edmonton Symptoms Assessment Scale (ESAS), in which there are eight visual analogue scales (VAS) of 0 to 10, indicating the levels of pain, activity, nausea, depression, anxiety, drowsiness, appetite, and sensation of well-being, sometimes with the addition of shortness of breath.[473] On the scales, 0 means that the symptom is absent and 10 that it is of worst possible severity.[474] It is completed either by the patient alone, by the patient with nurse's assistance, or by the nurses or relatives.

Symptom Management

Medications used for palliative patients are used differently than standard medications, based on established practices with varying degrees of evidence.[475] Examples include the use of antipsychotic medications to treat nausea, anticonvulsants to treat pain, and morphine to treat dyspnea (shortness of breath).

Routes of administration may differ from acute or chronic care, as many patients lose the ability to swallow. A common alternative route of administration is subcutaneous

---

[473] E. Bruera, N. Kuehn, M. J Miller, P. Selmser, K. MacMillan, "The Edmonton Symptom Assessment System (ESAS): A simple method for the assessment of palliative care patients", *Journal of Palliative Care* 7 (2), 1991, pp. 6–9. Also: Edmonton Symptom Assessment System (ESAS) from Cancer Care Ontario (Revised February 2005).

[474] E. Bruera, N. Kuehn, M. J Miller, P. Selmser, K. MacMillan, "The Edmonton Symptom Assessment System (ESAS): A simple method for the assessment of palliative care patients", *Journal of Palliative Care* 7 (2), 1991, pp. 6–9.

[475] D. Currow, M. R. Agar, A.P. Abernethy, "Tackling the Challenges of Clinical Trials in Palliative Care". *Pharmaceutical Medicine* 25 (1), 2011, pp. 7–15.

(beneath the skin), as it is less traumatic and less difficult to maintain than intravenous medications. Other routes of administration include sublingual, intramuscular and transdermal.[476] Family or nursing support often manages medications at home.[477]

Dealing with Distress

The key to effective palliative care is to provide a safe way for the individual to address their physical and psychological distress, that is to say their total suffering, a concept first thought up by Cicely Saunders, and now widely used, for instance by authors like Twycross or Woodruff.[478] Dealing with total suffering involves a broad range of concerns, starting with treating physical symptoms such as pain, nausea and breathlessness. The palliative care teams have become very skilful in prescribing drugs for physical symptoms, and have been instrumental in showing how drugs such as morphine can be used safely while maintaining a patient's full faculties and function. However, when a patient exhibits a physiological symptom, there are often psychological, social, or spiritual symptoms as well. The interdisciplinary team, which often includes a registered nurse, a licensed mental health professional, a licensed social worker or a counsellor and spiritual support such as a chaplain, can play a role in helping the patient and family cope with these symptoms, rather than depending on the medical/pharmacological interventions alone.

---

[476] Entering the bloodstream by absorption through the skin.

[477] Caresearch: Palliative Care Knowledge Network, "Palliative Medications"

[478] P. Strang, S. Strang, R. Hultborn, S. Arnér, "Existential pain—an entity, a provocation, or a challenge?" *Journal of Pain Symptom Management* 27 (3), March 2004, 241–50.

Usually, a palliative care patient's concerns are pain, fears about the future, loss of independence, worries about their family, and feeling like a burden. While some patients will want to discuss psychological or spiritual concerns and some will not, it is fundamentally important to assess each individual and their partners' and families' need for this type of support. Denying an individual and their support system an opportunity to explore psychological or spiritual concerns is just as harmful as forcing them to deal with issues they either don't have or choose not to deal with.

There are five principal methods for addressing patient anxiety in palliative care settings. They are counselling, visualisation, cognitive methods, drug therapy and relaxation therapy. Palliative pets can play a role in this last category. For animal lovers approaching the end of life, contact with the familiar positive interactions with pets helps to normalise the hospice environment and reduce anxiety. Even for patients whose cognitive abilities have been hampered by illnesses such as Alzheimer's disease, clinical research has shown that the presence of a therapy dog enhanced nonverbal communication as shown by increases in looks, smiles, tactile contact and physical warmth.[479]

Provision of Services

Because palliative care sees an increasingly wide range of conditions in patients at varying stages of their illness it follows that palliative care teams offer a range of care. This may range from managing the physical symptoms in patients receiving treatment for cancer, to treating depression in patients with advanced disease, to the care of patients in their

---

[479] Kathryn Batson et al., "The Effect of a Therapy Dog on Socialization and Physiological Indicators of Stress in Persons Diagnosed with Alzheimer's Disease", in Companion Animals in Human Health', Editors - Cindy C. Wilson and Dennis C. Turner, Sage Publications 1998.

last days and hours. Much of the work involves helping patients with complex or severe physical, psychological, social, and spiritual problems. In the UK over half of patients are improved sufficiently to return home. Most hospice organisations offer grief counselling to the patient's partner or family should he die.

In the United States, hospice and palliative care represent two different aspects of care with similar philosophy, but with different payment systems and location of services. Palliative care services are most often provided in acute care hospitals organised around an interdisciplinary consultation service with or without an acute inpatient palliative care ward. Palliative care may also be provided in the dying person's home as a "bridge" programme between traditional USA home care services and hospice care or provided in long-term care facilities.[480] In contrast, over 80% of hospice care in the USA is provided in a patient's home with the remainder provided to patients residing in long-term care facilities or in free standing hospice residential facilities. In the UK hospice is seen as one part of the specialty of palliative care and no differentiation is made between "hospice" and "palliative care".

In the UK palliative care services offer inpatient care, home care, day care, and outpatient services, and work in close partnership with mainstream services. Hospices often house a full range of services and professionals for both paediatric and adult patients.

---

[480] "In-Home Palliative Care Allows More Patients to Die at Home, Leading to Higher Satisfaction and Lower Acute Care Utilization and Costs", Agency for Healthcare Research and Quality, 3 April, 2013.

People Involved

In most countries hospice and palliative care is provided by an interdisciplinary team consisting of physicians, pharmacists, nurses, social workers, hospice chaplains, physiotherapists, occupational therapists, complementary therapists, volunteers, and, most important, the family. The team's focus is to optimise the patient's comfort. Additional members of the team are likely to include nursing assistants or home health care aides, volunteers from the community (largely untrained but some being skilled medical personnel), and housekeepers.

Palliative care provides for the holistic needs of patients with life-limiting, advanced disease and catastrophic injury; the relief of distressing symptoms; the coordination of interdisciplinary patient and family-centred care in diverse settings; the use of specialised care systems including hospice; the management of the imminently dying patient; and legal and ethical decision-making in end-of-life care.[481]

Caregivers, both family and volunteers, are crucial to the palliative care system. Caregivers and patients often form lasting friendships over the course of care. As a consequence caregivers may find themselves under severe emotional and physical strain. Opportunities for caregiver respite are some of the services hospices provide to promote caregiver well-being. Respite may last a few hours up to several days (the

[481] American Board of Medical Specialties, ABMS Establishes New Subspecialty Certificate in Hospice and Palliative Medicine [1], October 6, 2006. Also: American Board of Medical Specialties, ABMS Guide to Physician Specialties [2], 2011, p. 2.

latter being done usually by placing the patient in a nursing home or in-patient hospice unit for several days).[482]

In the USA, many fellowship programmes provide 1–2 years of specialty training in palliative care. In the UK palliative care has been a full specialty of medicine since 1989 and training is regulated by the Royal College of Physicians - as with any other medical specialty.[483]

Funding

Funding for hospice and palliative care services varies. Although in the UK and Ireland hospice care is offered free to the patient, it is only partly state funded, the larger part is funded through charitable donations. In many other countries all palliative care is offered free to the patient and their family, either through the National Health Service (as in the UK) or through charities working in partnership with the local health services.

Palliative care services in the USA are paid by philanthropy, fee-for service mechanisms, or from direct hospital support while hospice care is provided as Medicare benefit; similar hospice benefits are offered by Medicaid and most private health insurers. The hospice agency, together with the patient's primary physician, is responsible for determining the Plan of Care. All costs related to the terminal illness are paid from a *per diem* rate that the hospice agency receives from Medicare - this includes all drugs and equipment, nursing, social service, chaplain visits, and other

---

[482] Dr T. T. Jayakrishnan and J.M, Cherumanalil, "Assessment of status of patients receiving palliative home care and services provided in a rural area-Kerala, India", *Indian Journal of Palliative Care.* 18, 2012, pp. 213–218.
[483] American Academy of Hospice and Palliative Medicine.

services deemed appropriate by the hospice agency; Medicare does not pay for custodial care.

Acceptance

Physicians practicing palliative care do not always receive support from patients, family members, healthcare professionals, or their social peers for their work to reduce suffering and follow patients' wishes for end-of-life care. More than half of physicians in one survey reported that a patient's family members, another physician, or another health care professional had characterised their work as being "euthanasia, murder, or killing" during the last five years. A quarter of them had received similar comments from their own friends or family member, or from a patient.[484]

Palliative Sedation

In medicine, specifically in end-of-life care, palliative sedation (also known as terminal sedation, continuous deep sedation, or sedation for intractable distress in the dying/of a dying patient) is the palliative practice of relieving distress in a terminally ill person in the last hours or days of a dying patient's life, usually by means of a continuous intravenous or subcutaneous infusion of a sedative drug. This is an option of last resort for patients whose symptoms cannot be controlled by any other means. This should be differentiated from euthanasia, as the goal of palliative sedation is to control symptoms through sedation but not shorten the patient's life, while in euthanasia the goal is to shorten (terminate) life.

---

[484] N. E. Goldstein; L. M. Cohen; R. M. Arnold; E. Goy; S. Arons; L. Ganzini, "Prevalence of Formal Accusations of Murder and Euthanasia against Physicians", *Journal of Palliative Medicine* 15 (3), March 2012, pp. 334–339.

According to 2009 research, 16.5% of all deaths in the United Kingdom during 2007-2008 took place after continuous deep sedation.[485] On the other hand, a 2009 survey of almost 4000 UK patients whose care had followed the Liverpool Care Pathway for the dying patient found that while 31% had received low doses of medication to control distress from agitation or restlessness, only 4% had required higher doses.[486]

The Liverpool Care Pathway

The Liverpool Care Pathway (LCP) was abolished in 2013 following a government-commissioned review which heard that hospital staff wrongly interpreted its guidance for care of the dying, leading to stories of patients who were drugged and deprived of fluids in their last weeks of life.

The government-commissioned review, headed by Lady Neuberger, found it was not the pathway itself but poor training and sometimes a lack of compassion on the part of nursing staff that was to blame, while junior doctors were expected to make life-and-death decisions beyond their competence after hours and at weekends. The review says individualised end-of-life care plans must be drawn up for every patient nearing that stage. Neuberger said, "Caring for the dying must never again be practised as a tickbox exercise and each patient must be cared for according to their

---

[485] C. Seale, "End-of-life decisions in the UK involving medical practitioners", *Palliative Medicine*, 23(3), 2009, pp. 198-204. C. Seale "Continuous Deep Sedation in Medical Practice: A Descriptive Study", *Journal of Pain and Symptom Management*, 39(1), 2010, pp. 44-53. Adam Brimelow, "The alternative to euthanasia?", BBC News, 12 August 2009. Daniel Martin, "Doctors admit to practising 'slow euthanasia' on terminally-ill patients, *Daily Mail*, 29 October 2009.

[486] National Care of the Dying Audit 2009, Royal College of Physicians, 14 September 2009.

individual needs and preferences, with those of their relatives or carers being considered too."[487]

She said it was too late to turn the clock back and salvage the LCP, which was devised to try to extend the positive experiences of dying hospice patients into the hospital setting. But in replacing it, the NHS must make care of the dying part of its core business: "What we have also exposed in this review is a range of far wider, fundamental problems with care for the dying – a lack of care and compassion, unavailability of suitably trained staff, no access to proper palliative care advice outside of 9-5, Monday to Friday."[488] The care minister, Norman Lamb said:

> I have personally heard families describe staff slavishly following a process without care or compassion and leaving people suffering at the end of their lives. This is something we cannot allow to go on. "People's final days should be as comfortable and dignified as possible. That is why there is a place for thoughtful and careful end-of-life care that involves patients and their families, but it is clear what we have now needs to be replaced so we can create a better way of doing this.[489]

The review listened to harrowing stories from families who had not been told their loved one was expected to die and, in some cases, were shouted at by nurses for attempting to give them a drink of water. Nursing staff had wrongly thought, under the LCP guidance, that giving fluids was wrong. Some patients were put on the pathway and treatment was withdrawn, only for them to make a recovery, albeit temporarily. Communication was very poor and

---

[487] Sarah Boseley, health editor. *The Guardian*, 15 July 2013.
[488] Sarah Boseley, health editor. *The Guardian*, 15 July 2013.
[489] Sarah Boseley, health editor. *The Guardian*, 15 July 2013.

medical staff sometimes dodged painful discussions with patients and families, the review found.[490]

General Practice

Palliative sedation is often initiated at the patient's request. The physician who would discuss the option with the patient and family can also initiate it. Palliative sedation can be used for short periods with the plan to awaken the patient after a given time period, making terminal sedation a less correct term. The patient is sedated while symptom control is attempted, then the patient is awakened to see if symptom control is achieved. In some cases, palliative sedation is begun with the plan to not attempt to reawaken the patient. One such common example is a patient with an enlarging cancer in the throat that compresses the trachea in a patient who does not want intubation or a tracheostomy, so that eventually symptom control is impossible. Instead of experiencing death by suffocation, once symptoms are intolerable some patients will request palliative sedation to ease their symptoms as death approaches.

Drugs Used

A typical drug is midazolam, a short acting benzodiazepine. Opioids such as morphine are not used as the primary medicine since they are not effective sedative medications compared to benzodiazepines. However, if a patient was already on an opioid for pain relief, this is continued for pain relief while sedation is achieved. Other

---

[490] Sarah Boseley, health editor, *The Guardian*, 15 July 2013.

medications to be considered include haloperidol, chlorpromazine, pentobarbital, propofol or phenobarbital.[491]

Nutrition and Fluids

As patients undergoing terminal sedation are typically in the last hours or days of their lives, they are not usually eating or drinking significant amounts. There have not been any conclusive studies to demonstrate benefit to initiating artificial nutrition (TPN, tube feedings, etc.) or artificial hydration (subcutaneous or intravenous fluids). There is also the risk that IV fluids or feedings can worsen symptoms, especially respiratory secretions and pulmonary congestion. If the goal of palliative sedation is comfort, IV fluids and feedings are often not consistent with this goal.[492] Before initiating terminal sedation, a discussion about the risks, benefits and goals of nutrition and fluids is encouraged, and is mandatory in the United Kingdom.

Sedation vs. Euthanasia

There is no evidence that titrated (i.e. varied) sedation causes the death of the patient and sedation does not equate with euthanasia.[493] At the end of life sedation is only used if the patient perceives their distress to be unbearable, and

---

[491] To avoid confusion a distinction should be made between midazolam, commonly used in palliative care to relieve anxiety, (another is levomepromazine) or older drugs such as haloperidol or chlorpromazine, and those that might be used in euthanasia such as the anaesthetic drugs propofol or phenobarbital. Pentobarbital is not available in the UK.

[492] Maltoni, M. et al., "Palliative sedation therapy does not hasten death: results from a prospective multicenter study", *Annals of Oncology* 20(7), 2009, pp. 1163–1169.

[493] Maltoni, M. et al., "Palliative sedation therapy does not hasten death: results from a prospective multicenter study", *Annals of Oncology* 20(7), 2009, pp. 1163–1169.

there are no other means of relieving that distress. In palliative care the doses of sedatives are titrated to keep the patient comfortable without compromising respiration or hastening death. Death results from the underlying medical condition.

Once unconsciousness begins, as the patient is no longer able to decide to stop the sedation or to request food or water, the clinical team can act in the patient's best interests. A Living Will, made when competent, can under UK law, give a directive that they refuse palliative care or terminal sedation or any drug likely to suppress respiration. In 2008, the American Medical Association Council on Ethical and Judicial Affairs approved an ethical policy regarding the practice of palliative sedation.[494]

Slippery Slope

The introduction of euthanasia and assisted suicide as alternatives to palliative and hospice care will lead to a slippery slope. It is naïve to believe the law can provide safeguards against such slippery-slope effects. If the Netherlands teaches us anything it teaches us that. Legalising any form of euthanasia leads to a slippery slope effect, resulting eventually in non-voluntary or even involuntary euthanasia. The slippery slope argument has been present in the euthanasia debate since at least the 1930s.[495]

---

[494] Kevin B. O'Reilly, AMA meeting: AMA OKs palliative sedation for terminally ill, *American Medical News*, 7 July 2008. *Report of the Council on Ethical and Judicial Affairs: Sedation to Unconsciousness in End-of-Life Care* American Medical Association, 2008.

[495] D. M. Pappas, "Recent historical perspectives regarding medical euthanasia and physician assisted suicide". *British Medical Bulletin* 52 (2), April 1996, pp. 386–393.

Lawyer Eugene Volokh argued in his article "The Mechanism of the Slippery Slope", that judicial logic could eventually lead to a gradual break in the legal restrictions for euthanasia.[496]

Acceptance of certain practices, such as physician-assisted suicide or voluntary euthanasia, will invariably lead to the acceptance or practice of concepts, which are currently, deemed unacceptable, such as non-voluntary or involuntary euthanasia. In order to prevent these undesirable practices from occurring it is important to resist taking the first step.[497]

There are two basic forms, which the argument may take, each of which involves different arguments for and against.[498] The first of these, referred to as the logical version, argues that the acceptance of the initial act, A, logically entails the acceptance of B, where A is acceptable but B is an undesirable action. This version is further refined into two forms based on how A entails B. In the first, it is argued that there "is no relevant conceptual difference between A and B" – the premises that underlie the acceptance of A logically entail the acceptance of B.

Within the euthanasia debate, van der Burg identifies one of Richard Sherlock's objections to Duff and Campbell as fitting this model. Duff and Campbell had presented an argument for the selective non-treatment of new-borns suffering from serious defects. In responding to Duff and Campbell's stance, Sherlock argued that the premises, which

---

[496] Eugene Volokh, "The Mechanisms of the Slippery Slope", *Harvard Law Review* 116 (4), February 2003, pp. 1026–1137.

[497] Penney Lewis, "The empirical slippery slope from voluntary to non-voluntary euthanasia", *The Journal of Law Medicine and Ethics* 35 (1), 2007, pp. 197–210.

[498] Wibren van der Burg, "The slippery slope argument", Ethics 102 (1), October 1991, pp. 42–65.

they employed in order to justify their position would be just as effective, if not more-so, in justifying the non-treatment of older children: In short, if there is any justification at all for what Duff and Campbell propose for new-borns then there is better justification for a similar policy with respect to children at any age.[499]

The second logical form of the slippery slope argument is referred to as the "arbitrary line" version.[500] This argues that the acceptance of A will lead to the acceptance of A1, as A1 is not significantly different to A. A1 will then lead to A2, A2 to A3, and eventually the process will lead to the unacceptable B.[501] As Glover argues, this version of the argument does not say that there is no significant difference between A and B, but instead argues that it is impossible to justify accepting A while also denying B – drawing a line at any point between the two would be creating an arbitrary cut-off point that would be unjustifiable.[502] Glover provides the example of infanticide (or non-voluntary euthanasia) and severely deformed children:

> If it is allowable at birth for children with some grave abnormality, what will we say about an equally grave abnormality that is only detectable at three months? And another that is only detectable at six months? And another that is detectable at birth

---

[499] Richard Sherlock, "Selective non-treatment of newborns". *Journal of Medical Ethics* 5 (3), 1979, p. 140.

[500] "Voluntary Euthanasia", *Stanford Encyclopedia of Philosophy*.

[501] Wibren van der Burg 1991, p. 44.

[502] Jonathan Glover, *Causing Death and Saving Lives: The Moral Problems of Abortion, Infanticide, Suicide, Euthanasia, Capital Punishment, War, and Other Life-or-Death Choices*, Penguin Books, 1991 (first published 1977) p. 166.

only slightly less serious? And another that is slightly less serious than that one? [503]

The second primary form of the slippery slope argument is that of the "Empirical" or "Psychological" argument.[504] The empirical version does not rely on a logical connection between A and B, but instead argues that an acceptance of A will, in time, lead to an acceptance of B.[505] The process is not a logical necessity, but one which will be followed through a process of moral change.[506] Enoch describes the application of this form of the argument thus:

> Once we allow voluntary euthanasia...we may (or will) fail to make the crucial distinction, and then we will make the morally unacceptable outcome of allowing involuntary euthanasia; or perhaps even though we may make the relevant distinction, we will not act accordingly for some reason (perhaps a political reason, or a reason that has to do with weakness of will, or some other reason).[507]

More generally, it has been argued that in employing the slippery slope there can be an "implicit concession" as it starts from the assumption that the initial practice is acceptable – even though it will lead to unacceptable outcomes in the future.[508]

---

[503] Glover, 1977, p. 165.

[504] Lewis 2007, p. 197 van der Burg 1991, p. 43
"Voluntary Euthanasia", Stanford Encyclopedia of Philosophy.

[505] Lewis 2007, p. 197

[506] van der Burg 1991, p. 51

[507] Enoch, David "Once You Start Using Slippery Slope Arguments, You're on a Very Slippery Slope". *Oxford Journal of Legal Studies* 21 (4), 2001, p. 631.

[508] Frederick Schauer, "Slippery slopes". *Harvard Law Review* 99 (2), 1985, pp. 368–369.

Initially it may be possible to support voluntary euthanasia while denying non-voluntary euthanasia but ultimately such a position weakens opposition to involuntary and non-voluntary euthanasia.

Action T4

Leo Alexander, in examining the events of the Holocaust during the Nuremberg Trials, stated that the origins of the Nazi programmes could be traced back to "small beginnings" and presented a slippery slope argument.[509] Others have argued that Action T4 is not an example of the empirical slippery slope as there is "no record of the Nazi doctors either killing or assisting in the suicide of a patient who was suffering intolerably from a fatal illness."[510]

Euthanasia historian Ian Dowbiggin linked the Nazis' Action T4 to the resistance in the West to involuntary euthanasia. He believes that the revulsion inspired by the Nazis led to some of the early advocates of euthanasia in all its forms in the USA and UK removing non-voluntary euthanasia from their proposed platforms.[511]

Permitting voluntary euthanasia to occur could lead to the support and legalisation of non-voluntary and involuntary euthanasia. Some studies of the Netherlands after

---

[509] Walter Wright, "Historical Analogies, Slippery Sloped, and the Question of Euthanasia", *Journal of Law, Medicine and Ethics*. 28:2, 2000, pp. 176–186.
[510] "Voluntary Euthanasia", *Stanford Encyclopedia of Philosophy*. See also D. M. Pappas, "Recent historical perspectives regarding medical euthanasia and physician assisted suicide", British Medical Bulletin. 52 (2), April 1996, p. 390.
[511] Ian Robert Dowbiggin, *A Merciful End: The Euthanasia Movement in Modern America*, New York: Oxford University Press, 2002.

the introduction of voluntary euthanasia suggest that there is sufficient evidence to support this claim.[512]

A study from the Jakobovits Center for Medical Ethics in Israel argued that a form of non-voluntary euthanasia such as the Groningen Protocol has "potential to validate the slippery-slope argument against allowing euthanasia in selected populations".[513] Anaesthesiologist William Lanier says that the "on-going evolution of euthanasia law in the Netherlands" is evidence that a slippery slope is "playing out in real time."[514]

A study by Jochemsen and Keown, from the Dutch Lindeboom Institute published in the peer reviewed *Journal of Medical Ethics*, argued that euthanasia in the Netherlands is not well controlled and that there are still a significant percentage of cases of euthanasia practiced illegally.[515] Raanan Gillon, from the Imperial College School of Medicine, University of London commented that: "...what is shown by the empirical findings is that restrictions on euthanasia that legal controls in the Netherlands were supposed to have implemented are being extensively ignored and from that point of view it is surely justifiable to conclude, as Jochemsen

---

[512] H. Jochemsen and J. Keown, "Voluntary euthanasia under control? Further empirical evidence from The Netherlands", *Journal of Medical Ethics* 25 (1), February 1999, 16–21.

[513] Alan Jotkowitz; S. Glick; B. Gesundheit, "A Case Against Justified Non-Voluntary Active Euthanasia (The Groningen Protocol)", *The American Journal of Bioethics* 8 (11), 2008, p. 25.

[514] William Lanier and K. H. Berge, "Physician Involvement in Capital Punishment: Simplifying a Complex Calculus", *Mayo Clinic Proceedings* 82 (9), September 2007, pp. 1043–1046.

[515] "Lindeboom Instituut Studiecentrum voor medische ethiek vanuit de christelijke levensbeschouwing", www.lindeboominstituut.nl. H, Jochemsen and J. Keown "Voluntary euthanasia under control? Further empirical evidence from The Netherlands", *Journal of Medical Ethics* 25 (1), February 1999, pp. 16–21.

and Keown do conclude, that the practice of euthanasia in the Netherlands is in poor control."[516]

A similar conclusion was presented by Herbert Hendin, who argued that the situation in the Netherlands demonstrated a slippery slope in practise, changing the attitudes of doctors over time and moving them from tightly regulated voluntary euthanasia for the terminally ill to the acceptance of euthanasia for people suffering from psychological distress, and from voluntary euthanasia to the acceptance of non-voluntary and potentially involuntary euthanasia.[517]

It would seem eminently more sensible for society to invest in palliative care as the best approach to end of life issues.

---

[516] Gillon Raanan, "Euthanasia in the Netherlands - down the slippery slope?" *Journal of Medical Ethics* 25 (1), February, 1999, pp. 3–4.

[517] Herbert Hendin, "The Slippery Slope: The Dutch Example", *Duquesne Law Review*, 35:1, 1996-1997, p. 427.

CHAPTER 16 A Biblical View of Life and Death

According to the Bible humanity was created in the image of God (Genesis 1:26-28). Sadly, we are living in a world where human life has become a cheap commodity. Murder is common. Abortion on demand is now a form of post-sex contraception for many societies. The right of a woman to have an abortion is seen as a fundamental human right. Countries that do not offer legal abortion are seen as underdeveloped in terms of human rights. In addition, it is becoming easier to discard those individuals that are seen as worthless and as being a drain on society.

While there are times when it becomes necessary to withhold further medical treatment and just allow nature to take its course at the end of life, in the Netherlands the so-called liberal agenda is taking society into a dystopian nightmare. The elderly, the sick, the mentally ill, babies, young children, teenagers are being euthanized many without their consent. Doctors of death deem the quality of their lives to be unworthy of treatment. Many elderly are now carrying cards to say they do not want to be euthanized. One almost has to opt out of what is becoming the normal practice. Is Western society is going Dutch?

Assisted suicide workshops (hosted by Exit International) are held regularly in many cities in Europe. These have been publicly advertised. The only legitimate Christian position on this issue is that God is sovereign in the creation of life and every human is a special being. One of the primary truths of

Scripture is that man (to use the word in its generic sense) is the product of God's creative power. The human species is not the result of random evolution. Mankind did not evolve from a single-cell organism over the space of millions of years. People are the special creation of God. There is a vast difference between humans and the rest of the animal kingdom. If mankind is nothing more than the product of random selection then human life loses its value. If people simply evolved then they are no different than dogs or cats and death is the end of existence. There is no God in this worldview. According to this bleak worldview, people do not have souls or spirits that live on. There is no heaven to be gained or hell to be shunned. People are nothing more than animals and they can be eliminated if it becomes necessary. Those who hold to this view believe that people should live until their quality of life is over and then they should be put out of their misery. Advocates of euthanasia and assisted suicide actually argue that the euthanasia available to animals should be made available to people.

Once society starts down this slippery slope, there will be no turning back. Babies and brain-damaged people, the mentally and physically challenged as well as the old and the infirm become increasingly vulnerable. That is exactly where society is headed.

If the evolutionary theory is correct, there is no moral problem with euthanasia and assisted suicide, though it would still pose serious social problems, especially for vulnerable groups. However, it is a false view of life, death and eternity. Every human being bears the image of God. That means that each person has a body, soul and spirit. Each person has intellect, will and emotions.

The body is the obvious, visible physical entity that provides a home for the soul and the spirit during this life on earth. The soul is the seat of the will, the character, the intellect, thoughts, and emotions. The soul is where we reason, love, desire, etc. The soul is what we refer to when we speak of the mind (not to be confused with the brain). The soul animates the body and allows the person to interact with their world and with other people in a unique way. In short, the soul is that part of the person that makes them who they are. The Bible says, "The spirit returns to God who gave it" (Ecclesiastes 12:7),[518] the redeemed to glory (John 14:1-3). The lost to Hell (Psalm 9:17; 2 Thessalonians. 1:8-9).[519]

Men and women are the special creation of God. They were made in the image of God and have the capacity to know God. God is in charge of when life is created within the womb. Conception is not just the product of a physical union between a man and a woman. Behind physical issues is the sovereign will of God. He opens the womb and he closes the womb according to his will. He is the author of life and he has special plans for his people: "Before I formed you in the womb I knew you, and before you were born I consecrated you." (Jeremiah 1:5). The Lord had a plan for the prophet's life before he was ever born. The same was true in the life of John the Baptist. The Bible speaks about what he would be before he was ever born:

Luke 1:13-17 English Standard Version (ESV)

---

[518] Christian Publishing House would suggest the following article, so as to have a balanced view, http://www.christianpublishers.org/soul-what-is-it

[519] Christian Publishing House would suggest the following articles, so as to have a balanced view,

(1) http://www.christianpublishers.org/hellfire-eternal-torment **(2)** http://www.christianpublishers.org/hellfire-is-it-just

¹³ But the angel said to him, "Do not be afraid, Zechariah, for your prayer has been heard, and your wife Elizabeth will bear you a son, and you shall call his name John. ¹⁴ And you will have joy and gladness, and many will rejoice at his birth, ¹⁵ for he will be great before the Lord. And he must not drink wine or strong drink, and he will be filled with the Holy Spirit, even from his mother's womb. ¹⁶ And he will turn many of the children of Israel to the Lord their God, ¹⁷ and he will go before him in the spirit and power of Elijah, to turn the hearts of the fathers to the children, and the disobedient to the wisdom of the just, to make ready for the Lord a people prepared."

What people are in this life is not the product of random chance and hapless genetics rather they are the product of divine sovereignty. We are what we are because God determined it to be the way that it is. This was the conviction of David:

Psalm 139:13-16 English Standard Version (ESV)

¹³ For you formed my inward parts;
  you knitted me together in my mother's womb.
¹⁴ I praise you, for I am fearfully and wonderfully made.
Wonderful are your works;
  my soul knows it very well.
¹⁵ My frame was not hidden from you,
when I was being made in secret,
  intricately woven in the depths of the earth.
¹⁶ Your eyes saw my unformed substance;
in your book were written, every one of them,
  the days that were formed for me,
  when as yet there was none of them.

Job also held this view:

Job 10:9-12 English Standard Version (ESV)

⁹ Remember that you have made me like clay;
  and will you return me to the dust?
¹⁰ Did you not pour me out like milk
  and curdle me like cheese?
¹¹ You clothed me with skin and flesh,
  and knit me together with bones and sinews.
¹² You have granted me life and steadfast love,
  and your care has preserved my spirit.

Even modern atheistic science, which tries so hard to destroy the very thought of God, unwittingly confirms that people cannot be the product of mere chance. The average body contains some 7.5 trillion cells. It is far more complex than the most advanced computer. Each cell has 200 trillion tiny groups of atoms called protein molecules. The largest molecule is called DNA. This carries hereditary information from the parents to the offspring, a genetic code. It determines if a person will be a man or a butterfly. DNA in one cell is six feet long. Total DNA in a body would fill a box the size of an ice cube. However, if it were joined together, it would reach to the sun and back 400 times! If the coded DNA information and instructions of one human were translated into English, it would fill a 1000 volume encyclopaedia. Every human that is conceived in the womb is special. Every human life is precious and not to be discarded. Life must be protected and preserved. The unborn child in the mother's womb is precious. The mentally incapacitated person in that institution is precious. The terminally ill individual is precious. Regardless of their condition, every human life is precious in the sight of God. Life must be defended from those who divest it of sanctity and consider it to be disposable.

Just as surely as God is sovereign in the creation and the continuation of human life he is also sovereign in the end of life. God appoints the time of a person's death. This is the clear teaching of Scripture. Job declared, "In his hand is the life of every living thing and the breath of all mankind." (Job 12:10). Job went on to say:

Job 14:1-5 English Standard Version (ESV)

¹ "Man who is born of a woman
  is few of days and full of trouble.
² He comes out like a flower and withers;
  he flees like a shadow and continues not.
³ And do you open your eyes on such a one
  and bring me into judgment with you?
⁴ Who can bring a clean thing out of an unclean?
  There is not one.
⁵ Since his days are determined,
  and the number of his months is with you,
  and you have appointed his limits that he cannot pass,

Some people die suddenly in tragic circumstances, in infancy, youth or adulthood. Most die because of disease in old age but God determines the place, time and manner of death. People must not play God, whether we are talking about murder, assisted suicide, euthanasia or abortion. Such sin will be judged and punished by God.

Many people don't like the idea that God will vent his wrath in judgement. The popular hymn "In Christ Alone" will be left out of the new hymnal of the Presbyterian Church in the USA. That is because songwriters Keith Getty and Stuart Townend said they will not change the lyrics. Some members objected to the line that says "On that cross as Jesus died, the wrath of God was satisfied." Spokesperson and chair of the Presbyterian Committee Mary Louise Bringle wrote in *The Christian Century*. She said most of the committee wanted the lyrics changed to "The love of God was magnified." They said they didn't want to suggest in the new hymnal that Jesus' death on the cross was an atoning sacrifice needed "to assuage God's anger" over sin. The hymn writers refused. Getty said they wrote "In Christ Alone" to tell "the whole gospel."

Human life is precious. It is so precious that God sent His Son Jesus into this world to save life through his death on the cross (John 3:16-17). Christian voices must be raised on behalf of the helpless, voiceless people who face death in the name of convenience, money and godless indifference in what is euphemistically called "euthanasia".

If the human species simply evolved, then we are no different than other animals and death merely means the end of existence. Consequently many who hold to this view believe that people should live until their quality of life is diminished and then they should be put out of their misery. But in many instances that "choice" is being made by others for dubious reasons.

Body, Mind and Spirit

The evolutionary theory is a false view of life, death and eternity. The Bible gives spiritual perspective concerning the origin, purpose and ultimate destiny of mankind. Humans are special beings because they are spiritual beings. The soul is that part of a person that makes them who they are. The soul makes people self-conscious. There is a sense in which it can be said that animals have souls. That is, they are sentient beings, they have life within them, and they are able to interact with the world around them.

Here is where the similarities between humans and animals end. While the soul makes people self-conscious; the spirit allows them to be God-conscious. Both soul and spirit refer to the immaterial part of humanity. People have been created by God to live in harmony with each other and to enjoy living, dynamic relationship with the Lord.

Help for the Hopeless

It is heart breaking to think that many who present themselves as candidates for euthanasia and physician-assisted suicide are having their lives terminated. The legal criteria for these interventions are being either liberally interpreted or completely ignored so that people who suffer from depression are frequently not offered counselling or medication to alleviate their mental anguish. These hopeless people need help.

Many people who choose euthanasia or physician-assisted suicide suffer from terrible illnesses. These physiological conditions and their psychological impact cause a great deal of distress not only for the sufferers themselves but also for their loved ones. Of particular concern are the psychological factors that would cause people to opt for death instead of life. There is also a spiritual dimension to this issue, which can be illuminated by Scripture.

Biblical Perspective

Some biblical characters despaired of life: Job wished he had never been born and longed for death, the Old Testament prophet Elijah prayed for death and the apostle Paul once wrote, "For we were so utterly burdened beyond our strength that we despaired of life itself."—2 Corinthians 1:8.

Discouragement, depression and despair are feelings to which no human being is immune. Not everybody suffers from depression but many people do, irrespective of their religious beliefs. As a Baptist pastor, I am very aware of the fact that many Christians struggle with depression. Pastoral ministry involves drawing alongside people who face many discouragements and disappointments. It also means preaching prophetically and pastorally, which involves proclaiming the sanctity of life. Medical doctors and pastors ought to be involved in helping terminally ill people to die but not killing them. Some people who opt for euthanasia are depressed. There are many causes of depression but often it is related to specific circumstances, particularly as a stage of grief, which may be caused by bereavement, divorce, catastrophic injury and so on.

Depression is a direct result of human imperfection, as result of the fall of Adam's rebellion, which can be used to sculpt our character in God's image, depending on how we respond.[520] In spite of significant advances in understanding that many people suffer from depression there is still a great deal of stigma attached to this form of suffering. Some people tend to think that all suffering comes from sin or immaturity in the life of the believer. However, this is not so.[521] Nevertheless, a godly response to potentially depressing circumstances can glorify God, adorn the sufferer and attract non-believers to Christ, thereby giving credibility to the gospel message.

---

[520] Christian Publishing House would completely agree with this statement, and would offer the following free articles, so as to have a deeper understanding, **(1)** http://www.christianpublishers.org/prayer-does-god-answer **(2)** http://www.christianpublishers.org/suffering-evil-why-god

[521] See John's Gospel chapter 9 where Jesus addresses this issue.

The Purpose of Pain

Paul wrote the second letter to the Corinthian church from Macedonia on his third missionary journey in the middle 50's A.D. This letter gives a very interesting insight into the personality and emotions of this seemingly tireless servant of God. One major theme in this epistle is "suffering" and its tremendous value in the life of the believer. The central truth of 2 Corinthians 1:3-7 may be summarised by saying that the God of all comfort teaches those who suffer to become comforters to others. Those who have endured certain afflictions can offer more than sympathy to others; they can offer empathy, which is more meaningful. Thus, the preacher's experience of suffering enables him to preach pastorally to wounded people. Dying people have to go through that turnstile on their own but the pastor and the caring Christian can accompany them along the way, ministering comfort.

Paul learned something about God's limitless compassion and never-failing comfort. God's purpose was for Paul to become dependent on God and to shed the spirit of self-reliance. That is God's purpose for every Christian.

The Vulnerability of the Mind

When people get deeply depressed they sometimes want to die. At such a time, what they need and what they want are two different things. In a world that values personal autonomy so highly this sounds arrogant. Whereas one understands the value of "non-directive" counselling there are situations where people need a nudge in a particular direction. In fact, in some situations non-directive counselling would be negligent. What is needed is a proactive intervention based on the sanctity of life. The depressed person needs support, not to terminate their life but to find meaning and value again. The mind is vulnerable.

In 214 B.C., the emperor of China, Shi Huang Ti, began to build the Great Wall of China. The work went on for generations until this rampart stretched for 1,200 miles across the north of China. It seemed as if everything was secure behind it. The wall was intended to keep out the Mongol enemy. But it didn't do so, because the enemy finally bribed a gatekeeper and just walked through the gate!

The mind is a citadel with a gateway and it is there in times of difficulty that doubt, discouragement, depression and despair gain access. These trespassers will intrude wherever possible and cause damage to the soul.

Becoming Equipped as Comforters

God accomplishes his best work through people who are aware of their own inadequacies and conscious of their utter dependence on God. Depression can actually be a tool God uses to purify people. Scripture helps a person to be more reflective about their experiences and such self-awareness is necessary in developing a coping strategy in difficult situations. Central to that coping strategy is fleeing into the presence of the Lord and resting in his power, provision and protection.

Ultimately, Paul understood his suffering as personally beneficial, driving him to a deeper trust in God. He also sees it as beneficial to others. To experience God's help, consolation and encouragement in the midst of one's affliction is to become equipped to communicate comfort to others in distress.

Triumphant in Trouble

There are psychological, sociological and spiritual factors, which contribute to depression. People who are stranded on such islands of discouragement need to be rescued not abandoned to their despair. People in that condition are deluded into thinking that they are unique in their particular struggle. When they are alone these assumptions begin to seem like absolute truth.

When people are facing present difficulties or future uncertainty they need to be reassured that they can get through this. They need to be told of others who have done so. People who become weary with this world need to be helped to understand that they can be triumphant in trouble. If somebody stood on a sixth floor window ledge and threatened to jump it would be considered highly inappropriate to encourage that person to do so. Yet that is what is happening in some places with people who are tired of living. They go to the doctor, express the desire to jump into the abyss and the doctor nudges him over the edge!

The psalms are a great comfort in times of discouragement. They were not written in a vacuum. They came out of the crucible of the real life experiences of the people of God and as such they have an appealing authenticity. They are not the detached, theoretical reflections of religious philosophers. They are the prayers of real believers in the midst of real problems. They are the praises wrung out of real situations. They are quarried from real experience of God and they have much to offer by way of comfort in times of discouragement. They are a deep reservoir that will refresh the weary.

Regaining Perspective

The great apostle Paul experienced discouragement. But that discouragement was a momentary and relatively light affliction in comparison to the joy that awaits the redeemed in the eternal presence of the Lord. Paul was honest in his correspondence with the Corinthians. He unashamedly told them that he was discouraged to the point of despair in Asia. Paul wrote, 'For we were so utterly burdened beyond our strength that we despaired of life itself." (2 Corinthians 1:8). There is no need to read between the lines here! However, he regained perspective and that is reflected in the verses immediately following:

2 Corinthians 1:9-10 English Standard Version (ESV)

⁹ Indeed, we felt that we had received the sentence of death. But that was to make us rely not on ourselves but on God who raises the dead. ¹⁰ He delivered us from such a deadly peril, and he will deliver us. On him we have set our hope that he will deliver us again.

Although believers may experience affliction, anxiety and discouragements they should not be driven into a permanent state of despair. The Christian has an eternal perspective and this gives hope. Hope may burn dimly but that flame should never be allowed to go out. God can surround that flickering light with his loving hands and protect the vulnerable from the winds that blow in the dark and bleak places.

At one time when I was in a foreign city, a local believer tried to explain where certain places of historical and architectural interest were in relation to each other. I found what he was saying difficult to remember and even more difficult to imagine. Then I saw a tower where one could go to have an elevated view of the city. When I climbed the tower and looked out over the area it all made sense. I could see everything that had been described to me earlier. It is beneficial to get an elevated vantage point in order to understand the infrastructure of the physical landscape and this also applies to the spiritual landscape. We need to get above the things that obstruct our vision and hinder our understanding. This is what happens when we get close to God in prayer and the reading of his Word. From that lofty place, we have a panoramic view that enables us to see further and better.

I have wondered around many cities trying to find certain places of interest to me, mostly with success but there have been times when I got lost. Being lost is a miserable experience that deprives us of enjoyment. But if we live in the moment, even in times of confusion there is much to be experienced that can be pleasant.

On one occasion in Venice, I was standing outside a shop at the Rialto Bridge looking at some beautiful hand-made, leather-bound journals, when a tourist approached me and asked, in a slightly distressed tone, if I could tell her how to get to the Rialto Bridge. Initially I thought she was joking but soon realised her question was earnest. I told her she was standing on it and we laughed.

Sometimes there is an oasis in the wilderness that we can miss if we are looking for an ocean. Sometimes we live in the inner landscape of our minds and dwell on the past with regret. Other times we think too much about the future and this can cause anxiety. We need to learn to live, not *for* the moment, but *in* the moment.

Injuries of the Soul

We are complex and vulnerable people and our emotional, physical and spiritual lives are interconnected. We are all susceptible to injuries of the soul. Somewhere along the way we can lose our vigour and confidence and find ourselves discouraged, depressed, lonely and isolated. Few can boast of never feeling down. Few are without dark moods and periods of anxiety. Shadows creep into our souls. Even if today we feel on top of the world we will meet people who are drowning in a sea of despair. And tomorrow it could be you.

Sometimes people feel plagued by fatigue, loneliness, a sense of defeat, and the burden of too much responsibility. Emotional struggles are often due to neglect of the need for rest and recreation but they can also have a spiritual dimension. People are fragile and can be easily overexerted. The connection between fear and fatigue might not be immediately evident but when we are tired, we can suffer anxiety and stress. It is tragic to think that people, who are physically exhausted, emotionally drained, fearful, isolated, stressed and spiritually depressed might be assisted in their desire for euthanasia or assisted suicide when counselling, therapy and/or medication can help them find equilibrium again.

Depression produces distorted thinking. When a person is depressed he does not want to face anyone or talk to anyone. He does not want any responsibility. He can even lose the will to live. It is morally wrong to assist such a person to die and yet that is exactly what is happening in the Netherlands and other places. Depressed people are confused and in such a state of mind, their judgement is impaired. The Christian must bring hope and help to a world where so many people are overwhelmed by problems, defeated by fear and feel there is no purpose in life.

Transcending our Limitations

God wants us to be victorious and transcend the debilitating limitations of our circumstances. In order to do this we need to have that divine perspective. This is attained not only from the summit of Christian experience but also from the valley of despair. For it is often in the "slough of despond" that our experience of God is deepened. Here we come to realise that although we would prefer to live without affliction and even pray to that end (as Paul did three times) that God says: "My grace is sufficient for you, for my power is made perfect in weakness." (2 Corinthians 12:9). When we realise this we come to the same conclusion as the apostle Paul by being content with our afflictions and weaknesses, knowing that, "when I am weak, then I am strong."—2 Corinthians 12:10.

Death is Inevitable

Death is inevitable for everybody. Life on earth is temporary.[522] This is a reality that many people do not like to contemplate. The apostle Paul wrote to Christian believers in Corinth in the first century A.D. about the temporary nature of mortal existence:

2 Corinthians 5:1-8 English Standard Version (ESV)

¹ For we know that if the tent that isour earthly home is destroyed, we have a building from God, a house not made with hands, eternal in the heavens. ² For in this tent we groan, longing to put on our heavenly dwelling, ³ if indeed by putting it on we may not be found naked. ⁴ For while we

---

[522] Christian Publishing House would suggest the following article, so as to have a balanced view,

http://www.christianpublishers.org/resurrection-hope-where

are still in this tent, we groan, being burdened—not that we would be unclothed, but that we would be further clothed, so that what is mortal may be swallowed up by life. ⁵ He who has prepared us for this very thing is God, who has given us the Spirit as a guarantee.

⁶ So we are always of good courage. We know that while we are at home in the body we are away from the Lord, ⁷ for we walk by faith, not by sight. ⁸ Yes, we are of good courage, and we would rather be away from the body and at home with the Lord.

Paul was a tentmaker and here he likens the human body to a tent. In other words a temporary dwelling that can at any moment be easily dismantled. This passage gives a sense of the frustrations of the limitations of mortal existence. Paul's message here relates directly to the previous chapter where he pointed out that even in the midst of affliction, perplexity, persecution and the possibility of death the believer has the consolation of knowing that he is going to a better place. The believer is going to be with the Lord.

The Christian is one who realises he is a sinner in need of salvation and has repented of his sins. The true (biblical) Christian understands that such salvation is by grace alone, through faith alone, in Christ alone. Such a believer is going to a home prepared for him where he will enjoy more intimate fellowship with the Lord. Death merely marks the end of the process of weakness and decay already at work in the body. The believer is assured of a permanent heavenly home and his existence is merely a change of location and a change in the quality of fellowship with the Lord. This is not to diminish the pain of parting with loved ones in this world.

Upgraded

When my children were younger my wife and I took them on a family camping holiday near Biarritz in the south of France. When we arrived I did not notice that the tent allocated to us was pitched on a very slight incline. The weather had been hot and dry and the ground was hard. In the middle of our first night there was an almighty thunder storm with torrential downpours of rain resulting in a veritable river of water (unable to penetrate the sun-baked soil) flowing into the tent and quickly flooding it. Thankfully we all had raised beds but the water was quickly rising in the tent. There was no real danger of drowning but we had to evacuate the tent and salvage whatever we could as quickly as possible. My daughter, the youngest of the three kids was crying, the middle son, being the quintessential boy, wanted to go out and play in the storm and the eldest son (a young teenager at the time) typically slept through it and had to be roused. With the children bundled into the car and our soggy goods packed into the boot (trunk) we drove around for a few hours until the office of the campsite opened in the morning. When we reported what had happened, the manager upgraded the rest of our three-week stay to a mobile home. What seemed at the time to be a negative event turned out to be a very positive thing as we were much more comfortable in the mobile home!

When a Christian dies, he is upgraded, from the tent of this life, not to a mobile home, but to a mansion prepared for him by Jesus. The Lord said to his disciples "In my Father's house are many rooms...I go to prepare a place for you" (John 14:2). Followers of Jesus are "pilgrims and strangers" in this world (1 Peter 2:11). They are citizens of a place called Heaven (Philippians 3:20), the ultimate and glorious destination of the redeemed in Christ.

There are times in this life with all its burdens and sorrows that we long for our heavenly home. Life is temporary; a tent is a temporary dwelling. It is a metaphor for these human bodies, which are a temporary home for the soul. At death, that tent is taken down.

This life and its possibilities and problems will not last forever. Life, with all its thrills and trials, blessings and burdens, will end one day. We watch our loved ones leave this world, and we must prepare to leave it ourselves. This life is filled with many joys as well as tragedies, trials, traumas, diseases, infirmities, aging, and death. Thank God that this life is temporary!

One day, a preacher who was burdened with many problems was walking through town. He came to a construction site where a cathedral was being built. He watched the men work and noticed one man carving a small triangle out of granite with a chisel and a hammer. The preacher called out to the stonemason and asked him what he was making. The workman stopped and pointed to a place near the top of that great cathedral. He said, "Do you see that tiny, open triangle near the top of the roof?" The preacher answered, "Yes." "Well", said the workman, "I am carving this out down here so that it will fit in up there." Then the preacher understood what God was doing. The Lord was merely carving him out down here so that he would fit in up there. Our trials were not sent to destroy us, but to shape us for God's glory.

Longing for Home

The believer has a comforting *home* and comforting *hope*. Paul has already told the Corinthian believers that this life, with all its ups and downs, will not last forever. Now he tells them (and all true believers) that they have some things to look forward to in the future. Our bodies are aging. Someone has said that you know you are aging when it takes longer to rest up than it did to get tired; when your knees buckle, but your belt won't; when you sink your teeth into a steak and they stay there; when everything hurts, and what doesn't hurt doesn't work. The Bible says that man came from dust and will return to dust.

I heard about a little boy that came running downstairs, scared to death. His mother said, "What's wrong?" The boy said, "Mother, didn't the preacher say that the body comes from dust?" She said, "Yes." He said, "Didn't he also say that one day the body will go back to dust?" She said, "Yes". He said, "Mamma, you better come upstairs quick and look under my bed, somebody's either going or coming." That's the way life is, somebody's either coming or going all the time. Thank God, there is a comforting hope, for all those who trust the completed work of Christ, as we pass through this world. Our lives *commence* by the power of God, they *continue* by the power of God and they are brought to *completion* by the power of God. Paul said to the believers at Philippi "...he who began a good work in you will bring it to completion."—Philippians 1:6.

The heavenly home prepared for the believer is a *perfect* place where there will be no death, no tears, no burdens, and no sadness. The heavenly home prepared for the believer is a *permanent* place. This earthly life is temporary but, the place the believer is headed for is permanent. The heavenly home prepared for the believer is *precious*. The Bible says that Heaven is a place of golden streets, jasper walls, angelic hosts, pearly gates and foundations of precious stones. But it is the presence of Jesus Christ that will make Heaven heavenly! It will be his glory that will light that city (Revelation 21:23).

Beyond the Horizon

In the ancient world, men used to sail in and around the Mediterranean Sea. It is called the Mediterranean because the word literally means "the middle of the earth." Sometimes they would go to the Straits of Gibraltar and venture out a little way into that open sea. That great Rock of Gibraltar, rising up there out of the sea had some caves and some mariners went up into these caves and chiselled these words in Latin: "*Ne plus ultra*" which means "nothing more beyond". As far as they knew, that was the end of the world. Then one day a man by the name of Christopher Columbus sailed west and discovered the Americas. After this some mariners went back to the Rock of Gibraltar and chiselled off the word "*Ne*" and left the words "*plus ultra*". The inscription which had read, "Nothing more beyond," now simply said, "More beyond". When the Christian dies he does not come to what some might think is the end of the journey. There is more beyond, more than anyone could ever imagine. The apostle Paul wrote to the believers in Corinth, "But, as it is written, '...no eye has seen, nor ear heard, nor the heart of man imagined, what God has prepared for those who love him'" (1 Corinthians 2:9). The end of human life is like a boat sailing beyond the horizon where it goes out of sight but not out of existence.

The Resurrection

Everybody is going to die. Though we know it is true, we do not like to talk about it, because the thought of dying is unpleasant to us. The apostle Paul presents a view on facing death that enables people to confront it, not morbidly or fearfully, but positively and with confidence.

We are all composed of recycled atoms, genes, chromosomes and we have our unique DNA, but there is something a little offensive about this, because we believe our lives have more significance than simply being a complex mixture of physical matter. Hamlet asks the universal question about the nature of our being, "...what is this quintessence of dust?"[523]

In the Old Testament Solomon addresses the significance of life in Ecclesiastes where he wrote from the perspective of a life lived under the sun. He is looking at it from the end of his nose; what he could see, touch, hear, smell and taste. Only what is tangible is reality to him. Having experienced this, he repeats thirty-six times in Ecclesiastes that life is meaningless...utterly meaningless. All the things he pursued; pleasure, wealth, women, food, drink, knowledge - all of it was meaningless. However, right in the middle of the book, he makes a profound statement about something he cannot escape. He says of his Creator, "he has put eternity into man's heart"—Ecclesiastes 3:11.

Solomon was a man who had experienced life with God and life without God. Though he concludes that everything under the sun is meaningless, he acknowledges there is something greater outside of ourselves that gives life meaning, purpose and significance. It is a universal truth. In his book, *Mere Christianity*, C.S. Lewis writes:

> Creatures are not born with desires unless satisfaction for those desires exists. A baby feels hunger: well, there is such a thing as food. A duckling wants to swim: well, there is such a thing as water. Men feel sexual desire: well, there is such a thing as sex. If I find in myself a desire which no experience in this world can satisfy, the most probable explanation

---

[523] William Shakespeare, *Hamlet, Prince of Denmark* (Act II, Scene ii, ll. 296-297).

is that I was made for another world. If none of my earthly pleasures satisfy it that does not prove that the universe is a fraud. Probably earthly pleasures were never meant to satisfy it, but only to arouse it, to suggest the real thing. If that is so, I must take care, on the one hand, never to despise, or to be unthankful for, these earthly blessings, and on the other, never to mistake them for the something else of which they are only a kind of copy, or echo, or mirage. I must keep alive in myself the desire for my true country, which I shall not find till after death; I must never let it get snowed under or turned aside; I must make it the main object of life to press on to that country and to help others to do the same.[524]

There is something inherent in us that cannot be satisfied apart from God. Paul talks about the transient nature of the body, but what lies beyond that? Hinduism believes in reincarnation as do other religions. If you live your life well, you will come back in a higher position, but if you live it badly, you will come back less than what you were before. Within that belief is the idea of perpetuity.

Buddhism has the concept that one life lights the candle of another, and the light is passed on and on. Though you physically die, your light is perpetuated, which also gives a sense of continuity.

There are also various animistic ideas where people are understood as extensions of their parents and grandparents and so on. A continuation of the person exists in their ancestors and is passed on to future generations. It all gives a

---

[524] C. S. Lewis, *Mere Christianity*, Collins Fontana Religious, 1974 (23rd impression, first published 1952), p. 118.

sense of perpetuity in that our lives live on in some way, but the big question is: Are these beliefs true?

Paul first talks about the human body as earthly tents wherein one dwells. They are mortal and temporary, but then he talks about the eternal home in Heaven, a building from God, which is strong, secure and eternal. That creates restlessness, because he writes, "For while we are still in this tent, we groan, being burdened - not that we would be unclothed, but that we would be further clothed, so that what is mortal may be swallowed up by life."—2 Corinthians 5:4.

Paul openly and clearly states the reason for his confidence, "knowing that he who raised the Lord Jesus will raise us also with Jesus and bring us with you into his presence." (2 Corinthians 4:14). The resurrection of Jesus Christ is a precedent for the resurrection of all those who are in Christ. In other words, the future resurrection of the Christian is based on the historicity of Christ's resurrection.

The resurrection of Jesus Christ is not a peripheral issue, but is central and crucial to the Christian faith and cannot be ignored. The resurrection of Jesus Christ is the main thrust of the Gospel and it is what guarantees our own resurrection. Paul says "And if Christ has not been raised, then our preaching is in vain and your faith is in vain." (1 Corinthians 15:14).

After Christ had been raised from the dead, he appeared to all his disciples and to a crowd of more than five-hundred, many of whom were alive at the time Paul was writing, and would have testified to the risen Christ. One of the great proofs of the fact and transforming power of the resurrection is that the disciples were transformed from weaklings to witnesses. It caused them to emerge from fear and hiding and to proclaim the message of the gospel with boldness and authority. They were persecuted and ultimately executed for their faith. If the resurrection was a lie they would certainly not have laid down their lives for proclaiming it.

In our era, books have been written by atheists who set out to demolish belief in the resurrected Christ, but their work resulted in their becoming professing Christians because they could not find an acceptable explanation for the empty tomb other than the divine intervention of God.[525] The Christian faith is neither groundless nor mindless. There is much evidence for the veracity of the Resurrection and the inspiration of Scripture for those who are willing to read the apologetic literature. There is an abundance of historical textual sources for those who care to know.

For example, the historical authenticity of the New Testament is worthy of consideration. Approximately 5,700 Greek manuscripts of the New Testament are available in the world today (in addition to other witnesses, such as the Latin, Coptic and Syriac versions), in contrast to one copy of Velleius Paterculus' *History of Rome*, or an incomplete

---

[525] See Antony Flew, *There is a God: How the World's Most Notorious Atheist Changed His Mind*, New York: HarperOne, 2007. Flew was a prominent atheist who decided to follow the argument wherever it leads. It led him to God as creator. See also Frank Morison, *Who Moved the Stone? A Skeptic Looks at the Death and Resurrection of Christ*, Zondervan; reprint edition, 1987. This is a classic text on examining the evidence for the Resurrection. Convinced that the story wasn't true, Frank Morison started to write about Jesus' last days. However, as he studied this crucial period he became convinced by the evidence and was converted. First published in 1930, this is an in-depth exploration of what happened between the death of Jesus and the resurrection as recorded in the Bible. Using many information sources, this is crammed with vital detail that every Christian should know and is also a powerful tool for persuasion of those questioning Christianity.

collection of the 14 books of *Histories* and 16 of *Annals* by Latin historian Cornelius Tacitus.[526]

The fact that Jesus is alive does not only change our perspective on the next life, but also in this life, because until we are ready to face death, we will never really know how to live freely. Lurking in the background is always the fear of death, as this unknown poet writes:

Death is part of life, they say;

And true, it haunts me everyday –

Silently creeping up to my door,

Patiently waiting to settle the score.

To share Paul's perspective, death loses its sting because on the cross over two thousand years ago, Jesus Christ conquered death. Paul says, "to be absent from the body is to be present with the Lord." The Christian faith is not about escapism, but about life here and now, lived in the love, strength and wisdom of the presence of God within us. And with the indwelling presence of God we have the assurance of the one who was raised from the dead raising us up to our eternal home with him.

Reasons to Believe in the Bible

Many great leaders and thinkers in history have affirmed the truth and impact of the Bible. Abraham Lincoln said: "I believe the Bible is the best gift God has ever given man. All the good from the Savior of the world is communicated to us

---

[526] Bruce M. Metzger and Bart D. Ehrman, *The Text of the New Testament: Its Transmission, Corruption and Restoration*, 4th edition, New York: Oxford University Press, 2005, pp. 50-51.

through this book. But for it we could not know right from wrong."

Good arguments can be made for the credibility of the Bible. As already stated there is convincing manuscript evidence. There are way more copies of the biblical manuscripts, with remarkable consistency between them, than there are for any of the classics like Plato, Aristotle and Socrates. F. F. Bruce has said, "There is no body of ancient literature in the world which enjoys such a wealth of good textual attestation as the New Testament."[527] In his modern classic (*The New Testament Documents: Are They Reliable?*) Bruce offers a compelling defence of biblical truth. He is a respected scholar who makes a clear case for the historical trustworthiness of the Christian Scriptures, drawing on evidence from the New Testament documents themselves as well as extra-biblical sources he provides archaeological and literary evidence for the trustworthiness of the Bible.

There is significant archaeological evidence corroborating biblical places, people and events. Again and again archaeological discoveries have verified the accuracy of the historical and cultural references in the Bible. The more they dig, the more it confirms the Bible. E.M. Blaiklock says, "It is important to note that Near Eastern archaeology has demonstrated the historical and geographical reliability of the Bible in many important areas."[528] *The New International Dictionary of Biblical Archaeology* surveys the findings and methods of Biblical archaeology. It offers information about specific sites, ancient cultures, extra-biblical literature and historical figures, all affirming the trustworthiness of scripture.

---

[527] F.F. Bruce, *The New Testament Documents: Are They Reliable?* First published 1943 by Wm. B. Eerdmans Publishing Company.

[528] E.M. Blaiklock, *The New International Dictionary of Biblical Archaeology*, Regency Reference Library, Zondervan, 1983.

The Bible was written by people who witnessed the events it describes and as such offers valuable eye-witness accounts. Many of these people were persecuted or martyred but never changed their story. It is unlikely they would die for something they knew was untrue. John Calvin said, "It is no moderate approbation of Scripture that it has been sealed by the blood of so many witnesses, especially when we reflect that they died to render testimony to the faith ...with a firm and constant, yet sober, zeal toward God."[529]

There are plenty of corroborating accounts with many references in non-biblical sources to the events described in the Bible. The *New Bible Dictionary* says that the Jewish historian Josephus (born in 37 AD), "provides indispensable background material for the student of...New Testament history. In them, we meet many figures well known to us from the New Testament. Some of his writings provide direct commentary on New Testament references."[530]

The Bible is remarkable for its literary consistency. It contains sixty-six books written over 1,500 years by forty different writers but it tells one "big story" of God's plan of salvation that culminated in Jesus Christ. People can't even pass a secret around a circle of twelve and get the same message at the end. John Stott says, "There is indeed a wide variety of human authors and themes...Yet behind these...there lies a single divine author with a single unifying theme."[531]

---

[529] John Calvin, *Institutes of the Christian Religion*, Hendrickson, 2007.

[530] J.D. Douglas (ed.) *The New Bible Dictionary*, Edited By: I. Howard Marshall, J.I. Packer, D.J. Wiseman, A.R. Millard, Inter Varsity Press, 1996.

[531] John R.W. Stott, *Understanding the Bible*, Zondervan, 1999.

There are over three-hundred specific prophecies in the Old Testament that are fulfilled in the life, death and resurrection of Jesus Christ in the New Testament. R.C. Sproul says, "The very dimension of the sheer fulfilment of prophecy of the Old Testament Scriptures should be enough to convince anyone that we are dealing with a supernatural piece of literature....God has himself planted within the scriptures an internal consistency that bears witness that this is his Word."[532] The Bible has had a greater influence on the laws, art, ethics, music and literature of world civilisation than any other book in history.[533] Craig Blomberg says that Christianity, as set forth in the Bible, "is responsible for a disproportionately large number of the humanitarian advances in the history of civilization—in education, medicine, law, the fine arts, working for human rights and even in the natural sciences...."[534] In *Christian Apologetics: A Comprehensive Case for Biblical Faith* it is affirmed that the Christian worldview proposes reliable answers to the most enduring human questions. In this work Douglas Groothuis makes a comprehensive apologetic case for Christian theism-- proceeding from a defence of objective truth to a presentation of the key arguments for God from natural theology to a case for the credibility of Jesus, the incarnation and the resurrection. Throughout, Groothuis considers alternative views and how they fare intellectually.

---

[532] R.C. Sproul, *Now That's a Good Question*, Tyndale House, 1996.

[533] The King James Version of the Bible has had a more profound influence on the development of the English language than any other work.

[534] Craig L. Blomberg, "Jesus of Nazareth: How Historians can know Him and Why it Matters", in Douglas Groothuis, *Christian Apologetics: A Comprehensive Case for Biblical Faith*, IVP Academic, 2011.

From St. Augustine to Martin Luther to Joni Eareckson Tada to countless everyday men, women and children, the words of the Bible have transformed lives unmistakably and forever. Countless numbers of Christians down through the ages have shown that the Bible is the most reliable place to turn for finding the key to a meaningful spiritual life. Honest seekers who investigate the trustworthiness of the Bible will not be disappointed.

Does Science Contradict the Bible?

Whenever science has "contradicted" the Bible, it has always been science, which has changed. New discoveries are constantly forcing science to change. For example, the word "atom" is derived from *tomas*, which means, "to cut" and "a" which means "not". A little over 100 years ago it was the view of science that the atom could not be split. But today the splitting of atoms is the basis of atomic energy, as an enormous amount of energy is released when atoms are split.

Jeremiah 33:22 states that the stars "cannot be numbered". This was written approximately 2600 years ago when the prevailing view was quite different. The Greek astronomer Hipparchus, in 150 B.C. said there were "less than 3,000 stars." Hebrews 11:12 (written in the first century A.D.) describes the stars as being "innumerable as the sand which is by the seashore." Science did not agree with the Bible until the telescope was invented in 1608 and used by Galileo to peer into space.

Job 38:25 states that "the path of the thunderbolt" causes it to rain. In 1964, science discovered this same fact. The discharge of lightning changes the electrical polarity of water molecules, which causes the water molecules to coalesce into raindrops.

One of the great discoveries of modern physics is that time had a beginning. We see this fact clearly stated almost 2,000 years ago:

2 Timothy 1:8-12 English Standard Version (ESV)

[8] Therefore do not be ashamed of the testimony about our Lord, nor of me his prisoner, but share in suffering for the gospel by the power of God, [9] who saved us and called us to a holy calling, not because of our works but because of his own purpose and grace, which he gave us in Christ Jesus before the ages began, [10] and which now has been manifested through the appearing of our Savior Christ Jesus, who abolished death and brought life and immortality to light through the gospel, [11] for which I was appointed a preacher and apostle and teacher, [12] which is why I suffer as I do. But I am not ashamed, for I know whom I have believed, and I am convinced that he is able to guard until that Day what has been entrusted to me.

The apostle Paul wrote this book when he was on death row (after the Roman Empire turned against Christians). From his perspective death was merely a doorway from time to eternity in heaven – "immortality" as he put it. In some translations the word "history" is used instead of time, but the word in the original Greek is *chronos*.

Hebrews 4:3 states, "The works were finished from the foundation of the world". No more matter or energy was created after the beginning. Science did not embrace this fact until 1841 when Mayer formulated the law of mass and energy conservation, also known as "The First Law of Thermodynamics", which states: the sum total of all mass and energy in the universe remains constant. One form of energy or mass may be changed into another form, but the total amount cannot increase or decrease.

The Second Law of Thermodynamics states: there is a constant amount of energy, but in all energy transfers there is a loss in the amount of usable energy and an increase in the amount of useless energy. That means that everything is growing older, wearing out. In 700 B.C. God revealed this same fact to the prophet Isaiah –

Isaiah 51:6 English Standard Version (ESV)

⁶ Lift up your eyes to the heavens,
  and look at the earth beneath;
for the heavens vanish like smoke,
  the earth will wear out like a garment,
  and they who dwell in it will die in like manner;
but my salvation will be forever,
  and my righteousness will never be dismayed.

The Bible is accurate about these facts of science as it is accurate about our need for the forgiveness of sins that is available to us through Jesus Christ. "For the wages of sin is death, but the gift of God is eternal life in Christ Jesus our Lord."—Romans 6:23.

True science does not contradict the Bible. The revelation of science is not the purpose of the Bible. Its object is the revelation of the origin and destiny of man, and to reveal the will of the creator. The Bible is truth, and though its language is not scientific (in the academic sense of the term), every reference in the Bible to science is scientifically accurate. Every mention of things geological is geologically correct and every word in it touching things astronomical is astronomically true. Thus while science searches and revises its findings, the Word of God is settled and fixed.

The Bible, though not a revelation of science, anticipates the discoveries of science. Therein lays the incontrovertible proof of inspiration. The scientific truth and accuracy of the

Bible are witnesses to its divine origin as the inspired word of God. In the cosmogony of the Bible it never mistakes fables for facts. For instance, the delusions of astrology are not confused with the researches of astronomy. The former is superstition the latter is science. In all the writings of men, certain errors and misconceptions of the times in which they lived are found in their books. What kept those errors and superstitions out of the Bible? No endorsement of such is to be found in it.

On the contrary, in times of such misconceptions, the Bible anticipates with scientific accuracy the truth in whatever realm the reference is made. The examples of this fact are numerous. Time was when men believed that the "firmament" was solid. But in Psalms 19, the Spirit of God had David to use the Hebrew word "expanse" for our word "firmament" in that passage, thus anticipating science. When men thought the earth rested on some sort of a foundation such as huge rock pillars, Job declared that it was suspended in space or hanging "on nothing."—Job 26:7.

The same is true of the geology of the Bible. The geological order of the scientist is the exact creative order of Moses. Geology teaches that a vast, watery waste existed. Moses said the earth was void and without form and that darkness was upon the face of the deep (Genesis 1:1-2). Geology claims that watery vapours were lifted and formed into an expanse. Moses ascribes the same procedure to the creative act of God. Geology asserts that the earth pushed itself up from below or beneath the waters, and vegetation followed. Moses wrote that the dry land appeared and yielded grass, herb and tree.

Geology says that the heavens then were cleared of the dense atmospheric expanse hanging over them, and that the luminaries of the heavens began to shine on the earth. Moses records that on the fourth day of creation God made these luminary bodies of the heaven to give light upon the earth, to divide the day from the night, for seasons, for days and for years.

In the order of animal creation, geology gives the order from the lower to the higher — fish, reptiles, birds and mammals, which the geologist lists according to the "proportion of brain to spinal cord". However, Moses records the exact order of animal creation. What did Moses know about the comparative anatomy (that fish are lower than reptiles, and reptiles lower than birds and lower than mammals) of the geological discoveries?

The record of creation in Genesis, centuries before science was born and ages before geology was known, tabulates the order without a geological error or a scientific blunder. This undeniable agreement between the Bible record of creation and the modern discoveries of science is indisputable proof that God made the world and wrote the Book.

The efforts of some of the critics to create contradictions between geology and the Bible on the basis of the age of the earth and the date of fossils have proven presumptive and futile.[535]

Preparing for Death

We all want to die mentally competent and alert, without physical pain or emotional distress, at peace with God and with family and friends. We all want to die with dignity, courage and hope. We all desire this good death. It would be immensely wise to prepare for death by coming to faith in Christ. It is not how we live that prepares us for death

---

[535] Christian Publishing House would suggest the following article, so as to have a balanced view, http://www.christianpublishers.org/creation-days-how-long

rather it is how and why he (Christ) died. Scripture is crystal clear about this and deserves our full attention: "The saying is trustworthy and deserving of full acceptance, that Christ Jesus came into the world to save sinners, of whom I am the foremost" (1 Timothy 1:15). Recognising this is the best way to prepare for death.

Good News for Dying People

The shadow of the cross lengthens in the light of history and touches us today. Three people were taken that day to a hill outside Jerusalem to be crucified. One died *in* sin. One died *to* sin. One died *for* sin. Two were guilty. One was innocent. Two were paying their debt to society. One was paying our debt of sin. Consider, for a moment, the one who died to sin: the repentant thief. He made some remarkable observations. His was a remarkable conversion. Of all the converts among the rich, the religious and the rejected, his is the most amazing.

The story is recorded in Luke's Gospel (23:32-43). Both of these men asked Jesus to save them. One of the men being crucified said, "Are you not the Christ? Save yourself and us!" (v.39). His words were sarcastic and sneering. The other man said, "Jesus, remember me when you come into your kingdom." (v.42). His words were simple and sincere. Hear the response of Christ: "Truly, I say to you, today you will be with me in Paradise." The repentant thief rebukes the other criminal. He recognises his own guilt and admits that he and the other man both fully deserve death, "we are receiving the due reward of our deeds; but this man has done nothing wrong" (v.41). Pilate and Herod said this but did not respond appropriately to that knowledge. There was one essential difference between these two convicted criminals. One sought to be saved from his *situation*, the other sought to be saved from his *sin* and he would hear the best news ever, "...today you will be with me in Paradise."

Conviction Comes before Conversion

Notice how conviction comes before conversion. The repentant thief says, "...we are receiving the due reward of our deeds" (v.41). What was happening in this man's life? Was he afraid of falling into the hands of the living God? The Bible says "It is a fearful thing to fall into the hands of the living God." (Hebrews 10:31). He understood what was happening. He sensed the eternal significance of the occasion. Scripture also says, "The fear of the LORD is the beginning of wisdom, and the knowledge of the Holy One is insight" (Proverbs 9:10). Here in this unfolding drama there are two very different attitudes to Christ. The repentant thief admits his own sinfulness. What led to his conviction and conversion? Was it fear or was it that he heard Jesus say "Father, forgive them, for they know not what they do" (v.34). Was it the fact that Jesus forgave his tormentors? Maybe he had heard about Jesus. God was certainly working in his heart. Not only did he rebuke the other thief. Not only did he admit his guilt. However, he confessed Jesus as the innocent one.

However, he did one more thing for which he will always be remembered. He said, "Jesus, remember me when you come into your kingdom" (v.42). He looked at the battered and bruised body of Jesus and saw a king! What a remarkable insight! He didn't ask for a place of honour. All he dared to ask was to be remembered. But he was speaking to the one who is able to do immeasurably more than we can imagine. In all his agony and anguish Jesus had time to win one more soul. The promise of paradise is great news.

The Great Exchange

There is much we don't know about this man (his name and age). But we do know that at this point in his life he knew he was a sinner and that Jesus could help him. That is all he needed to know. Astonishingly, he anticipates the Resurrection. This is evident when he asks Jesus to remember him. Here is a man who was saved in his dying hour, probably after a life of wrongdoing. A very important question was answered that day, it is this: can a person be sure of heaven after death? The answer is "yes"! Jesus said, "Truly, I say to you, today you will be with me in Paradise." He did not deserve a place in Paradise. He could not earn it. Yet the promise was extended to him on the same basis that it is extended to all who will believe: by grace alone, through faith alone, in Christ alone. Salvation is not secured by good deeds or religious rites, rituals and ceremonies.

Both men faced eternity. One turned to Christ. His prayer was answered. He had the assurance of sins forgiven and the promise of eternal life from the Lord. It was a personal word from Jesus ("with me"). This man cried out for personal help. Christ's promise to this man casts light on some important issues. First, eternity is just a step away. It is not several steps away. There is no reincarnation. The issue of our spiritual condition needs to be sorted out now. Second, salvation is not by works or religious acts. Third, believers are going to a better place. Heaven and hell met at Calvary. There was a great exchange: the prince of heaven for the prisoner of hell. Surely, this adds up to the best news ever!

Two Responses to Christ and the Cross

We all tend to have our personal prejudices and perhaps we even write people off as "not salvageable". Perhaps we have our petty excuses for not reaching out to others. But in all the discomfort of the cross Jesus reaches out to this undeserving man. This shows the selfless nature of Christ. It makes our (Christian) excuses, for not reaching out to others, seem petty. We should never give up on sinners. The paths of three men met in death. Much of humanity is represented in these two responses to Christ and the cross. The cross is not good news for everybody. One of the dying men mocked Christ. The words of the hymn, by Helen Franzee Bower, put this idea beautifully:

Three Crosses

Three crosses on a lonely hill,

A thief on either side,

And, in between, the Son of God...

How wide the gulf, how wide!

Yet one thief spanned it with the words,

"Oh Lord, remember me";

The other scoffed and turned aside

To lost eternity.

Forsaken is the hilltop now,

And all the crosses gone,

But in believing hearts of men

The centre cross lives on.

And still, as when these sentinels

First met earth's wondering view,

The presence of the Lord divides.

Upon which side are you?

The Commonwealth of Christ

This repentant thief looked at Jesus and saw himself as he really was. When we look to Jesus we too see ourselves as we really are. This thief was deemed unfit to live in the Roman Empire but God gave him a place in his empire, in the commonwealth of Christ. Remarkably, the man who asked to be remembered expects Jesus to complete his work. All those who trust in the completed work of Christ can have the same assurance, "...today you will be with me in Paradise." This passage of Scripture shows us that it is possible to have (in this life) the assurance of sins forgiven and that we can be sure of heaven after death. This must be the best news ever! The words of the William Cowper hymn put's the cross of Christ in context for all who put their trust in Jesus as Saviour and Lord.

There is a fountain filled with blood drawn from Emmanuel's veins;

And sinners plunged beneath that flood lose all their guilty stains.

The dying thief rejoiced to see that fountain in his day;

And there have I, though vile as he, washed all my sins away

The words of the psalmist seem apt: "What shall I render to the LORD for all his benefits to me? I will lift up the cup of salvation and call on the name of the LORD, I will pay my vows to the LORD in the presence of all his people." (Psalm 116:12-14). We can give nothing in payment for salvation. To try to do so would be an offence to Christ. He offers the free gift of eternal life, in his presence both now and hereafter, forever. People who scoff and sneer at what they think is a pathetic figure and spent force will have to face him in the final judgement. The cross divides and this begs the question: which side are we on? Those who look to him in faith will inherit the promise of paradise. Christ's life did not end at Calvary. He rose from the dead. Our lives do not end in death.

The future certainty of our resurrection depends on the historicity of Christ's Resurrection. Belief in the resurrection is reasonable. Unless we are prepared to die we are unprepared to live.

Conclusion

Euthanasia and assisted suicide are issues that have profound sociological implications. We have traced its origins (or at least its earliest manifestations) and the historical development of debate surrounding these issues. We have examined the legal status of such activity in different countries (see "Appendix C") and explored the medical and moral issues surrounding this emotive and controversial matter in various cultural contexts.

This work has profiled the key advocates and pioneers of this agenda-driven movement (such as the late Jack Kevorkian, popularly known as "Dr Death" and Philip Nitschke, founder of Exit International). The organisations involved in facilitating euthanasia and assisting suicide are popularly understood as champions of human rights and the personalities involved in this grim reality are thought to be heroes. But contemporary heroism needs to be reimagined and a spirit of altruism cultivated so that it produces a new generation of noble souls who aspire to achieve great things rather than merely wear the mantle of fame.

This book utilises empirical material from cross-national and cross-cultural perspectives. It addresses questions about social attitudes to mortality and the social nature of death and dying. Importantly it addresses the vital role of physicians as healers in society.

The forensic analyses of real-case scenarios which have been outlined are profoundly disturbing. Not only are the elderly and disabled becoming increasingly vulnerable but children, psychiatric patients, the depressed and those who are simply tired of life are now on a slippery slope into a dystopian nightmare. The spotlight has been brought to bear on the Netherlands, in particular, where palliative care and the hospice movement are greatly underdeveloped as a result of legalising euthanasia and assisted suicide. These dubious "services" are now offered as part of "normal" medical care in Holland where it is deemed much more cost-effective to be given a lethal injection than to provide palliative care.

Euthanasia and assisted suicide are not just geriatric issues and they are not strictly reserved for the terminally ill. The debate is well underway in the UK and has an important but neglected spiritual dimension. Thus, a biblical view of human life has been presented.

Death is a reality that everybody must face. The public management of end-of life issues are not merely matters for clinicians, lawyers and accountants. There is a vital spiritual perspective, which must be presented. This is where chaplaincy and pastoral ministry play a vital role in the holistic approach to palliative care. Dying, death and bereavement are universal phenomena and people of all faiths and those of none have a legitimate right to comment. The historic Christian tradition is struggling to be heard in the clamour for personal autonomy and civil liberties in a world that is becoming increasingly secular.

I trust this work offers some small contribution to honest investigation and response by offering an investigative analysis of the issues and an ethical framework in which they might be evaluated.

I hope that this work will challenge readers to examine (or perhaps re-examine) their cherished assumptions about human existence and the immortality of the soul. Although euthanasia and assisted suicide are complex issues I hope this work is an accessible introduction to a matter of crucial importance. End-of-life issues are becoming increasingly relevant to many disciplines with a multiplying range of professional roles associated with death and dying.

Is death the end? Are people immortal? These are questions of a philosophical and theological nature that everybody considers on some level. But most people are not philosophers or theologians and they do not want to think too much about such "morbid" matters. Nevertheless, mankind has an insatiable hunger for knowledge and that appetite has a spiritual dimension which is reflected in spiritual curiosity. To deny this sense of immortality and transcendent connectedness to something "other" beyond ourselves is to deny that universal, intuitive and instinctive sense that there is life after death.

It would be a welcome development to see Christian script-writers making television documentaries, soap operas and films about euthanasia and assisted suicide because it is here that the battle for hearts and minds is won. In fact that is where the battle is being fought. These issues will continue to be discussed in philosophical societies among intellectual elites and in parliament with those entrusted with enacting legislation. Medical associations, legal bodies and the judiciary are important participants in the debate about euthanasia and assisted suicide. The battle for the minds and hearts of ordinary people is well underway. Every organisation knows that it cannot bring about substantial and sustainable change merely with a top-down approach. Rather it is through bottom-up, grassroots, support that radical change comes about.

Euthanasia and assisted suicide are now on the radar indicating a collision course with Christian values. This means it is time for Christians to be alert and to present the case that euthanasia and assisted suicide are not satisfactory solutions to the serious social issues related to death and dying.

APPENDIX A The Sixth Commandment in the 21st Century

Some people feel that they have never broken any of the commandments but they are seriously deluded souls. However, most people feel that there are a few commandments they have not broken and this one concerning murder is one of that number. It is quite sobering, therefore, to consider the words of Jesus on this matter:

Matthew 5:17-22 English Standard Version (ESV)

[17] "Do not think that I have come to abolish the Law or the Prophets; I have not come to abolish them but to fulfill them. [18] For truly, I say to you, until heaven and earth pass away, not an iota, not a dot, will pass from the Law until all is accomplished. [19] Therefore whoever relaxes one of the least of these commandments and teaches others to do the same will be called least in the kingdom of heaven, but whoever does them and teaches them will be called great in the kingdom of heaven. [20] For I tell you, unless your righteousness exceeds that of the scribes and Pharisees, you will never enter the kingdom of heaven.

[21] "You have heard that it was said to those of old, 'You shall not murder; and whoever murders will be liable to judgment.' [22] But I say to you that everyone who is angry with his brother will be liable to judgment; whoever insults his brother will be liable to the council; and whoever says, 'You fool!' will be liable to the hell of fire.

I think we would agree that our observance of the law hardly matches, let alone exceeds, that of the Pharisees. Jesus is saying here that it is futile to depend on our own righteousness as a means of gaining access to the kingdom of heaven. He is saying that even the Pharisees determined and detailed adherence to the law was not sufficient grounds to warrant entry to the kingdom of heaven. This must have rocked the listening Scribes and Pharisees back on their heels. They prided themselves on keeping the commandments and saw themselves as innocent of violating them.

However, nobody is innocent of violating the commandments. Jesus referred to the sixth commandment, "You shall not murder" but points out that to harbour hatred or anger in your heart is where murder begins. In this sense many who feel they are innocent of murder are in fact guilty before the law and will face judgement. The law is a standard which must be observed inasmuch as possible but it cannot save. Only Christ can save and the law drives us to God for mercy and grace.

What are the commandments? Are they outward technical rules to be ticked off? Or do they express spiritual principles? Surely the commandments are not just about our *actions* but also about our *attitudes*. This principle runs right throughout the *Sermon on the Mount*. Jesus mentions anger as a violation of this commandment, which would incur judgement. Anger in some circumstances is proper. Jesus was angry when he drove traders out of the temple courts. In one parable he calls a man a "fool". But Christ's anger was a righteous indignation without sin. Paul said to the Ephesians, '"Be angry, and do not sin": do not let the sun go down on your wrath' (Ephesians 4:26).[536]

---

[536] "Be angry, and do not sin" is a quotation from Psalm 4:4.

Jesus demolished the interpretation, which the Scribes and Pharisees put on the sixth commandment. He extended it in a most uncomfortable way as far as all of us are concerned.

Confusion

There is some confusion and misunderstanding about this commandment. There are some people who say that it forbids the taking of any life, animal or human and so they practice vegetarianism or adopt a vegan position. People are free to be vegetarians if they wish but it is not wrong to eat animals. This is not condemned in Scripture. Whatever the reason for vegetarianism may be it has no biblical warrant. Meat eating is normal in Scripture. One may have certain sensibilities about eating meat and one may adopt a sentimental diet to accommodate such a way of thinking but it is wrong to seek to justify such a position as a biblical view.

Death Penalty and War

What about the death penalty or war? Are there any circumstances where we are permitted to kill fellow human beings? Does this commandment rule out all wars or are there just wars? We have to go to the Bible for the answers.

God made it clear that the tribes and nations that inhabited the Promised Land were to be wiped out. Is this "genocide" and "ethnic cleansing"? It was authorised by God and is one of the most difficult issues of the Old Testament to understand. It is disturbing to read of such incidents in Scripture. Our hearts are frequently moved to pity the peoples who were exterminated in these accounts. We wonder how God could condone, commend and command such action. However, it should be borne in mind that many of these peoples indulged in extremely evil practices and the only way of eradicating these was to stamp out the culture in which they thrived.

We might even question God's benevolence. How are we to understand such things? Here we fall back on our faith and trust that he is omnipotent, omniscient and benevolent. Who are we to question God? His ways are not our ways (Isaiah 55:8-9). He is infinitely wise and we cannot expect to comprehend all his doings. We cannot be so arrogant as to assume we know better. We should not be so deluded that we think we are more compassionate than him. How dare we suggest that he is malevolent! We need to have enough humility to accept that there are things we do not and cannot understand. We need to have enough faith to believe that his ways are good and best. We ought to have enough personal experience of him to realise that his integrity is beyond question or doubt.

Most violence, including wars come from the wrong attitudes of people's hearts. Ungodly attitudes and actions are at the core of civil and international wars. Greed is the reason for most conflicts. The lust for power has caused many wars in history. However, the alternative; pacifism, is not a biblical position. Christianity is not pacifist. There may be a necessity for war to prevent greater evil.

However, war is a terrible thing. The Christian church has a responsibility and opportunity to offer a radically different alternative to the current trigger-happy approach to solving conflict in our world. We are not promoting absolute pacifism as the ideal Christian position because there is no scriptural warrant for such a stance. Sadly there have been times in history (and there will likely be such times again) when war becomes necessary. There are evil despots who brutalize and terrorize their own people and abuse their power by invading neighbouring countries. There are regimes that harbour hatred against other countries and seek to accumulate weapons of mass destruction with the intention to annihilate others. There are powers that would engage in "ethnic cleansing" and policies of genocide.

Nevertheless, war must always be the last and least favoured option. War should never be declared unless and until every other avenue has been thoroughly explored and exhausted. War should be defensive rather than offensive. Even then those who declare a "just war" should do so with the purest motives, the greatest reluctance and the heaviest of hearts. Because the human cost (military and civilian) in terms of the suffering that will inevitably result from war is so truly awful, the ultimate objective of war must, ironically, be sustainable peace itself. War must always be the last resort, in a cause that is just, where the intention is noble and likely to succeed in its goals.

The means must be proportionate and non-combatants should be guaranteed immunity. The rules of the Geneva Convention on Human Rights governing the rules of engagement in times of war must be upheld and no nation on earth should be exempt from accountability for war crimes. Admittedly, the post-cold-war world where Islamic fundamentalism issues *fatwa* and declares *jihad* needs to be factored in to an appropriate Christian response.

Christians ought to be a people who are essentially committed to non-violence. We are to offer the other cheek to those who would strike us so that peace may prevail. Jesus calls the Christian not only to non-violence but also to proactive peace making. Christ demands that his disciples love their enemies and do good to those who hate them. Furthermore we are to pray for those who persecute us. Jesus practiced what he preached. He was gentle to the point of not resisting betrayal, arrest, trial, sentence, flogging, mocking and execution. He did not retaliate: 'He was led as a lamb to the slaughter' (Isaiah 53:7). In his agony Christ prayed for those who nailed him to the cross, "Father, forgive them". This is the way of the cross and Christ invites us to follow him by taking up our cross daily. The teaching and example of Jesus call upon the Christian to be gentle in all his relationships.

Abortion

The sixth commandment forbids such deliberate and avoidable killing. We should speak up for those who cannot speak up for themselves. We should have compassion for women who have had abortions. I have no doubt that it is emotionally detrimental and damaging to their mental health. Nevertheless it has to be said that countless millions of babies have been murdered in the womb in our so-called "civilised" societies. The termination of a pregnancy may be acceptable if the mother's health is genuinely at risk but such instances are comparatively few.

Thoughts, Words and Deeds

This commandment forces us to recall some of the things we have said or done or thought. Have we harboured and nurtured hatred in our hearts? If we engage in character assassination then we have broken the principle of this commandment. Martin Luther presents us with these challenging words:

This commandment is violated, not only when he does evil but when he fails to do good to his neighbour. Or, though he has the opportunity, fails to prevent, protect and save him from suffering bodily harm or injury. If you send a person away naked when you could clothe him, you have let him freeze to death. If you see anyone suffer hunger and do not feed him you have let him starve. It will do you no good to plead that you did not contribute to his death by word or deed for you have withheld your love for him and robbed him of the service by which his life might have been saved. Therefore God rightly calls all persons murderers who do not offer counsel and aid to men in need and in peril of body and life. He will pass a terrible sentence upon them in the Day of Judgement.[537]

And Christ had strong words for those who ignore the hungry, the destitute, the sick and those languishing in prison:

Matthew 25:41-45 English Standard Version (ESV)

[41] "Then he will say to those on his left, 'Depart from me, you cursed, into the eternal fire prepared for the devil and his angels. [42] For I was hungry and you gave me no food, I was thirsty and you gave me no drink, [43] I was a stranger and you did not welcome me, naked and you did not clothe me, sick and in prison and you did not visit me.' [44] Then they also will answer, saying, 'Lord, when did we see you hungry or thirsty or a stranger or naked or sick or in prison, and did not minister to you?' [45] Then he will answer them, saying, 'Truly, I say to you, as you did not do it to one of the least of these, you did not do it to me.'

We can take this commandment and turn it in a positive direction. Not only are we not to kill but we are to love others. We are to be kind and compassionate to others. This commandment challenges us and searches our hearts. We are made in God's image and that is not something to be violated.

Capital Punishment

Does this commandment forbid capital punishment? The answer is it neither forbids it nor requires it. Historically, the

---

[537] Albrecht Peters, *Commentary on Luther's Catechisms: Ten Commandments*, Concordia Publishing House, 2009.

execution of criminals and political opponents was used by nearly all societies—both to punish crime and to suppress political dissent. In most places that practice capital punishment today, the death penalty is reserved as punishment for premeditated murder, espionage and treason, or as part of military justice. In some countries sexual crimes, such as rape, adultery and sodomy, carry the death penalty, as do religious crimes such as apostasy (renunciation of the state religion). In many retentionist countries (countries that use the death penalty), drug trafficking is also a capital offence.

In China, human trafficking and serious cases of corruption are also punished by the death penalty. In militaries around the world, court-martials have imposed death sentences for offences such as cowardice, desertion, insubordination and mutiny.

Among countries worldwide, almost all European and many Pacific Area states (including Australia and New Zealand) have abolished capital punishment. In Latin America most countries have completely abolished the use of capital punishment, while some countries, such as Brazil allow for capital punishment only in exceptional situations, such as treason committed during wartime. Canada has got rid of it but the U.S.A. (the federal government and 36 of the states) retain it.

The majority of democracies in Asia (Japan and India) retain it. In Africa Botswana and Zambia retain it but South Africa, which is probably the most developed African nation, and which has been a democracy since 1994, does not have the death penalty.

Capital punishment is a contentious issue in some cultures. Supporters of capital punishment argue that it deters crime, prevents recidivism, that it is less expensive than life imprisonment and is an appropriate form of punishment for some crimes. Opponents of capital punishment argue that it has led to the execution of the wrongfully convicted, that it discriminates against minorities and the poor and that it does not deter criminals more than life imprisonment. They argue that it encourages a culture of violence, that it is more expensive than life imprisonment and that it violates human rights.

Does the sixth commandment require the death penalty for murder? Does the sixth commandment forbid the execution of convicted murderers? Capital punishment for murder was part of the judicial law. There were three dimensions to the law: moral, judicial and ceremonial. The moral law is absolute. It is transcendent and applies to all peoples in all cultures at all times, past present and future. In other words it still applies today. This sixth commandment, "you shall not kill", is part of God's timeless moral law. However, the penalty for that crime belongs to the judicial aspect of the law and is, therefore, not *necessarily* required today. The judicial aspect of the law applied to a particular culture at a specific time in its history. Not all aspects of the law of God are timeless. For example, the ceremonial requirements of the law are no longer relevant because they were fulfilled in Christ. The judicial penalty for murder is a matter for the state. Some will argue that Scripture demands it but that is not so. It is true that Scripture demanded it then and there but that is not to say that it demands it here and now. Understanding the three dimensions of the law (moral, judicial and ceremonial) is the key to unlocking a truly biblical position on this issue.

However, the Bible does not prohibit capital punishment. The penalty commanded by God for murder at that time was death. That is unequivocal. Whether a society wishes to exercise that penalty today is another matter. The death penalty was also imposed for adultery in ancient Jewish society. We cannot say because the death penalty was imposed then that it therefore follows that it should also be imposed now. Who would want those who do not honour their father and mother to be stoned? Stoning to death was the judicial penalty for a breach of the absolute law, "honour your father and mother". In many Muslim countries today, people can be stoned to death for adultery. However repugnant adultery may be to our religious sensibilities most decent people would not want to see adulterers executed. In decent society this is considered to be barbaric. Many Christians today are confused about this matter and they think that Scripture demands the death penalty for murder. Sadly they have been misled by their spiritual leaders who do not fully understand the difference between the moral and judicial aspects of the law. They understand how the ceremonial aspect of the law has passed away but fail to separate the moral and judicial elements of the law regarding murder. Yet they have no difficulty separating these two dimensions of the law when it comes to adultery and failure to honour parents because both of these also required the death penalty.

What can be said on this matter, therefore, about countries that exercise the death penalty for the crime of murder? The apostle Paul wrote about the necessity of submitting to government.

Romans 13:1-7 English Standard Version (ESV)

¹ Let every person be subject to the governing authorities. For there is no authority except from God, and those that exist have been instituted by God. ² Therefore whoever resists the authorities resists what God has appointed, and those who resist will incur judgment. ³ For rulers are not a terror to good conduct, but to bad. Would you have no fear of the

one who is in authority? Then do what is good, and you will receive his approval, [4] for he is God's servant for your good. But if you do wrong, be afraid, for he does not bear the sword in vain. For he is the servant of God, an avenger who carries out God's wrath on the wrongdoer. [5] Therefore one must be in subjection, not only to avoid God's wrath but also for the sake of conscience. [6] For because of this you also pay taxes, for the authorities are ministers of God, attending to this very thing. [7] Pay to all what is owed to them: taxes to whom taxes are owed, revenue to whom revenue is owed, respect to whom respect is owed, honor to whom honor is owed.

The clear implication is that in certain situations it is legitimate for the civil authorities to exercise the sword. Not just brandishing it as a threat but using it as an instrument of execution. The sword is the emblem of death and the authorities, by divine ordination, have that sword placed in their hands.

Nevertheless, it should be pointed out that Christians do not submit to all governments on all matters. Up until the recent past the former communist countries of the United Soviet Socialist Republics (USSR) had laws which forbade the reading and distribution of the Scripture. These laws were ignored, circumvented and broken by Christians. There are repressive regimes today (notably, North Korea and Islamic states where Sharia Law is in force) where Christians have clandestine ministries and operate under the radar. It is not sinful because some of the anti-Christian laws of these repressive regimes are morally wrong and God's law is a higher law. In a democracy we do not submit passively to the laws of the state, rather we participate in enacting and reforming legislation for the governance of society. Scripture does not demand the death penalty. We do not have to accept *all* norms of the then culture as normative for us today. Scripture does not oppose slavery but that does not mean that we should be in favour of slavery. Yet that is the very argument of some believers with regard to the death penalty. They are misguided.

Christians disagree on the issue of the death penalty out of ignorance and sometimes because of arrogance. It is a controversial matter. There is no consensus on this issue because there is no clarity about the biblical perspective. So, in the absence of consensus we must try to examine the implications of this commandment, "You shall not murder".

In the history of Ireland under British rule there were hundreds of offences for which a person could be hanged. There is no way that such a thing can be justified. It was legitimised state execution often for the most trivial of crimes. But Ireland has changed and its laws have changed to reflect that shift to self-government (from colonial rule).

It has already been mentioned that none of the European Union (EU) countries exercise capital punishment for murder. In fact it is a condition of entry for a country wishing to join the EU that the death penalty for murder be abolished. Ireland, like many European countries is a civilised society with its own sovereign laws as well as European legislation which governs its affairs.

Wherever capital punishment is retained it needs to be safeguarded with judicial procedures so as to err on the safe side of caution.

God Himself commanded the death penalty for murder eight to nine hundred years before the commandments were given at Sinai. Immediately after the flood, the Almighty said to Noah, "Whoever sheds the blood of man, by man shall his blood be shed, for God made man in his own image." (Genesis 9:6). Some people say that this statute has never been rescinded. But surely we no longer adhere to the eye-for-an-eye and a tooth-for a-tooth principle. A state may exercise it and others may lobby for its abolition. It is at least a good thing that society is reluctant to take a human life and that there is debate about the issue.

It could be argued that the injunction given to Noah was later incorporated in the judicial Law of Moses where it categorically states that the death penalty is the *only* punishment for murder. It could be argued from this that there is no other form of just restitution. The Pentateuch says, "If anyone kills a person, the murderer shall be put to death on the evidence of witnesses. But no person shall be put to death on the testimony of one witness" (Numbers 35:30). Those who argue for the death penalty are not so insistent about the number of witnesses. In this they are inconsistent in expositing Scripture and not being faithful exegetes of the texts. The next verse in Numbers says, "Moreover, you shall accept no ransom for the life of a murderer, who is guilty of death, but he shall be put to death" (Numbers 35:31). The argument here is that a person should not be able to buy their way out of the sentence. It clearly says the murderer should be put to death but elsewhere, as already pointed out, the death penalty also applied to people for disobeying their parents and in cases of adultery. Consistency of argument would necessitate the reintroduction of capital punishment for disobedient children and adulterers and I don't know of any lobby for this.[538]

Cain

Cain was the first man ever to be born and he murdered his brother Abel. God cursed but did not kill Cain, nor did he allow anybody to kill him. It could be argued that Cain was

---

[538] And I sincerely hope that I don't accidentally kick-start one by my argument! Thankfully my words are not that influential.

not put to death probably because of the unique situation as this murder occurred at a crucial juncture in the human race. Early civilisation was to issue from the first offspring of Adam and Eve. Cain was allowed to live, but as a murderer he was cursed of God; henceforth he would exist, but only as a fugitive. The men and women of early civilisation lived to very great ages. He had to flee from place to place as a vagabond because he was a murderer. Every man and woman living at that time knew that he should not have done such a thing. But where did this knowledge come from? The sixth commandment had not been written upon the tablets of stone at this point in history. Neither had this statute been communicated to Noah, for he was not yet born. These commandments, as contained in the Moral Law of God, are creation institutions. The monogamy of marriage, the sacredness of the Sabbath and the sanctity of human life were known from the beginning.

Cain's life was spared but it was not a ruling for all time. Importantly, therefore, we can conclude that some of God's rulings are not intended for permanent duration. God's moral laws, including, "You shall not murder", is enduring and undeviating. The ceremonial aspect of the law has been abolished. Under the judicial aspect of the law murderers were to be put to death for the deliberate killing of another person but this punishment comes under the judicial aspect of the law and that was temporary. Murder is always wrong, a serious violation of God's permanent moral law but the punishment for it came under the Jewish judicial system, and that is no longer applicable. Nevertheless, murder must be punished severely.[539]

---

[539] Christian Publishing House, addition insights, http://www.christianpublishers.org/death-penalty-biblical

In Ireland it carries a mandatory life sentence but that usually means not more than fifteen years' (often just ten years) incarceration and many people rightly feel this is too lenient. Many people in Ireland and the UK feel that there is too much emphasis on the human rights of the murderer and not enough emphasis on the human rights of the victims and their families. Murder destroys the lives of the victim's family. A person who commits murder is given a certain tariff whereby he is entitled to a parole board hearing after a certain number of years (say ten years). It is the duty of the parole board to decide if that person is still a threat to society or not. If the person, in their opinion, no longer poses a threat then they will be released. Often the murderer is released within ten to fifteen years and this rankles with the families and friends of the victims and is an issue that society on this side of the Atlantic needs to address.[540]

In his defence before Festus, the apostle Paul said, "If then I am a wrongdoer and have committed anything for which I deserve to die, I do not seek to escape death" (Acts 25:11). Paul readily conceded that if he had done anything demanding capital punishment, then the just punishment should take effect. He did not object to the God-ordained judgement of the death penalty as it pertained in the ancient world. The state today also has the right to exercise the death penalty for murder. However, it also has the right to *not* execute murderers if it so wishes.

I have accused the pro capital punishment camp of ignorance and arrogance but it has to be said that the same can be said for the anti-capital punishment camp with regard to how they use (or rather abuse) Scripture. This latter group says that the sixth commandment, "you shall not kill", forbids

---

[540] Sentences for murder in the USA (where the death penalty is not imposed) are usually much longer than those issued in Ireland and the UK.

the death penalty. This is a foolish basis for the abolition of the death penalty. The words that Jesus spoke to the Sadducees in a discussion about the resurrection seem apt, "You are wrong, because you know neither the Scriptures nor the power of God." (Matthew 22:29). The section of the Decalogue which states "You shall not murder" does not apply to the punishment required by God in the Jewish judicial system for those who committed murder. This sentence when carried out today is not murder.

APPENDIX B Religious Views

There are many views among Buddhists on the issue of euthanasia, but most are critical of the procedure. An important value of Buddhist teaching is compassion. Some Buddhists use compassion as a justification for euthanasia because the person suffering is relieved of pain.[541] However, it is still immoral "to embark on any course of action whose aim is to destroy human life, irrespective of the quality of the individual's motive."[542]

Buddhism

In Theravada Buddhism, a layperson recites daily the simple formula, "I undertake the precept to abstain from destroying living beings."[543] For Buddhist monastics (*bhikkhu*) however the rules are more explicitly spelled out. For example, the monastic code (*Patimokkha*) states:

> Should any bhikkhu intentionally deprive a human being of life, search for an assassin for him, praise the advantages of death, or incite him to die (thus): 'My good man, what use is this wretched, miserable life to you? Death would be better for you than life,' or with such an idea in mind, such a purpose in mind, should in various ways praise the

---

[541] Damien Keown, "End of life: the Buddhist View," *Lancet* 366, 2005, p. 953.

[542] Op. cit. p. 954.

[543] This is the first of the Five Precepts. It has various interpretations.

advantages of death or incite him to die, he also is defeated and no longer in communion.[544]

Roman Catholicism

The *Declaration on Euthanasia* is the Roman Catholic Church's official document on the topic of euthanasia, a statement that was issued by the Sacred Congregation for the Doctrine of the Faith in 1980.[545]

Roman Catholic teaching condemns euthanasia as a "crime against life" and a "crime against God".[546] This teaching rests on several core principles of Catholic ethics, including the sanctity of human life, the dignity of the human person, concomitant human rights, due proportionality in casuistic remedies, the unavoidability of death, and the importance of charity.[547]

Protestantism

Protestant denominations vary widely in their approach to euthanasia and physician assisted death. Most evangelical churches if they have any explicit policy at all on these issues adopt a "sanctity of life" approach. Mainstream ecumenical Protestantism tends to have a sort of co-belligerency policy with Roman Catholicism that acknowledges certain intersections and overlaps with regard to social morality. Most evangelicals would tend to adopt a more exception-less opposition to physician-assisted suicide and euthanasia. While

---

[544] Damien Keown "End of life: the Buddhist View," *Lancet* 366, 2005, p. 953.
[545]Declaration on Euthanasia", Sacred Congregation for the Doctrine of the Faith, 5 May 1980.
[546] Op. cit.
[547] Op. cit.

liberal Protestant denominations have largely eschewed euthanasia, some individual advocates (such as Joseph Fletcher) and euthanasia society activists have been Protestant clergy and laity. As physician-assisted dying has obtained greater legal support, some liberal Protestant denominations have offered religious arguments and support for limited forms of euthanasia.

Hinduism

There are two Hindu points of view on euthanasia. By helping to end a painful life, a person is performing a good deed and so fulfilling their moral obligations. On the other hand, by helping to end a life, even one filled with suffering, a person is disturbing the timing of the cycle of death and rebirth. This is a bad thing to do, and those involved in the euthanasia will take on the remaining karma of the patient.[548] It is clearly stated in the *Vedas* that man has only two trustworthy friends in life, the first is called *Vidya* (Knowledge), and the second is called *Mrityu* (Death). The former is something that is beneficial and a requirement in life and the latter is something that is inevitable.

Islam

Islam categorically forbids all forms of suicide and any action that may help another person to kill themselves.[549] It is forbidden for a Muslim to plan, or come to know through self-will, the time of his own death in advance – which in

---

[548] "Religion & Ethics - Euthanasia", BBC. Retrieved 2009-02-14.

[549] *Translation of Sahih Bukhari, Book 71*, University of Southern California, Hadith 7.71.670.

Translation of Sahih Muslim, Book 35, University of Southern California, Hadith 35.6485.

itself is an interesting comment on suicide bombing.[550] The precedent for this comes from the Islamic prophet Muhammad having refused to bless the body of a person who had committed suicide. If an individual is suffering from a terminal illness, it is permissible for the individual to refuse medication and/or resuscitation. Other examples include individuals suffering from kidney failure who refuse dialysis treatments and cancer patients who refuse chemotherapy.

Jainism

Mahavira Varadhmana explicitly allows a *sharavak* (follower of Jainism) full consent to put an end to his or her life if the *sharavak* feels that such a stage is near that *moksha* (liberation from *samsara*, the cycle of death and rebirth) can be achieved this way, liberation from the cycles of lives being the primary objective in the religion.

Judaism

Like the trend among Protestants, Jewish medical ethics has become divided, partly on denominational lines, over euthanasia and end of life treatment. Generally, Jewish thinkers oppose voluntary euthanasia, often vigorously.[551] However, there is some backing for voluntary passive euthanasia in limited circumstances.[552] Within Conservative Judaism there has been increasing support for passive euthanasia.[553] In Reform Judaism, the preponderance of anti-

---

[550] *Translation of Sahih Muslim, Book 35*, University of Southern California, Hadith 35.6480.

[551] For example, J. David Bleich and Eliezer Waldenberg.

[552] Such as the writings of Daniel Sinclair, Moshe Tendler, Shlomo Zalman Auerbach, Moshe Feinstein.

[553] See Elliot Dorff and, for earlier speculation, Byron Sherwin.

euthanasia sentiment has shifted in recent years to increasing support for certain passive euthanasia options.[554] A study performed in 2010 investigated elderly Jewish women who identified themselves as Hasidic Orthodox, non-Hasidic Orthodox, or secularised Orthodox in their faith. The study found that all of the Hasidic Orthodox responders disapproved of voluntary euthanasia whereas a majority of the secularised Orthodox responders approved of it.[555]

Shinto

In Japan, where the dominant religion is Shinto, 69% of the religious organisations agree with the act of voluntary passive euthanasia.[556] In Shinto, the prolongation of life using artificial means is a disgraceful act against life.[557] Views on active euthanasia are mixed, with 25% Shinto and Buddhist organisations in Japan supporting voluntary active euthanasia.

---

[554] Reform Judaism is a phrase that refers to various beliefs, practices and organisations associated with the Reform Jewish movement in North America, the United Kingdom and elsewhere. In general, Reform Judaism maintains that Judaism and Jewish traditions should be modernised and compatible with participation in the surrounding culture. This means many branches of Reform Judaism hold that Jewish law should undergo a process of critical evaluation and renewal. Traditional Jewish law is therefore often interpreted as a set of general guidelines rather than as a list of restrictions whose literal observance is required of all Jews. Similar movements that are also occasionally called "Reform" include the Israeli Progressive Movement and its worldwide counterpart.

[555] Goedele Baeke, Jean-Pierre Wils and Bert Broeckaert, "'We are (not) the master of our body': elderly Jewish women's attitudes towards euthanasia and assisted suicide," *Ethnicity and Health* 16, no. 3, 2011, pp. 259-278.

[556] "9.3. Implications of Japanese religious views toward life and death in medicine". www.eubios.info. Retrieved 14 February, 2009.

[557] Op. cit.

APPENDIC C Legality of Euthanasia

The legality or illegality of euthanasia and assisted suicide varies from culture to culture but these practices are generally (in most places in the world today) deemed to be illegal and immoral actions. *West's Encyclopedia of American Law* states "a 'mercy killing' or euthanasia is generally considered to be a criminal homicide" and is normally used as a synonym of homicide committed at a request made by the patient.[558]

The judicial sense of the term "homicide" includes any intervention undertaken with the express intention of ending a life, even to relieve intractable suffering.[559] Not all homicide is unlawful.[560] Two designations of homicide that carry no criminal punishment are *justifiable* and *excusable* homicide.[561] The term "euthanasia" is usually confined to the active variety and generally means that the physician would act directly, for instance by giving a lethal injection, to end the patient's life. Physician-assisted suicide is not classified as euthanasia by the US State of Oregon, where it is legal under

---

[558] The legal-dictionary.thefreedictionary.com says: "... If a person kills another person in order to end the other person's pain or suffering, the killing is considered a homicide. It does not matter if the other person is about to die or is terminally ill just prior to being killed; the law generally views such a killing as criminal. Thus, a "mercy killing", or act of Euthanasia, is generally considered a criminal homicide ..."

[559] Manoj Kumar Mohanty (August 2004). "Variants of homicide: a review", *Journal of Clinical Forensic Medicine* 11 (4): pp. 214–8. See http://legal-dictionary.thefreedictionary.com/homicide

[560] http://dictionary.reference.com/browse/homicide

[561] http://dictionary.reference.com/browse/homicide

the Oregon Death with Dignity Act, and despite its name, it is not legally classified as suicide either.[562] Unlike physician-assisted suicide, withholding or withdrawing life-sustaining treatments with patient consent (voluntary) is almost unanimously (in the USA, at least) considered to be legal and acceptable.[563] The use of pain medication in order to relieve suffering, even if it hastens death, has been upheld as legal in several court decisions.[564] Efforts to change government policies on euthanasia in the 20th and 21st centuries have met limited success in Western countries. Euthanasia policies (opposing) have also been developed by a variety of NGOs, most notably medical associations and advocacy organisations. Today euthanasia is legal in the three Benelux countries: the Netherlands, Belgium, and Luxembourg. In Europe it is also legal in Switzerland. In the USA it is legal in the states of Montana, Oregon, Vermont and Washington. In Latin America it is legal in Columbia.

Australia

Euthanasia is now illegal in Australia. As noted earlier it was once legal in the Northern Territory, by the Rights of the Terminally Ill Act 1995. In 1997, the Australian Federal Government overrode the Northern Territory legislation through the introduction of the Euthanasia Laws Act 1997.[565] Unlike the states, legislation in the Northern Territory is not

---

[562] http://www.leg.state.or.us/comm/commsrvs/background_briefs20 04/Health%20Care/FG_Physician_Assisted_Suicide2004.pdf

[563] "Legal Aspects of Withholding and Withdrawing Life Support from Critically Ill Patients in the United States and Providing Palliative Care to Them", *American Journal of Respiratory and Critical Care Medicine*, Volume 162, Number 6, December 2000.

[564] http://depts.washington.edu/bioethx/topics/pas.html

[565] Inquiry into the Rights of the Terminally Ill (Euthanasia Laws Repeal) Bill 2008. Law Council of Australia, April 2008.

guaranteed by the Australian constitution. Before this law was passed by the Australian Government Dr Philip Nitschke helped three people by assisting them in using his "Deliverance" machine. Organisations such as Exit International, founded by Nitschke, want the government to bring back euthanasia "rights" to Australia. Exit International made TV commercials, which were banned before they made it to air in September 2010.[566]

Although it is a crime to assist in euthanasia, prosecutions have been rare. In 2002, police extensively investigated relatives and friends who provided moral support to an elderly woman who committed suicide, but no charges were brought. The Commonwealth government subsequently tried to hinder euthanasia with the passage of the Criminal Code Amendment (Suicide Related Materials Offences) Bill of 2004. In Tasmania in 2005 a nurse was convicted of assisting in the death of her elderly father, who had terminal cancer, and trying to kill her mother, who was in the early stages of dementia.[567] She was sentenced to two and a half years in jail but the judge later suspended the conviction because he believed the community did not want the woman put behind bars. This sparked debate about decriminalising euthanasia.[568] The Australian Greens, the Secular Party of Australia, the Australian Sex Party, the Australian Democrats, and the Liberal Democratic Party support decriminalisation of euthanasia in Australia.

In 2008 Shirley Justins and Caren Jennings, were found guilty of manslaughter and accessory to manslaughter

---

[566] Cathy Alexander "Pro-euthanasia TV ad ban 'a violation of free speech'", *The Age* (Melbourne), 13 September 2010.

[567] "Legal case reopens euthanasia debate", *Australian Broadcasting Corporation*, 20 December 2005.

[568] "Assisted suicide case prompts calls for euthanasia law review", *Australian Broadcasting Corporation*, 20 December 2005.

respectively for providing Nembutal to former pilot Graeme Wylie in 2006. Justins claims that Wylie wanted to die "with dignity." The prosecution argued that Graeme Wylie did not have the mental capacity to make the crucial decision to end his life, classing it as involuntary euthanasia.[569] In August 2009 the Supreme Court of Western Australia ruled that it was up to Christian Rossiter, a 49 year old quadriplegic, to decide if he was to continue to receive medical care (tube feeding) and that his carers had to abide by his wishes. Chief Justice Wayne Martin also stipulated that his carers, Brightwater Care, would not be held criminally responsible for following his instructions. Rossiter died on 21 September 2009 following a chest infection.[570]

Legalisation in the Northern Territory

When euthanasia was legalised in Australia's Northern Territory, by the Rights of the Terminally Ill Act 1995, it passed by a vote of 15 to 10 and a year later, a repeal bill was brought before the Northern Territory Parliament in August 1996, but was defeated by 14 votes to 11.[571] Soon after, the Commonwealth to the Northern Territory (Self-Government) Act 1978 voided the law in an amendment. However, before the Commonwealth government made this amendment, three people had already died through physician-assisted suicide under the legislation, aided by Dr Philip Nitschke. The first person was a carpenter, Bob Dent, who died on 22 September, 1996.

---

[569] Kim Arlington, "Graeme Wylie's partner Shirley Justins guilty of manslaughter", *The Daily Telegraph*, 20 June 2008.

[570] "Quadriplegic Christian Rossiter dies from chest infection", News.com.au, 21 September 2009.

[571] "Euthanasia and Assisted Suicide in Australia." The World Federation of Right to Die Societies.

Reaction to Act

The passage of the bill — one of the first of its kind in the world — provoked a furore in Australia, and indeed in much of the rest of the world. The Act received both widespread support from "death with dignity" and right to die groups who saw it as a model to be followed elsewhere, and widespread condemnation from euthanasia opponents, such as right to life groups, who sought to overturn it. Opponents also included the Australian Medical Association.[572]

Organisations

The euthanasia advocacy group YourLastRight.com is an organisation nationally representing the "Dying with Dignity" associations of Queensland, New South Wales, Victoria and Tasmania, as well as the South Australian Voluntary Euthanasia Society (SAVES), the Western Australian Voluntary Euthanasia Society (WAVES) and the Northern Territory Voluntary Euthanasia Society (NTVES).[573]

Other Australian groups include Christians Supporting Choice for Voluntary Euthanasia and Doctors for Voluntary Euthanasia Choice.[574]

---

[572] C. Zinn "Australia passes first euthanasia law". BMJ 310 (6992), June 1995, pp. 1427–1428.

[573] http://www.yourlastright.com/ ; ^
http://www.dwdv.org.au/Links.html;
http://www.saves.asn.au/
http://www.waves.org.au/; http://www.ntves.org.au/

[574] http://www.christiansforve.org.au/ http://drs4vechoice.org/ It is clear from the content of this website that these people are nominal rather than biblical Christians.

Christians Supporting Choice for Voluntary Euthanasia

One might be surprised to learn that some Christians support voluntary euthanasia; one such organisation is the Australian, Christians Supporting Choice for Voluntary Euthanasia. Their statement of belief says, "We are Christians who believe that, as a demonstration of love and compassion, those with a terminal or hopeless illness should have the option of a pain-free, peaceful and dignified death with legal voluntary euthanasia."[575]

Belgium

The Belgian parliament legalised euthanasia in late September 2002.[576] A survey published in 2010 showed that those who died from euthanasia (compared with other deaths) were more often younger, male, cancer patients and more often died in their homes. In almost all cases, unbearable physical suffering was reported. Euthanasia for nonterminal patients was rare.[577]

Canada

In Canada as in the UK, Australia and New Zealand, assisted suicide and voluntary euthanasia are illegal. There have been several attempts to change the legislation.

While it was illegal to "aid and abet suicide" under Section 241(b) of the Criminal Code of Canada, which states

---

[575] www.christiansforve.org.au

[576] M. Adams and H, Nys, "Comparative reflections on the Belgian Euthanasia Act 2002". *Med Law Rev* 11 (3), 2003, pp. 353–376.

[577] T. Smets, J. Bilsen, J, Cohen, M.L. Rurup, L. Deliens, "Legal euthanasia in Belgium: characteristics of all reported euthanasia cases", *Med Care* 48 (2), February 2010, pp.187–92.

that this is an indictable offence with a potential fourteen-year sentence if the appellant is found guilty, British Columbia's Supreme Court struck down the section, arguing that it imposed unconscionably discriminatory burdens on severely disabled individuals that were not valid under Sections 7 and 15 of the Charter of Rights and Freedoms on 15 June 2012. Thus, Canadian euthanasia and assisted suicide law are currently in legal limbo.

Quebec

However, the Canadian situation is changing. In Quebec a landmark right-to-die bill was adopted in June 2014, making it the first legislation of its kind in Canada and setting up a potential legal challenge from Ottawa. Bill 52 was carried by a sweeping 94-22 majority in a free vote for members of the national assembly. The legislation is officially dubbed "an act respecting end-of-life care." It specifies that patients would have to repeatedly ask a doctor to end their lives on the basis of unbearable physical or psychological suffering. They would have to be deemed mentally sound at the time of the requests.

The federal government has said it could challenge the legality of the legislation. Assisted suicide and euthanasia are illegal under Canada's Criminal Code and Ottawa has insisted it has no intention of changing that. Quebec politicians have argued that delivery of health-care services falls under provincial jurisdiction and has said it is on solid legal footing.

The bill was originally introduced by the previous Parti Quebecois government in 2013 but wasn't passed by the time then-premier Pauline Marois called the April 7 election in early March. The legislation, which had all-party support, was resurrected when the national assembly resumed sitting following the Liberals' election victory. The bill had already passed numerous hurdles, including highly divisive public hearings in 2010 and 2011.

A report from members of the legislature in 2012 suggested doctors be allowed in exceptional circumstances to help the terminally ill die if that is what the patients want. A panel of experts later concluded that provinces had the legal jurisdiction to legislate in matters of health.

The legislation has three main components — it aims to expand palliative care; sets protocols for doctors sedating suffering patients until they die naturally; and offers guidelines to help patients who want to end their pain. It refers to medically assisted death with a doctor administering medication to a terminally ill patient if they meet certain of requirements, including filling out a consent form and gaining the written approval of two doctors.

China

Euthanasia is illegal in China. There are a rapidly growing number of elderly people who feel abandoned in a society that has traditionally treated its elders with a respect bordering on reverence. For generations, elderly Chinese citizens could count on having a place in multi-generational households, where their children could take care of them in infirmity. But today this ancient social contract is giving way as the Chinese economy booms, prying apart families with job opportunities in distant cities or abroad

New law

Non-governmental organisations, nursing homes and provincial governments are increasingly picking up the slack. China's government has taken notice of the trend. But now a new law allows parents to take their children to court for not visiting them "often." The law was passed in July 2012 after state media reported mistreatment of the elderly, including the story of a grandmother in her 90s who was forced to live in a pigpen for two years.

The tradition in China has been that the son is responsible for care of elderly parents. But sons are now moving to the cities or abroad to work and this weakens that link. China's one-child policy, instituted in the 1970s and ruthlessly enforced until recently, has made aging more difficult for the elderly and this is likely to get worse in the coming decades because there are fewer children. Though popular support is declining for the population-control effort, the damage has been done for China's post retirement-age citizens.

About 1.3 billion people live in China, including about 180 million people over sixty years old, the latest retirement age. By 2050, the United Nations projects, those sixty-five and older will represent more than 25% of China's population. That is more than 333 million people, which would far outnumber the elderly of the United States, Canada, Japan and all of Europe combined!

Respect for elders is a central tenet of Confucianism, the system of values that's been the foundation of traditional Chinese society. But it began to fall out of favour when Mao Zedong's communists seized power in 1949.

The high-rise apartment buildings that clutter Shanghai are very different from the traditional siheyuan-style housing of dynastic China. In a siheyuan (quadrangle) three generations would live in buildings that surrounded a common courtyard. Elders lived in the northern building; the oldest son and his family lived in the eastern building. They stood as practical symbols of an extended family's wealth and power.

The new parental-visitation law may indicate that the government is looking for ways to offset the costs of its expanding public-pension system by appealing to Confucian ethics. Until then, in the absence of children to keep them company, China's elderly find other ways to occupy themselves.

Some NGOs are focusing on care for the elderly and sick people and those with disabilities and many of the volunteers are retirement-age people looking to help others. It is sad to think of so many elderly people gathered around televisions or walking about aimlessly in public parks. It is not surprising, therefore that many of them struggle with loneliness and depression. As one can imagine the oldest without children or without their children nearby often hurt the most.

Retiree volunteers run many of the NGO centres almost entirely. These centres offer resources that include a psychological help line, weekly group meetings and routine visits from medical professionals.

Colombia

In a 6-3 decision, Colombia's Constitutional Court ruled (20 May 2002) that "no person can be held criminally responsible for taking the life of a terminally ill patient who has given clear authorisation to do so." The court defined "terminally ill" persons as those with diseases such as "cancer, AIDS, and kidney or liver failure if they are terminal and the cause of extreme suffering." The ruling specifically refused to authorise euthanasia for people with degenerative diseases such as Alzheimer's, Parkinson's, or Lou Gehrig's disease.[578]

Ironically, the court's decision came in a case brought by a euthanasia opponent who sought to tighten Colombia's

---

[578] Motor Neurone Disease

1980 law against euthanasia. Under that law, a person found guilty of assisting in a suicide could receive a prison sentence of six months to three years. Jose Euripedes Parra, who brought the case to the court, said that the ruling went far beyond the bounds of the court's mandate. The ruling also surprised pro-euthanasia activists.

The court directed the country's Congress to develop procedures to regulate the practice of euthanasia, leaving it up to the legislators to determine "how the terminally ill who want to die may express their consent and how they should be killed."

The Catholic Church, at both the local level and the Vatican, denounced the ruling and filed a petition asking the court to nullify its decision. The majority of Colombia's population of 36 million people belong to the Catholic Church.[579]

France

In July 2013, French President Francois Hollande stated his personal support for decriminalisation of voluntary euthanasia in France, which had been one of his presidential campaign promises ("introduction of the right to die with dignity") despite objections from France's National Consultative Ethics Committee (*Comite National Consultatif d'Ethique*) which alleged "abuses" in adjacent jurisdictions that have decriminalised and regulated either voluntary

---

[579] Many Roman Catholics are a la carte Catholics who pick and choose what they will believe from official teaching. This fact prompted Hans Küng to say that there are more heretics sitting on the pews of the Catholic Church than there are outside the church. Küng himself was considered to be a maverick, if not a heretic by the Roman Catholic Church authorities.

euthanasia or physician-assisted suicide (Belgium, Switzerland, the Netherlands and Luxembourg).

It remains to be seen whether President Hollande will be successful in his objectives, given that the Catholic Church in France and other religious social conservatives have announced that after forthright opposition to the introduction of same-sex marriage in France, their next target may be any such decriminalisation of voluntary euthanasia.[580]

India

Euthanasia and assisted suicide are illegal in India. Passive euthanasia, however, is legal.[581] On 7 March 2011, the Supreme Court of India legalised passive euthanasia by means of the withdrawal of life support to patients in a permanent vegetative state.[582] Forms of Active euthanasia, including the administration of lethal compounds remain illegal.[583]

Ireland

In Ireland, it is illegal for a doctor (or anyone) to contribute actively to someone's death.[584] It is not, however, illegal to remove life support and other treatment (the "right

---

[580] "France aims to allow euthanasia despite ethics doubts": TVNZ News: 7 February, 2013. http://www.tvnz.co.nz/world-news/france-aims-allow-euthanasia-despite-ethics-doubts-5484055

[581] "India joins select nations in legalising "passive euthanasia"", *The Hindu*, 7 March 2011.

[582] "Supreme Court disallows friend's plea for mercy killing of vegetative Aruna", *The Hindu*, 7 March 2011. "Aruna Shanbaug case: SC allows passive euthanasia in path-breaking judgement", *The Times of India*, 7 March 2011.

[583] "India's Supreme Court lays out euthanasia guidelines", *LA Times*, 8 March 2011.

[584] Ireland, a small country, is included here because I am Irish and it would be remiss of me not to reflect on the situation in my own culture.

to die") should a person (or their next of kin) request it. A September 2010 *Irish Times* poll showed that a majority, 57% of adults, believed that doctor-assisted suicide should be legal for terminally ill patients who request it.[585] One suspects that if palliative care was properly understood that these statistics might reflect disfavour with euthanasia and assisted suicide.

The case of Marie Fleming, who suffered from multiple sclerosis, is interesting. She lost a landmark Supreme Court challenge for the right to an assisted suicide, in Ireland in 2013. The High Court had rejected her claim in January 2013.

She died peacefully at home on 20th December 2013 aged 59. She was a university lecturer who went to court "to be lawfully assisted to have a peaceful death at a time of her choosing without putting loved ones who helped her at risk of prosecution."[586] Ms Fleming's case attracted huge publicity in Ireland and further afield and "her courage drew widespread admiration."[587] She had challenged the absolute ban on assisted suicide in the Criminal Law (Suicide) Act 1993. She argued that, as a severely disabled person unable to take her own life unaided, the law disproportionately infringed her personal autonomy rights under the Constitution and the European Convention on Human Rights. She claimed that the ban was discriminatory in that an able-bodied person may take their own life lawfully but she could not be lawfully helped to do the same. Ms Fleming had perfect cognitive function but had lost almost all motor function.

---

[585] "Majority believe assisted suicide should be legal", *The Irish Times*, 17 September, 2010.

[586] Ruadhán Mac Cormaic, "Marie Fleming dies after long MS struggle", *Irish Times*, 21 December, 2013.

[587] Ibid.

This ruling puts the issue of assisted back into the hands of politicians. Many politicians don't seem to know the difference between what the public is interested in and what is in the public interest. Marie Fleming was not the first person to raise the issue of assisted suicide but her case has embedded the issue in the public consciousness. This issue is unlikely to go away. The debate is at a relatively early stage in Ireland. In the Fleming versus Ireland case, the seven-judge Supreme Court held that although suicide is no longer a crime in Ireland, this does not mean that there is a constitutional right to take one's own life or to determine the time of one's death. It also found that the principle of equal treatment did not confer on Ms Fleming, as a disabled person, the right to be helped in taking her own life. The judges stressed that they were conscious of Ms Fleming's suffering. Nevertheless, they said, "It is impossible to craft a solution specific to the needs of a plaintiff such as Ms Fleming without jeopardising an essential fabric of the legal system – namely respect for human life – and compromising these protections for others."[588] This echoed the earlier ruling of the High Court, which found it, could not rule in Ms Fleming's favour because "it could open a Pandora's box leading to the involuntary deaths of vulnerable others. Ms Fleming could have taken an appeal to the European Court of Human Rights but other decisions of the Strasbourg court are not supportive. It has tended to leave the decision up to individual states. In November 2013 the then Tánaiste (deputy Prime-Minister) Eamon Gilmore in the Dáil (the Irish Parliament) praised Ms Fleming's "brave and courageous campaign."[589] He went on to acknowledge that "There is a range of ethical, legal and

---

[588] Ruadhán Mac Cormaic, "Ruling batted problem back to politicians", Irish Times, 21 December, 2013.

[589] Ibid.

other issues associated with this topic."[590] However, he added that "The issue requires to be dealt with legislatively."[591] This campaign will not end here with Ms Fleming's death. There will be other challenges and legislators have indicated that change is needed to accommodate assisted suicide.[592]

Israel

The Israeli Penal Law forbids causing the death of another and specifically forbids shortening the life of another. Both Israeli law and Jewish law forbid active euthanasia. Passive euthanasia is forbidden by Jewish law but has been accepted in some cases under Israeli law.[593] In 2005, proposals were put forward to allow passive euthanasia to be administered using a switch mechanism similar to Sabbath clocks.[594] In 2006, the Steinberg Commission was set up to look into whether life and death issues could be rethought in the context of Jewish law, which suggested that hospitals could

---

[590] Ibid.

[591] Ibid.

[592] The Constitutional Review Committee has been commissioned to examine the issue of assisted dying.

[593] "Euthanasia: The Approach of the Courts in Israel and the Application of Jewish Law Principles", *Jewish Virtual Library*.

[594] Tim Butcher, "Israelis to be allowed euthanasia by machine", *Daily Telegraph*, 8 December, 2005. Various rabbinical authorities have pronounced on what is permitted and what is not, but there are many disagreements in detailed interpretation, both between different individual authorities and between branches of Judaism. Regarding Sabbath clocks: a clock may be used to view the time during Shabbat, since it is not touched or affected in any way by viewing it, and a watch may be worn during Shabbat. Some rabbis recommend alarm clocks should not be set before Shabbat, because one may forget upon awakening that it is Shabbat, and may turn it off. Some rabbis nonetheless permit the use of an alarm clock if the shutoff switch is covered or some other object is put in place that would remind the user that it is Shabbat.

set up committees to determine whether patients would be given passive euthanasia.[595]

Japan

The Japanese government has no official laws on the status of euthanasia and the Supreme Court of Japan has never ruled on the matter. Rather, to date, Japan's euthanasia policy has been decided by two local court cases, one in Nagoya in 1962, and another after an incident at Tokai University in 1995. The first case involved "passive euthanasia" (allowing a patient to die by turning off life support) and the latter case involved "active euthanasia" (by lethal injection). The judgements in these cases set forth a legal framework and a set of conditions within which both passive and active euthanasia could be legal. Nevertheless, in both of these particular cases the doctors were found guilty of violating these conditions when taking the lives of their patients. Further, because the findings of these courts have yet to be upheld at the national level, these precedents are not necessarily binding. Nevertheless, at present, there is a tentative legal framework for implementing euthanasia in Japan.

In the case of passive euthanasia, three conditions must be met. First, the patient must be suffering from an incurable disease, and in the final stages of the disease from which he/she is unlikely to make a recovery. Second, the patient must give express consent to stopping treatment, and this consent must be obtained and preserved prior to death. If the patient is not able to give clear consent, their consent may be determined from a pre-written document such as a living will or the testimony of the family. Third, the patient may be

---

[595] Shlomo Brody, "Ask the Rabbi: 'Passive euthanasia'", *Jerusalem Post*, 19 November 2009.

passively euthanized by stopping medical treatment, chemotherapy, dialysis, artificial respiration, blood transfusion, IV drip, etc.

For active euthanasia, four conditions must be met. First, the patient must be suffering from unbearable physical pain. Second, death must be inevitable and drawing near. Third, the patient must give consent. Unlike passive euthanasia, living wills and family consent will not suffice. Fourth, the physician must have (ineffectively) exhausted all other measures of pain relief.

The problems that arose from this, in addition to the problem faced by many other families in the country, has led to the creation of bioethics SWAT teams. These teams are available to the families of terminally ill patients in order to help them, along with the doctors, come to a decision based on the personal facts of the case. However, in its early stages, and relying on subsidies from the Ministry of Health, Labour and Welfare there are plans to create a non-profit organisation to allow this effort to continue.[596]

Luxembourg

The country's parliament passed a bill legalising euthanasia on 20 February 2008, in the first reading which passed on a margin of 59 to 30 votes in favour. On 19 March 2009, the bill passed the second reading, making Luxembourg the third European Union country, after the Netherlands and Belgium, to decriminalise euthanasia. Terminally ill people

---

[596] Jennifer Fecio McDougall and Martha Gorman, *Euthanasia: A Reference Handbook (Contemporary World Issues)*, ABC – CLIO, Inc., 2008, p. 90.

will be able to have their lives ended after receiving the approval of two doctors and a panel of experts.[597]

Mexico

In Mexico, active euthanasia is illegal but since 7 January 2008 the law allows the terminally ill (or closest relative if the patient is unconscious) to refuse medication or further medical treatment to extend life - in Mexico City, in the central state of Aguascalientes (since 6 April 2009) and since 1 September 2009, in the Western state of Michoacán.[598] The senate approved a similar law extending the same provisions at the national level on 13 April 2007.[599]

At pet shops across Mexico, there is a drug known as liquid pentobarbital that is used by owners to euthanize pets. When given to humans, the drug can give them a painless death in under one hour. As a result, elderly tourists from across the globe seeking to terminate their lives travel to Mexico.[600] There have been allegations that this can go

---

[597] *Loi du* 16 Mars 2009 sur l'euthanasie et l'assistance au suicide MEMORIAL, Journal Officiel du Grand-Duché de Luxembourg. http://www.legilux.public.lu/leg/a/archives/2009/0046/a046.pdf

[598] "Publica GDF Ley de Voluntad Anticipada", El Universal (in Spanish), Mexico City. Notimex. 2008-01-07.
Rodríguez, Susana; Salazar, Aníbal (2009-04-08). "Sólo falta reglamentar la voluntad anticipada para aplicarla: Ruvalcaba". La Jornada Aguascalientes (in Spanish). "Michoacán aprueba Ley de Voluntad Anticipada". El Economista (in Spanish) (Morelia, Mexico), Notimex, 1 September, 2009.

[599] "Senado México aprueba a enfermos terminales rehusar tratamientos". EcoDiario (in Spanish). Reuters, 2008-11-26. "Mexico moves to legalise euthanasia". Mexico City. Reuters. 2007-04-13.

[600] Robin Emmott, "Euthanasia tourists snap up pet shop drug in Mexico" Nuevo Laredo, Mexico, Reuters, 3 June, 2008.

wrong because the quality of the lethal drug is not controlled.[601]

Suicide and euthanasia tourism is taking place in Mexico. The pro-euthanasia and assisted suicide movement in other countries organise trips for potential suicide candidates. In doing this they hope to encourage the decriminalisation of the practice in other parts of the world.

Netherlands [602]

In the 1973 "Postma case," a physician was convicted for having facilitated the death of her mother following repeated explicit requests for euthanasia.[603] While upholding the conviction, the court's judgement set out criteria when a

---

[601] Julie-Anne Davies, "Nitschke DIY kit upsets British", *The Australian*, 20 April, 2009. They asked Dr. Philip Nitschke about it. "As revealed in The Australian last month, Exit members are obtaining Nembutal from an online mail order supplier in Mexico. Others travel to Mexico and smuggle the drug home in their luggage. The kits, which will retail for $50, include a syringe that allows users to extract half a millilitre of the solution. 'Clearly, sterility doesn't matter given that death is the desired outcome,' Dr Nitschke said. 'People want reassurance they've not just bought a bottle of water.'" "News briefs from home and abroad", The International Task Force on Euthanasia and Assisted Suicide, Year 2009, Volume 23, Number 3. "Australia's Dr Death, Dr Philip Nitschke, has been on the road proffering his latest invention, a do-it-yourself kit to test the quality and potency of the barbiturate Nembutal...So Nitschke tells the elderly and not-so-elderly that the drug is both available and cheap in Mexico. But not all Mexican vendors are reputable, so his euthanasia test kit is needed to make sure that people have the real thing and the potency is truly deadly..." *The Australian*, 20 April, 2009.

[602] The Netherlands is dealt with extensively throughout this work but also listed here in summary form for quick reference.

[603] Judith A. C. Rietjens, Paul J. van der Maas, Bregje D. Onwuteaka-Philipsen, Johannes J. M. van Delden and Agnes van der Heide, "Two Decades of Research on Euthanasia from the Netherlands: What Have We Learnt and What Questions Remain?", *Journal of Bioethical Inquiry* 6 (3), September 2009, pp. 271–283.

doctor would not be required to keep a patient alive contrary to their will. This set of criteria was formalised in the course of a number of court cases during the 1980s.

In 2002, the Netherlands passed a law legalizing euthanasia including physician-assisted suicide.[604] This law codified the twenty-year-old convention of not prosecuting doctors who have committed euthanasia in specific cases, under specific circumstances. The Ministry of Public Health, Wellbeing and Sports claims that this practice "allows a person to end their life in dignity after having received every available type of palliative care."[605] The United Nations has reviewed and commented critically and negatively on the Netherlands euthanasia law.[606]

In September 2004 the Groningen Protocol was developed, which sets out criteria to be met for carrying out child euthanasia without the physician being prosecuted.[607]

New Zealand

Assisted suicide and voluntary euthanasia remain illegal in New Zealand under Section 179 of the New Zealand Crimes Act 1961, which renders it a criminal offence to "aid and abet suicide." There have been two prior decriminalisation attempts- the Death with Dignity Bill 1995 and the Death with Dignity Bill 2003. Both failed, although the latter only did so by a three-vote margin. In May 2012, the Labour Party

---

[604]André Janssen, "The New Regulation of Voluntary Euthanasia and Medically Assisted Suicide in the Netherlands", *International Journal of Law Policy the Family*, Oxford Journals, 16 (2), 2002, pp. 260–269.

[605] Discussion of euthanasia on the site of the Dutch ministry of Health, Welfare and Sport.

[606] Observations of the UN Human Rights Committee.

[607] E. Verhagen and P.J. Sauer, "The Groningen protocol--euthanasia in severely ill newborns", New England Journal of Medicine, 352 (10), March 2005, pp. 959–962.

of New Zealand MP Maryan Street introduced a private member's bill into the ballot box, the End of Life Choices Bill, which may mean that such debate will be deferred for years, given that selection of private member's bills from the ballot box is a random process.

Norway

Euthanasia remains illegal, though a caregiver may receive a reduced punishment for taking the life of someone who consents to it or out of compassion, taking the life of a person that is "hopelessly sick".[608]

Switzerland

In Switzerland, deadly drugs may be prescribed to a Swiss person or to a foreigner, where the recipient takes an active role in the drug administration.[609] More generally, article 115 of the Swiss penal code, which came into effect in 1942 (having been written in 1918), considers assisting suicide a crime if (and only if) the motive is selfish.

Turkey

Euthanasia is strictly forbidden in Turkey. The aide who helps a person to suicide or other ways to kill one-self will be punished for assisting and encouraging suicide under the stipulation of article 84 of the Turkish Criminal Law. With regard to active euthanasia, article 81 of the same law sets forth that any person who carries out this act will be judged and punished with life imprisonment just like a simple murder.

---

[608] "Straffeloven", *Criminal Law* 1902-05-22.
[609] Leigh Lundin, "YOUthanasia", *Criminal Brief*, 2 August, 2009.

United Kingdom

Euthanasia is illegal in the United Kingdom. Any person found to be assisting suicide is breaking the law and can be convicted of assisting suicide or attempting to do so.[610] Between 2003 and 2006 Lord Joffe made four attempts to introduce bills that would have legalised voluntary euthanasia - all were rejected by the UK Parliament.[611] Currently, Dr Nigel Cox is the only British doctor to have been convicted of attempted euthanasia. He was given a 12 month suspended sentence in 1992.

A consultant rheumatologist from Hampshire, he was found guilty of attempted murder after injecting 70-year-old Lillian Boyes with a lethal drug. A nurse who read Miss Boyes medical notes discovered Dr Cox's act. She realised that the potassium chloride he had used would not alleviate pain, but instead stop Ms Boyes' heart. The charge of attempted murder was brought because it could not be proved conclusively that the injection had killed her. Despite the verdict, Winchester Crown Court imposed a suspended sentence, while the General Medical Council let him off with a reprimand. During Dr Cox's court case and subsequent appearance before the General Medical Council, Ms Boyes' family never wavered in their support for the doctor's actions.

Concerning the principle of double effect, in 1957 Judge Devlin in the trial of Dr John Bodkin Adams ruled that causing death through the administration of lethal drugs to a patient, if the intention is solely to alleviate pain, is not

---

[610] Suicide Act 1961 s.2.

Ursula Smartt "Euthanasia and the Law", Criminal Law & Justice Weekly, 173 (7), 2009, p. 100.

[611] "Assisted Dying Bill - latest", BBC News Online.

considered murder even if death is a potential or even likely outcome.[612]

Physician-assisted suicide is already being practiced in the UK, though it is not clear how widespread it is. Scottish GP Ian Kerr has admitted to helping four of his patients to end their lives. He gave an elderly couple enough sleeping pills to allow him or her to kill themselves and told another pensioner how many antidepressants to take to die.[613]

Dr Kerr was suspended from practising medicine for six months in 2008 after being found guilty of misconduct following a General Medical Council hearing that found that he had prescribed a businesswoman, only known as "Patient A", with sodium amytal in 1998 "solely for the purpose of ending her life." It is no wonder that people like sixty-six year-old Kerr, who used to work at the Williamwood Medical Centre in Clarkston, East Renfrewshire, feel free to operate outside the law with virtual impunity.

USA

Active euthanasia is illegal in most of the USA. Patients retain the right to refuse medical treatment and to receive appropriate management of pain at their request even if the patients' choices hasten their deaths. Additionally, futile or disproportionately burdensome treatments, such as life-support machines, may be withdrawn under specified circumstances, under federal law and most state laws only with the informed consent of the patient, or in the event of the incompetence of the patient, with the informed consent of the legal surrogate.

---

[612] Margaret Otlowski, *Voluntary Euthanasia and the Common Law*, Oxford University Press, 1997, pp. 175-177

[613] Emma Innes, *Daily Mail*, 13 March 2013.

While active euthanasia is illegal throughout the USA, assisted suicide is legal in four states: Montana, Oregon, Vermont and Washington.[614]

Non-Governmental Organisations

There are a number of historical studies about the euthanasia-related policies of professional associations. In the American Academy of Neurology (AAN) analysis, Brody et al. found it necessary to distinguish such topics as euthanasia, physician-assisted suicide, informed consent and refusal, advance directives, pregnant patients, surrogate decision-making (including neonates), DNR (Do Not Resuscitate) orders, irreversible loss of consciousness, quality of life (as a criterion for limiting end-of-life care), withholding and withdrawing intervention, and futility. Similar distinctions are found outside the USA.[615]

On euthanasia (narrowly-defined here as directly causing death), Brody sums up the USA medical NGO arena:

> The debate in the ethics literature on euthanasia is just as divided as the debate on physician-assisted suicide, perhaps more so. Slippery-slope arguments are often made, supported by claims about abuse of voluntary euthanasia in the Netherlands... Arguments against it are based on the integrity of medicine as a profession. In response, autonomy and quality-of-life-base arguments are made in support of euthanasia, underscored by claims that when the only way to relieve a dying patient's pain or suffering is terminal

---

[614] Kevin B. O'Reilly, "Physician-assisted suicide legal in Montana, court rules", *American Medical News*, 18 January, 2010.
[615] Baruch Brody, McCullough, Rothstein and Bobinski, *Medical Ethics: Analysis of the issues raised by the Codes, Opinions and Statements*, Bloomberg BNA, 2013.

sedation with loss of consciousness, death is a preferable alternative - an argument also made in support of physician-assisted suicide.[616]

Other NGOs that advocate for and against various euthanasia-related policies are found throughout the world. Among proponents, perhaps the leading NGO is the UK's Dignity in Dying, the successor to the Voluntary Euthanasia Society. In addition to professional and religious groups, there are NGOs opposed to euthanasia found in various countries.[617]

Oregon Ballot Measure 16 (1994)

Measure 16 of 1994 established the USA state of Oregon's Death with Dignity Act (ORS 127.800-995), which legalises physician-assisted dying (commonly referred to as physician-assisted suicide) with certain restrictions.[618] Passage of this initiative made Oregon the first USA state (and one of the first jurisdictions in the world) to permit some terminally ill patients to determine the time of their own deaths.

The measure was approved in the 8 November, 1994 general election (627,980 votes - 51.3% - were cast in favour, 596,018 votes - 48.7% - against.[619] Measure 51, referred in the wake of Washington v. Glucksberg by the state legislature in November 1997, sought to repeal the Death with Dignity act, but was rejected by 60% of voters. The act was challenged by the George W. Bush administration, but

---

[616] Brody et al., p.283.

[617] For a list of these see http://www.euthanasia.com/page10.html

[618] C. Zinn, "Australia passes first euthanasia law". BMJ 310 (6992), June 1995, pp. 1427–8.

[619] Seth Mydans, "Legal Euthanasia: Australia Faces a Grim Reality", New York Times, 2 February 1997.

was upheld by the Supreme Court of the United States in Gonzales v. Oregon in 2006.

The law

Under the law, a competent adult Oregon resident who has been diagnosed, by a physician, with a terminal illness that will kill the patient within six months may request in writing, from his or her physician, a prescription for a lethal dose of medication for the purpose of ending the patient's life. Exercise of the option under this law is voluntary and the patient must initiate the request. Any physician, pharmacist or healthcare provider who has moral objections may refuse to participate.

Two witnesses, at least one of whom is not related to the patient, is not entitled to any portion of the patient's estate, is not the patient's physician, and is not employed by a health care facility caring for the patient, must confirm the request. After the request is made, another physician must examine the patient's medical records and confirm the diagnosis. The patient must be determined to be free of a mental condition impairing judgement. If the request is authorised, the patient must wait at least fifteen days and make a second oral request before the prescription may be written. The patient has a right to rescind the request at any time. If either physician has concerns about the patient's ability to make an informed decision, or feel the patient's request may be motivated by depression or coercion the patient must be referred for a psychological evaluation.

The law protects doctors from liability for providing a lethal prescription for a terminally ill, competent adult in compliance with the statute's restrictions. Participation by physicians, pharmacists, and health care providers is voluntary. The law also specifies a patient's decision to end his or her life shall not "have an effect upon a life, health, or accident insurance or annuity policy."

Analysis of Impact

From the act's passage through 2011, a total of 935 people had prescriptions written and 596 patients have died from ingesting medications prescribed under the act. The average age of the 596 patients who died from ingesting medication was 71, with 80.9% of patients suffering from malignant neoplasms (cancer). Of the 596, 51.7% were male (48.3% female); 44.7% had a Baccalaureate degree or higher; 45.7% were married; primary end of life concerns were loss of autonomy (90.9%), inability to make life enjoyable (88.3%), and loss of dignity (82.7%).

An independent study published in the October 2007 issue of the *Journal of Medical Ethics* reports there was: "...no evidence of heightened risk for the elderly, women, the uninsured, people with low educational status, the poor, the physically disabled or chronically ill, minors, people with psychiatric illnesses including depression, or racial or ethnic minorities, compared with background populations.[620]

Attempts to Repeal

In addition to the standard arguments against physician-assisted dying, opponents feared that terminally ill people throughout the nation would flock to Oregon to take advantage of the law. This fear has not been realised, largely because drafters of the law limited its use to Oregon

---

[620] P. Battin, "Legal physician-assisted dying in Oregon and the Netherlands: evidence concerning the impact on patients in 'vulnerable' groups", *Journal of Medical Ethics*, 2007; 33: pp. 591–597.

residents.[621] Despite the measure's passage, implementation was tied up in the courts for several years.

In 1997, the Oregon Legislative Assembly referred Measure 51, which would have repealed the act, to the ballot. Proponents of Measure 51 argued that the Death with Dignity Act lacked a mandatory counselling provision, a family notification provision, strong reporting requirements, or a strong residency requirement. Measure 51 opponents argued that sending the measure back to voters was disrespectful considering they had already passed Measure 16. They also felt that the safeguards in the Death with Dignity Act were adequate. Measure 51 was defeated in the 4 November, 1997 special election with 445,830 votes in favour, and 666,275 votes against.

Some members of the United States Congress, notably Senator Don Nickles of Oklahoma, tried to block implementation of Measure 16, but failed.[622] In 2002, federal judge Robert E. Jones blocked a move by United States Attorney General John Ashcroft to suspend the license for prescribing drugs covered in the Controlled Substances Act of doctors who prescribed life-ending medications under the Oregon law. The Ninth Circuit Court of Appeals affirmed the block, stating that the "Attorney General lacked Congress' requisite authorization."

In October 2005, the U.S. Supreme Court heard arguments in the case of Gonzales v. Oregon to determine

---

[621] Joseph Howell, "Death With Dignity Act 2006 Annual Report", 2006,"State of Oregon. See

http://public.health.oregon.gov/ProviderPartnerResources/Evaluation Research/DeathwithDignityAct/Pages/index.aspx

[622] Patty Wentz, "Dignified suicide", *Willamette Week*.

"Senate Bill To Nullify Death With Dignity Act Also Threatens Pain Care Nationwide", *Compassion in Dying. Body Health Resources Corporation*, Spring 2000.

the fate of the Death with Dignity law. Arguing on behalf of the state was Oregon Senior Assistant Attorney General Robert Atkinson. Oregon's five Democratic members of Congress also filed a brief in support of the State's position.[623] United States Solicitor General Paul Clement argued on behalf of the Bush administration, which challenged Oregon's right to regulate the practice of medicine when that practice entails prescribing federally controlled substances. On 17 January 2006, the court ruled 6–3 in favour of Oregon, upholding the law.[624]

Documentary Film

How to Die in Oregon is a 2011 documentary film about the Oregon Death with Dignity Act, directed by Peter Richardson. It won the Grand Jury prize for documentary film at the 27th Sundance Film Festival.

Washington Death with Dignity Act

Initiative 1000 (I-1000) of 2008 established the USA state of Washington's Death with Dignity Act (RCW 70.245), which legalises physician-assisted dying with certain restrictions.[625] Passage of this initiative made Washington the second USA state to permit some terminally ill patients to determine the time of their own death. Former Governor, Booth Gardner, headed the effort.

The measure was approved in the 4 November, 2008 general election. 1,715,219 votes (57.82%) were cast in favour, 1,251,255 votes (42.18%) against. There were

---

[623] Matthew Daly, "Assisted suicide defended", Associated Press, *The Columbian*, 21 July, 2005.

[624] Ibid.

[625] "Chapter 70.245 RCW, The Washington death with dignity act", Washington State Legislature.

2,966,474 votes total.[626] Thirty of the state's thirty-nine counties voted in favour of the initiative.[627]

In 1991, Washington voters by a margin of 54% to 46% rejected the similar initiative 119. I-119 would have allowed doctors to prescribe a lethal dosage of medication, and to administer it if the terminally ill patient could not self-administer.[628] Unlike that initiative, I-1000 requires the patient to ingest the medication unassisted.[629] The initiative is based on Oregon Measure 16, which Oregon voters passed in 1994.

Specific Provisions in the Initiative

The official ballot summary for the measure was slightly amended following a February 2008 court challenge:

> This measure would permit terminally ill, competent, adult Washington residents medically predicted to die within six months to request and self-administer lethal medication prescribed by a physician. The measure requires two oral and one written request, two physicians to diagnose the patient and determine the patient is competent, a waiting period, and physician verification of an informed patient decision. Physicians, patients and

---

[626] "November 4, 2008 General Election", Washington Secretary of State, November 13, 2008.

[627] November 4, 2008 General Election". Secretary of State of Washington

[628] "Right-to-die initiative making its way to state ballot", *The Wenatchee World*. 14 July, 2008.

[629] Carol M. Ostrom, "Initiative 1000 would let patients get help ending their lives", *The Seattle Times*, 21 September, 2008.

others acting in good faith compliance would have criminal and civil immunity.[630]

Provisions in the law include that the patient must be an adult (18 or over) resident of the state of Washington. The patient must be mentally competent, verified by two physicians (or referred to a mental health evaluation). The patient must be terminally ill with less than 6 months to live, verified by two physicians. The patient must make voluntary requests, without coercion, verified by two physicians. The patient must be informed of all other options including palliative and hospice care. There is a 15-day waiting period between the first oral request and a written request. There is a 48-hour waiting period between the written request and the writing of the prescription. Two independent witnesses must sign the written request, at least one of whom is not related to the patient or employed by the health care facility. The patient is encouraged to discuss with family (not required because of confidentiality laws). The patient may change their mind at any time and rescind the request. The attending physician may sign the patient's death certificate, which must list the underlying terminal disease as the cause of death (not suicide).

Supporters

The campaign was run by a coalition that includes former Washington governor, Booth Gardner, Aid-in-Dying advocates from Oregon, the Death with Dignity National Center, Compassion & Choices (national), Compassion & Choices of Washington and Compassion & Choices of

---

[630] "Initiative Measure 1000 'The Washington Death with Dignity Act'", Secretary of State of Washington. 24 January, 2008.

Oregon.[631] The name of the official political advocacy group working on the campaign was changed from "It's My Decision" to "YES on 1000".

State Senator Darlene Fairley, who chaired the Death with Dignity Disabilities Caucus, said, "As a matter of personal control and autonomy, it makes sense to let patients themselves decide what kind of medical care they want to receive and how long they want to suffer with a terminal illness."

State Representative Jamie Pedersen, chair of LGBT (Lesbian, Gay, Bi-Sexual and Trans-Gender) for 1000, said "people facing terminal illnesses gain peace of mind from knowing that their end-of-life choices will be respected. Everyone deserves that respect and can appreciate its importance."[632] Organisations that supported I-1000 include the American Medical Student Association, the American Medical Women's Association, the Lifelong AIDS Association, the ACLU, the National Women's Law Center, the Washington Chapter of the National Association of Social Workers, and the Washington State Public Health Association.

The Washington State Psychology Association was neutral on I-1000, but found that patients choose aid in dying because of a desire for autonomy and the wish to avoid loss of dignity and control, not because of a poor mental state, lack of resources or social support.

The *Newcastle News* endorsed the measure in a 7 October 2008 editorial: "Some opponents of I-1000 will refer to the life-death option as assisted suicide, but this has no

---

[631] "My life does not belong to the state or the church", *Seattle Times*, 17 January, 2008. "Gardner revives discussion about assisted suicide", Longview, Washington: *The Daily News*, 22 January, 2008.

[632] LGBT is the acronym for Lesbian, Gay, Bi-sexual and Trans-gender.

resemblance to suicide. It is a humane end to a life that is already ending."[633]

Opposition

The Coalition Against Assisted Suicide opposed the measure. It included doctors and nurses, disability rights advocates and organisations, hospice workers, minorities, right-to-life organisations, the Catholic Church and other Christian organisations, and politicians.

The organisation held that the danger of making doctors the agents of a patient's death far outweighed any advantages to assisted suicide, or safeguards in the initiative's text. They felt that legalisation of assisted suicide would put pressure on minorities, the disabled, and the poor.

Actor Martin Sheen appeared in television ads opposing Initiative 1000.[634] There has been some debate over one of Sheen's statements that persons with depression can be given a lethal dose without prior professional assessment. According to the Washington Death with Dignity act: Medication to end a patient's life in a humane and dignified manner shall not be prescribed until the person performing the counselling determines that the patient is not suffering from a psychiatric or psychological disorder or depression causing impaired judgement.[635] This issue has been explored in the field of medical ethics.[636]

Not Dead Yet, a disabilities advocacy group which joined with the Coalition Against Assisted Suicide, objected to the

---

[633] "Death with Dignity initiative promotes a humane choice", Newcastle, Washington: Newcastle News, 7 October, 2008.

[634] "Martin Sheen to appear in ads against I-1000", *Yakima Herald*, 29 September, 2008.

[635] "Washington Death with Dignity Act, Page 4, Section 6".

[636] A. Rudnick, "Depression and competence to refuse psychiatric treatment", *Journal of Medical Ethics*, 28, 2002, pp. 151-155.

measure, arguing that it discriminates against and targets the disabled. They believe that disabled people who are worried they will become a burden to their families need help and pain relief for their conditions, not encouragement to die.[637]

Washington v. Glucksberg

Dr Harold Glucksberg, a physician—along with four other physicians, three terminally ill patients, and the non-profit organisation, Compassion in Dying, counselling those considering assisted-suicide—challenged Washington state's ban against assisted suicide in the Natural Death Act of 1979. They claimed that assisted suicide was a liberty interest protected by the Due Process Clause of the Fourteenth Amendment to the United States Constitution.

The District Court ruled in favour of Glucksberg, but the United States Court of Appeals for the Ninth Circuit reversed. Then, after rehearing the case *en banc*, the Ninth Circuit reversed the earlier panel and affirmed the District Court's decision.[638] The case was argued before the United States

---

[637] Steven Ertelt, "Spokesman's Son, Disability Groups Oppose Washington Assisted Suicide Prop", LifeNews.com, 18 June, 2008.

[638] En banc (Law French: "on [a] bench") is a legal term used to refer to a case heard or to be heard before all judges of a court – in other words, before the entire bench – rather than by a panel selected from them. *En banc* is often used for unusually complex cases or cases considered to be of greater importance. Appellate courts in the United States sometimes grant rehearing *en banc* to reconsider a decision of a panel of the court (generally consisting of only three judges) in which the case concerns a matter of exceptional public importance or the panel's decision appears to conflict with a prior decision of the court. In rarer instances, an appellate court will order hearing *en banc* as an initial matter instead of the panel hearing it first.

Some appellate courts, such as the Supreme Court of the United States and the highest courts of most U.S. states, do not sit in panels, but hear all of their cases *en banc* (with the exception of cases where a judge is ill or recused).

Supreme Court on 8 January 1997. The question presented was whether the protection of the Due Process Clause included a right to commit suicide, and therefore commit suicide with another's assistance.

Decision

Chief Justice Rehnquist wrote the majority opinion for the court. His decision reversed a Ninth Circuit Court of Appeals decision that a ban on physician-assisted suicide embodied in Washington's Natural Death Act of 1979 was a violation of the 14th Amendment's Due Process Clause. The Court held that because assisted-suicide is not a fundamental liberty interest, it was not protected under the 14th Amendment. As previously decided in Moore v. East Cleveland, liberty interests not "deeply rooted in the nation's history" do not qualify as being a protected liberty interest. Assisted-suicide, the court found, had been frowned upon for centuries and a majority of the States had similar bans on assisted suicide.

Rehnquist found the English common-law penalties associated with assisted suicide particularly significant. For example, in early common law, the state confiscated the property of a person who committed suicide. Like Blackmun in Roe v. Wade, Rehnquist used English common law to establish American tradition as a yardstick for determining what rights were "deeply rooted in the nation's history." Rehnquist cited Roe v. Wade and Planned Parenthood v. Casey in the opinion.

The Court felt that the ban was rational in that it furthered such compelling state interests as the preservation of human life and the protection of the mentally ill and disabled from medical malpractice and coercion. It also prevented those moved to end their lives because of financial or psychological complications. The Court also felt that if the

Court declared physician-assisted suicide a constitutionally protected right, they would start down the path to voluntary and perhaps involuntary euthanasia. Justice O' Connor concurred. Justices Souter, Ginsburg, Breyer, and Stevens each wrote opinions concurring in the judgement of the court.

In 2008 Washington State voters approved 58%–42% the Washington Death with Dignity Act, which established guidelines for using the services of a physician to terminate one's life.

Gonzales v. Oregon

Gonzales v. Oregon, 546 U.S. 243 (2006), was a decision by the United States Supreme Court, which ruled that the United States Attorney General could not enforce the federal Controlled Substances Act against physicians who prescribed drugs, in compliance with Oregon state law, for the assisted suicide of the terminally ill. It was the first major case heard under the leadership of Chief Justice John Roberts.

Background of the Case

In 1994, voters in the state of Oregon approved Measure 16, a ballot initiative that established the Oregon Death with Dignity Act, with 51.3% of voters supporting it and 48.7% opposing it. The Act legalised physician-assisted suicide. A 1997 referral by the Oregon Legislative Assembly aimed to repeal the Death with Dignity Act, but was defeated by a 60% margin, with 220,445 votes cast against it. The law permits physicians to prescribe a lethal dose of medication to a patient agreed by two doctors to be within six months of dying from an incurable condition. As of 29 February 2012, the Oregon Public Health Division reports that since "the law was passed in 1997, a total of 935 people have had DWDA prescriptions written and 596 patients have died from ingesting medications prescribed under the DWDA."[639]

On 9 November 2001, Attorney General John Ashcroft issued an Interpretive Rule that physician-assisted suicide was not a legitimate medical purpose, and that any physician administering federally controlled drugs for that purpose would be in violation of the Controlled Substances Act. The State of Oregon, joined by a physician, a pharmacist, and a group of terminally ill patients, all from Oregon, filed a challenge to the Attorney General's rule in the U.S. District Court for the District of Oregon. The court ruled for Oregon and issued a permanent injunction against the enforcement of the Interpretive Rule. The Ninth Circuit Court of Appeals affirmed the ruling.

The court's decision

In a 6-3 decision written by Justice Anthony Kennedy, the Court affirmed the Ninth Circuit's judgement, but employed different reasoning. The majority opinion did not dispute the power of the federal government to regulate drugs, but disagreed that the statute in place empowered the U.S. Attorney General to overrule state laws determining what constituted the appropriate use of medications that were not themselves prohibited. The court found that it was inappropriate to apply Chevron deference toward the Attorney General's "interpretive rule" that controlled substances could not medically be used for the purpose of physician-assisted suicide.[640]

---

[639] "Oregon's Death with Dignity Act--2011", Public.health.oregon.gov.

[640] Chevron U.S.A. Inc. v. Natural Resources Defense Council, Inc., 467 U.S. 837 (1984), was a case in which the United States Supreme Court set forth the legal test for determining whether to grant deference to a government agency's interpretation of a statute which it administers.

Scalia's dissent

Justice Scalia, in a dissent joined by Chief Justice Roberts and Justice Thomas, argued that under the Supreme Court precedent deference was due to the Attorney General's interpretation of the statute. He wrote, "If the term 'legitimate medical purpose' has any meaning, it surely excludes the prescription of drugs to produce death."

Thomas's dissent

In addition to joining Justice Scalia's dissent, Justice Thomas also filed a brief dissent in which he argued that the court's majority opinion was inconsistent with the reasoning in Gonzales v. Raich. Thomas also dissented in that decision in which five of the six justices in the majority in Oregon found broad federal authority under the Controlled Substances Act for Congress to forbid the growth of medical marijuana. Thomas had argued for a more limited congressional power under the Commerce Clause in Raich, which focused on intrastate vs. interstate commerce. In Oregon, by contrast, the case was instead a matter of the validity of an executive interpretation of that statute. However, given that the majority in Raich was willing to ignore federalism concerns to invalidate effectively a California law permitting intrastate possession of medical marijuana, it was questionable as to why those same federalism concerns should now be the basis for upholding an Oregon assisted suicide statute.

Baxter v. Montana

Baxter v. Montana was a Montana Supreme Court case, argued on 2 September 2009 and decided on 31 December

---

Chevron is the Court's clearest articulation of the doctrine of "administrative deference" to the point that the Court itself has used the phrase "Chevron deference" in more recent cases.

2009 that addressed the question of whether the state's constitution guaranteed terminally ill patients a right to lethal prescription medication from their physicians.[641]

Background of the Case

The original lawsuit was brought by four Montana physicians (Stephen Speckart, C. Paul Loehnen, Lar Autio, and George Risi, Jr., M.D.s), Compassion & Choices and Robert Baxter, a 76 year old truck driver from Billings, Montana, who was dying of lymphocytic leukaemia. The plaintiffs asked the court to establish a constitutional right "to receive and provide aid in dying."[642] The state argued that "the Constitution confers no right to aid in ending one's life."[643] Judge Dorothy McCarter, of Montana's First Judicial District Court, ruled in favour of the plaintiffs on 5 December 2008 stating that the "constitutional rights of individual privacy and human dignity, taken together, encompass the right of a competent terminally-ill patient to die with dignity."[644] Baxter died that same day.[645] The Montana Attorney General appealed the case to the state supreme court. Oral arguments were heard on 2 September 2009.[646]

Amicus briefs filed on behalf of those asking the court to grant the constitutional right to receive/provide aid in dying include human rights groups, women's rights groups, the American Medical Women's Association, American Medical

---

[641] Kirk Johnson, "Montana Court to Rule on Assisted Suicide Case", *New York Times*, 31 August, 2009.

[642] Original plaintiff's filing Baxter v Montana.

[643] Kirk Johnson, "Montana Court to Rule on Assisted Suicide Case", *New York Times*, 31 August, 2009.

[644] Montana District Court Judge Dorothy McCarter, decision to grant motion for summary judgement.

[645] Mike Dennison, Billings Gazette: "Personal choice vs. public interest: 'right to die' argued", 2 September, 2009.

[646] Ibid.

Students Association, clergy, legal scholars, thirty-one Montana state legislators and bioethicists, among others.[647]

Among the groups filing amicus briefs on behalf of the state were the Alliance Defense Fund on behalf of the Family Research Council, Americans United for Life, the American Association of Pro-Life Obstetricians and Gynaecologists, and the Catholic Medical Association.

The Montana Medical Association issued a statement opposing physician-assisted suicide, but refused to file an amicus brief in the appeal.

Controversy

Conservative lawyer Wesley J. Smith condemned the lower court ruling, stating:

> Judges are becoming too arrogant for our good as a nation...Culture-rending changes in law, morality should not be decided undemocratically by promoting a judge's own ideology through wrenching, and twisting constitutional terms to mean

---

[647] *Amicus Curiae* literally means friend of the court. A person with strong interest in or views on the subject matter of an action, but not a party to the action, may petition the court for permission to file a brief, ostensibly on behalf of a party but actually to suggest a rationale consistent with its own views. Such amicus curiae briefs are commonly filed in appeals concerning matters of a broad public interest; e.g., civil rights cases. They may be filed by private persons or the government. An *amicus curiae* educates the court on points of law that are in doubt, gathers or organises information, or raises awareness about some aspect of the case that the court might otherwise miss. The person is usually, but not necessarily, an attorney, and is usually not paid for her or his expertise. An *amicus curiae* must not be a party to the case, nor an attorney in the case, but must have some knowledge or perspective that makes his or her views valuable to the court.

things that were not intended when they were enacted.[648]

Verdict

On 31 December 2009, the Montana Supreme Court ruled in favour of Baxter. It stated that, while the state's Constitution did not guarantee a right to physician-assisted suicide, there was "nothing in Montana Supreme Court precedent or Montana statutes indicating that physician aid in dying is against public policy."[649]

---

[648] Steven Ertelt, "Montana Becomes Third State to Legalize Assisted Suicide as Judge Rules Again", LifeNews, 9 January, 2009.

[649] Kirk Johnson, "Montana Ruling Bolsters Doctor-Assisted Suicide", New York Times, 31 December, 2009.

Other Books by This Author

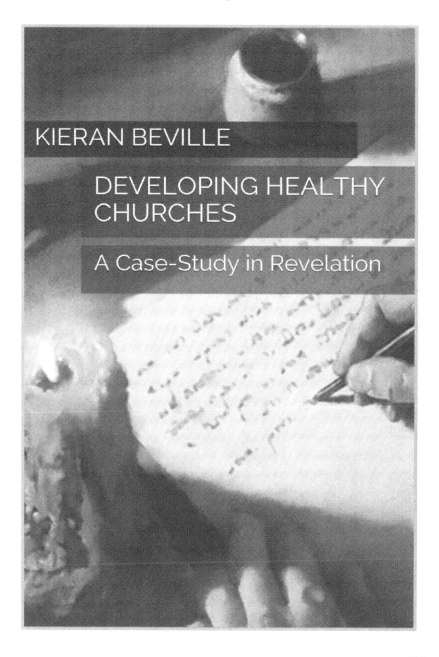

KIERAN BEVILLE

DEVELOPING HEALTHY CHURCHES

A Case-Study in Revelation

Kieran Beville

JOURNEY WITH JESUS THROUGH THE MESSAGE OF MARK

Experience the Ministry of Jesus in a Spiritually Captivating Way

Select Bibliography

Beville, Kieran. *The Commandments in Contemporary Culture* (ISPCK, 2010).

Blaiklock, E.M. *The New International Dictionary of Biblical Archaeology*, Regency Reference Library, Zondervan, 1983.

Bonett, Warren. (Editor), *The Australian Book of Atheism*, Melbourne, Victoria: Scribe, 2010.

Bruce, F.F. *The New Testament Documents: Are They Reliable?* First published 1943 Wm. B. Eerdmans Publishing Company.

Cavanaugh, T. A. *Double-Effect Reasoning: Doing Good and Avoiding Evil* - Oxford Studies in Theological Ethics - (Oxford University Press, USA, 2006).

Chadwick, Ruth (ed). *Encyclopedia of Applied Ethics* – second edition - (Academic Press, 2011).

Chermak, Steven M. and Frankie Y. Bailey. *Crimes and Trials of the Century*, (Greenwood Publishing Group, 2007).

Dowbiggin, Ian. *A Concise History of Euthanasia: Life, Death, God, and Medicine* (Rowman & Littlefield, 2007).

Dowbiggin, Ian. *A Merciful End: The Euthanasia Movement in Modern America*, (Oxford University Press. 2003).

Downing, A. B. and Barbara Smoker (eds). *Voluntary Euthanasia: Experts Debate the Right to Die* (Owen Publishers, 1986).

Flew, Antony. *There is a God: How the World's Most Notorious Atheist Changed His Mind*, New York: HarperOne, 2007.

Gomez, Carlos. *Regulating Death* (New York: Free Press, 1991).

Groothuis, Douglas. *Christian Apologetics: A Comprehensive Case for Biblical Faith*, IVP Academic, 2011.

Kemp, Nick. *Merciful Release* (Manchester University Press, 2002).

Keown, John (ed.) *Examining Euthanasia* (Cambridge University Press, 1997).

Kevorkian, Jack. *Beyond Any Kind of God* (Philosophical Library, 1966).

Kevorkian, Jack. *Medical Research and the Death Penalty: A Dialogue* (Vantage Books, 1960).

Kevorkian, Jack. *Prescription: Medicide, the Goodness of Planned Death*, (Prometheus Books, 1991).

Kohl, Marvin. *Beneficient Euthanasia* (Buffalo, New York: Prometheus Books, 1975)

Kohl, Marvin. *The Morality of Killing* (New York: Humanities Press, 1974)

Koop, C. Everett. *The Memoirs of America's Family Doctor*, Random House, 1991.

Kübler-Ross, Elisabeth. *On Death and Dying: What the Dying Have to Teach Doctors, Nurses, Clergy and their Own Families* (1969), First Scribner Trade Paperback Edition (1997).

Lewis, C. S. *Mere Christianity*, Collins Fontana Religious, 1974 (23rd impression, first published 1952).

Lifton, Robert Jay. *Medical Killing and the Psychology of Genocide: The Nazi Doctors* (Basic Books 1986) - 2000-Da Capo Press edition (1988).

Lynn, Joanne. *Sick To Death And Not going To Take It Anymore! Reforming Health Care for the Last Years of Life* (Berkeley: University of California Press and New York: Milbank Memorial Fund, 2004).

Marker, Rita L. *Deadly Compassion: The Death of Ann Humphry and the Truth about Euthanasia* (New York; William Morrow and Company, 1993).

McDougall, Jennifer Fecio and Martha Gorman. *Euthanasia: A Reference Handbook* (Contemporary World Issues, ABC – CLIO, Inc., 2008).

Metzger, Bruce M. and Bart D. Ehrman, *The Text of the New Testament: Its Transmission, Corruption and Restoration* (4th edition, New York: Oxford University Press, 2005).

Mill, John Stuart. *Utilitarianism* (London: Parker, Son and Bourn, West Strand, 1863).

Morison, Frank *Who Moved the Stone? A Skeptic Looks at the Death and Resurrection of Christ*, Zondervan; reprint edition, 1987.

Nicol, Neal and Harry Wylie. *Between the Dead and the Dying* (London: Satin Publications, 2006).

Otlowski, Margaret. *Voluntary Euthanasia and the Common Law* (Oxford University Press, 1997).

Peters, Albrecht. *Commentary on Luther's Catechisms: Ten Commandments*, (Concordia Publishing House, 2009).

Quill, T.E. and M.P. Battin. *Physician-Assisted Dying: The Case for Palliative Care & Patient Choice* (Johns Hopkins University Press, 2004).

Rachels, James. *The end of life: Euthanasia and Morality* (Oxford University Press, 1986).

Smith, Wesley J. *Forced Exit* (New York: Times Books, 1997).

Sproul, R.C., *Now That's a Good Question*, Tyndale House, 1996.

Stewart, William. *An A-Z of Counselling Theory and Practice* (Nelson Thornes, 2005).

Stott, John R.W., *Understanding the Bible*, Zondervan, 1999.

Timmons, Mark. *Moral Theory: An Introduction* (Rowman & Littlefield 2003).

Torr, James D. *Euthanasia: Opposing Viewpoints* (San Diego: Greenhaven Press, 2000).

Vickers, Brian. *Francis Bacon: The Major Works - Oxford World's Classics –* (Oxford University Press, USA, 2008).

Wells, Samuel and Ben Quash. *Introducing Christian Ethics* (John Wiley and Sons, 2010).

Zalta, Edward N. (ed.). (*Stanford Encyclopedia of Philosophy*, 2006 edition).